Bibliography of Feminist Criticism

Bibliographie de la critique féminist

Bibliography of Feminist Criticism

COMPILED BY BARBARA GODARD

Bibliographie de la critique féminist

ECW PRESS

Canadian Cataloguing in Publication Data

Godard, Barbara

    Bibliography of feminist literary criticism

ISBN 0-920763-97-9

1. Feminist literary criticism – Canada –
Bibliography. 2. Feminism and literature – Canada –
Bibliography. 3. Women authors, Canadian –
Bibliography. I. Title.

Z1377.F38G63 1987   016.810'9   C87-093328-0

This bibliography has been published with the help of a grant from the Canadian Federation for the Humanities, using funds provided by the Social Sciences and Humanities Council of Canada. Additional support has been provided by The Canada Council and the Ontario Arts Council.

Designed and typeset by ECW Production Services, Oakville, Ontario.

Cover by Bette Davies.

Printed and bound by Hignell Printing Limited, Winnipeg, Manitoba.

Published by ECW PRESS, 307 Coxwell Avenue, Toronto, Ontario.

TABLE OF CONTENTS

Bibliography of Feminist Criticism

WHILE NOT EXHAUSTIVE, this bibliography is more extensive than any presently available. In selecting material for inclusion, I have followed the principles outlined in my overview of literary criticism, so I have moved beyond the boundaries of academic periodicals. I have included many interviews which frequently raise the question of being a woman and a writer, even when these are conducted by men. Many book reviews have been included, because this is where much of the feminist criticism is being carried out. Many reviewers group the books of several women writers and seek that will-of-the wisp, female specificity. Others, in feminist periodicals addressed primarily to women readers, foreground thematic concerns with such an audience in mind. In this respect, I have tried to provide as inclusive an inventory as possible of material from Canadian feminist periodicals that are not indexed in the *Canadian Periodicals Index*. Included as well are the papers delivered at conferences and symposia. These are generally available from the author of the paper (as is the practice at the Modern Languages Association) or in specialized centres, such as the Women's Resource Centres at the Ontario Institute for Studies in Education and at York University, to which I have had access. Material is included up to May 1986.

Alphabetical listings by author, or by title where there is no author, have been arranged where applicable under the following headings: Bibliographies (including Books, Articles and Sections of Books, and Theses and Dissertations), Feminist Literary Theory (including Books, Articles and Sections of Books, Theses and Dissertations, and Reviews), General Studies of Several Writers (including Books, Articles and Sections of Books, Theses and Dissertations, and Reviews), Individual Writers (including Books, Articles and Sections of Books, Theses, Interviews, Reviews, and Miscellaneous), Images of Women in Men's Writing (including Books, Articles and Sections of Books, and Theses and Dissertations), Images of Men (including Articles and Sections of Books, and Reviews), Journalism (including Books, Articles and Sections of Books, Theses and Disserations, and Reviews), and Feminist Presses (including Articles and Sections of Books). Articles and reviews of several authors that include one female Canadian writer are listed in the appropriate section under Individual Writers.

When I began this bibliography, I expected to find a handful of articles. To my surprise, this has metamorphized into a giant's fist. While such expansion is an encouraging sign of the health in this new discipline, the invisibility of so much of it, even to such an interested party as I am, suggests that marginality is still the rule with women's artistic and intellectual productions. In this inventory, I hope to bring this considerable activity into public view, thus redrawing the circle.

Thanks to Freida Forman at the Ontario Institute for Studies in Education for organizing such a wonderful collection, making it easy to locate feminist periodicals, and to Mary Hudecki, at Inter-Library Loans, York University, for her excellent detective work in locating some of the more obscure journals.

Bibliographie de la critique féministe

BIEN QU'ELLE n'épuise pas toutes les ressources, cette bibliographie est la plus exhaustive actuellement disponible. En choissisant les entrées, j'ai suivi les principes tels que décrits dans mon introduction de la critique littéraire féministe. Ainsi, ai-je dépassé les frontières des revues académiques: j'ai inclu beaucoup d'entretiens qui soulèvent le problème d'être femme et ''écrivain,'' et cela, même quand ce sont des hommes qui signent les articles. J'ai inclu aussi beaucoup de comptes rendus de livres car c'est là que se fait une grande partie de la critique féministe. Beaucoup d'entre eux regroupent les livres de plusieures écrivaines et cherchent ce feu follet qu'est la spécificité féminine. D'autres, qui se trouvent dans des revues féministes, orientent leur thématique vers un public de femmes. C'est en puissant à ces revues que j'ai essayé d'établir un répertoire aussi compréhensif que possible de critiques féministes qui ne sont pas indexés dans Canadian Periodical Index. Il s'y trouve aussi, des communications présentées à différents colloques, celles-ci étant souvent disponibles auprès de l'auteure (suivant l'habitude de l'Association des Langues Modernes) ou dans des centres spécialisés, tel le Centre de documentation des femmes à l'Ontario Institute for Studies in Education et à l'Université York, où j'ai eu accès aux manuscrits. Toutes les entrées ont été publiées avant mai 1986.

Les entrées ont été cataloguées par ordre alphabétique d'auteurs ou de titres (lorsqu'il n'y a pas d'auteur-e) selon les catégories suivantes selon le cas: Bibliographies (comprenant Livres, Articles et sections de livres et Thèses), Théorie littéraire féministe (comprenant Livres, Articles et sections de livres, Thèses et Comptes rendus), Vue globale de plusieures auteures (comprenant Livres, Articles et sections de livres, Thèses et Comptes rendus), Écrivaines individuelles (comprenant Livres, Articles et sections de livres, Thèses, Entretiens, Comptes rendus et Matière diverse), La Représentation des femmes chez les écrivains masculins (comprenant Livres, Articles et sections de livres et Thèses), La Représentation des hommes (comprenant Articles et sections de livres et Comptes rendus), Journalisme (comprenant Livres, Articles et sections de livres, Thèses et Comptes rendus) et Les Presses féministes (comprenant Articles et sections de livres). Les articles et comptes rendus de plusieures auteures où figure une seule écrivaine canadienne sont indexé sous le nom de l'auteure dans la section des auteure individuelles.

Quand j'ai entrepris cette bibliographie, j'espérais trouver une dizaine d'articles. À ma grand surprise, j'en ai trouvée des centaines. Bien que voilà un indice encourageant par rapport à l'évolution de cette nouvelle discipline, il faut bien se dire que trop d'écrits — productions artistiques et intellectuelles des femmes — restent toujours invisibles. C'est pourquoi dans ce répertoire, j'espère dévoiler toute cette activité littéraire au public et, ainsi, redessiner le cercle.

Mes remerciements à Freida Forman pour son organisation de la collection manifique à Ontario Institute for Studies in Education, qui a rendu facile la tâche de repérer des périodiques féministes, et à Mary Hudecki, de La Service des prêts entre bibliothèques, de l'Université York, pour son travail excéllent détective en dénichant des périodiques obscurs.

Bibliographies (Books/Livres, Articles and Sections of Books/ Articles et sections de livres, and/et Theses and Dissertations/Thèses)

Books/Livres

The Atlantic Work Group. See/voir Gaskin, Geraldine, and The Atlantic Work Group.

Boucher, Andrée. Voir aussi/see also Cohen, Yolande, avec Andrée Boucher.

Canadian Women's Periodicals: KWIC Index/ Périodiques pour femmes canadiennes: mots-clés en contexte [Canadian Research Institute for the Advancement of Women/Institut canadien de recherche pour l'avancement de la femme], Trial Issue/Numéro expérimental (Oct./oct. 1984). N. pag.

Canadian Women's Periodicals: KWIC Index/ Périodiques pour femmes canadiennes: mots-clés en contexte [Canadian Research Institute for the Advancement of Women/Institut canadien de recherche pour l'avancement de la femme], Trial Issue, No. 2 (March 1985). N. pag.

Canadian Women's Periodicals: KWIC Index/ Périodiques pour femmes canadiennes: mots-clés en contexte [Canadian Research Institute for the Advancement of Women/Institut canadien de recherche pour l'avancement de la femme], Trial Issue, No. 3 (June 1985). N. pag.

Canadian Women's Periodicals: KWIC Index/ Périodiques pour femmes canadiennes: mots-clés en contexte [Canadian Research Institute for the Advancement of Women/Institut canadien de recherche pour l'avancement de la femme], 1, No. 1 (Oct. 1985). N. pag.

Cohen, Yolande, avec Andrée Boucher. *Les Thèses universitaires québécoises sur les femmes 1921–1981.* 2ᶜ ed. Institut Québécois de Recherches sur la Culture, 1983. 121 pp.

Collectif. *Les Québécoises: Guide biblio-graphique suivi d'une filmographie.* Le Conseil du statut de la femme/La Documentation québécoise, Ministère des communications, éditeur officiel du Quebec, 1976. 160 pp.

Commonwealth Institute and the National Book League. *Women and Women Writers in the Commonwealth.* London: National Book League, Commonwealth Institute, 1975. 52 pp.

Davidson, Evelyn, ed. *Who's Who of Canadian Women* (1983). 478 pp.

Gallant, Melvin, et Ginette Gould. *Portraits d'écrivains: Dictionnaire des auteurs acadiens* (1982). 174 pp.

Gaskin, Geraldine, and The Atlantic Work Group. *Women in Canadian Literature: A Resource Guide for the Teaching of Canadian Literature.* [Toronto]: Writer's Development Trust, [1977]. 93 pp.

Gelfand, Elissa D., and Virginia Thorndike Hules. *French Feminist Criticism: Women, Language and Literature. An Annotated Bibliography.* New York: Garland, 1985. 318 pp.

Germain-Samson, Marcelle, en collaboration avec Le Conseil du statut de la femme. *Des livres et des femmes.* Québec: Conseil du statut de la femme, Gouvernement du Québec, 1978. 254 pp.

Gould, Ginette. Voir/see Gallant, Melvin, et Ginette Gould.

Hamel, Reginald. *Bibliographie sommaire sur l'histoire de l'écriture féminine au Canada, 1769–1961.* Montréal: Univ. de Montréal, 1974. 133 pp.

Leonard, John William, ed. *Woman's Who's Who of America: A Biographical Dictionary of the Contemporary Women of the United States and Canada* (1914); rpt. (1974). 961 pp.

Morgan, Henry James, ed. *The Canadian Men and Women of the Time: A Hand-Book of Canadian Biography of Living Characters.* 1898; rpt. (revised) Toronto: William Briggs, 1912. 1218 pp.

———. *Types of Canadian Women and of Women Who Are or Have Been Connected with Canada.* Toronto: William Briggs, 1903. Vol. 1. 382 pp.

Articles and Sections of Books/
Articles et sections de livres

Ahearn, M. H. "Compilation." In *Women of Canada: Their Life and Work*. National Council of Women of Canada, 1900. 2nd ed., 1975, pp. 198–208.

Andersen, Marguerite. "Le Québec: féminisme contemporain et écrits de femmes (1970–1983): Une Bibliographie pilote." *Resources for Feminist Research/Documentation sur la recherche féministe,* 12, no 4 (Dec.–Jan./déc.–jan. 1983–84), 18–28.

Anthony, Geraldine, and Tina Usmiani. "A Bibliography of English Canadian Drama Written by Women." *World Literature Written in English* [Univ. of Texas at Arlington], [Women Writers of the Commonwealth], 17 (April 1978), 120–43.

Bellingham, Susan. "University of Waterloo Library Special Collection Related to Women." *Canadian Women's Studies/les cahiers de la femme* [Centennial College], 2, No. 2 (1980), 18–20.

Bentley, D. M. R., and Marylynn Wickens. "A Checklist of Women-Related Materials in *The Week* (1883–1896)." *Canadian Newsletter of Research on Women/Recherches sur la Femme — Bulletin d'Information Canadien*, 6, No. 3 (Oct. 1977), 106–23.

"Bibliographie commentée des femmes auteurs de langues français." BREFF (*Bulletin de recherches et d'études féministes francophone) [Dépt. de français, Univ. of Wisconsin]*, 1, no 1 (mai 1976)–[Dept. de français, Pennsylvania State Univ.], déc. 1985.

"Bibliographie des publications féministes canadiennes et internationales." *Des luttes et des rires de femmes,* 3, no 5 (juin 1980), pp. 49–51.

"Bibliography: Paid Work: Writers/Bibliographie: Travail Rémuneré: Ecrivains." In *Women and Work an Inventory of Research/La Femme et le travail un inventaire de recherches*. Ottawa: CRIAW/ICRAF, 1978, pp. 21–22.

Boucher, Andrée, Yolande Cohen et Ghislaine Desjardins. "Inventaire des thèses sur les femmes dans la société québécoise: Les thèses rédigés dans les universités montréalaises: présentation sommaire des résultats." Communication non-édit. Ontario Institute for Studies in Education, Toronto, n.d.

"Canadian Literature." *Women & Literature* [Rutgers Univ.], 4, No. 2 (Fall 1976)–, Supp.: Bibliography of Literature in English by and about Women. Annual.

Cohen, Yolande. "La Recherche universitaire sur les femmes au Québec (1929–1980): Répertoire de thèses de maîtrise et de doctorat déposées dans les universités du Québec: présentation thématique." *Resources for Feminist Research/Documentation sur la recherche féministe,* 10, no 4 (Dec.–Jan. 1981–82), 5–24.

——— . Voir/see Boucher, Andrée, Yolande Cohen et Ghislaine Desjardins.

Desjardins, Ghislaine. Voir/see Boucher, Andrée, Yolande Cohen et Ghislaine Desjardins.

Eddie, Christine. "Noir sur blanc (La lutte féministe: une parole qui s'imprime)." *Dérives*, [Idéologie, structuralisme & féminisme], no 27 (1981), pp. 58–67.

Eichler, Margaret. "Sociology of Feminist Research in Canada." *Signs: Journal of Women in Culture and Society,* 3 (Winter 1977), 413–14.

Emerson, Mary. "Women Writers." *The Canadian Magazine of Politics, Science, Art and Literature* [Toronto], Feb. 1905, pp. 379–80.

Godard, Barbara. "Francophone Canada." In *Women Writers in Translation: An Annotated Bibliography, 1945–1982*. Ed. Margery Resnick and Isabelle de Courtivron. Garland Reference Library of the Humanities, 288. New York: Garland, 1984, pp. 93–112.

Gottlieb, Lois C., and Wendy Keitner. "Bird at the Window: An Annotated Bibliography of Canadian Fiction Written by Women 1970–1975." *The American Review of Canadian Studies,* 9, No. 2 (Autumn 1979), 3–56.

———. "Reflections on Canadian Women's Writing of the 1970's: Preliminary Results of 'An Annotated Bibliography of Canadian Women Writers (in English): A Feasibility Study 1970–1975.'" *Canadian Newsletter of Research on Women/Recherches sur la Femme — Bulletin d'Information Canadien*, 7, No. 2 (July 1978), 22–26.

Houle, Ghislaine. "La femme et la littérature." Dans sa *La Femme et la société québécoise*. Bibliographies québécoises. Montréal: Ministère des Affaires culturelles, Gouvernement du Québec, 1975, pp. 141–72.

Keitner, Wendy. See/voir Gottlieb, Lois C., and Wendy Keitner.

Kessler, Carol Farley. See/voir Rudenstein, Gail M., Carol Farley Kessler, and Ann M. Moore.

Lefebvre, Janine. "L'Expressivité du féminin: bibliographie commentée." *Jeu: cahiers de théâtre*, [Théâtre-femmes], no 16 (1980), pp. 211–15.

Lemieux, Denise, et Lucie Mercier. *La Recherche sur les femmes au Québec: bilan et bibliographie*. Québéc: Institut Québécois de Recherche sur la Culture, 1982, pp. 290–95.

Linden, Marjorie, and Diane Teeple. "The Evolving Role of Canadian Women Writers." *Ontario Library Review*, 61 (June 1977), 114–31.

Lister, Rota Herzberg. "Canadian Plays in English about Older Women: A Bibliography." *Resources for Feminist Research/Documentation sur la recherche féministe*, [Women as Elders/Nos aînées], 11, No. 2 (July/juil. 1982), 238–40.

Maranda, Jeanne, et Maïr Verthuy. "Bibliographie des écrits féministes." *Canadian Women's Studies/les cahiers de la femme* [Centennial College], 1, no 1 (automne/Fall 1978), 135–36.

———. "Québec Feminist Writing." *Emergency Librarian*, [Québec Feminist Writing], 5, No. 1 (Sept.–Oct. 1977), 2–11. Repris trad. ("Les Écrits Féministes au Québec") dans *Emergency Librarian*, [Québec Feminist Writing], 5, no 1

(sept.–oct. 1977), 12–20.

Mazur, Carol, and Sheila Pepper. *Women in Canada: A Bibliography, 1965–1982*. 3rd ed. Toronto: OISE, 1984, pp. 154–58, 204–08.

McIntyre, Sheila. "A Bibliography of Scholarship on Literature by and about Canadian Women." *Canadian Newsletter of Research on Women/Recherches sur la Femme — Bulletin d'Information Canadien*, 6, No. 1, (Feb. 1977), 99–114.

Mercier, Lucie. Voir/see Lemieux, Denise, et Lucie Mercier.

Moore, Ann M. See/voir Rudenstein, Gail M., Carol Farley Kessler, and Ann M. Moore.

Pepper, Sheila. See/voir Mazur, Carol, and Sheila Pepper.

Rudenstein, Gail M., Carol Farley Kessler, and Ann M. Moore. "Bibliography: British and Commonwealth Fiction." In *The Lost Tradition: Mothers and Daughters in Literature*. Ed. Cathy N. Davidson and E. M. Broner. New York: Frederick Ungar, 1980, pp. 316–17.

Schwartz, Narda Lacey. *Articles on Women Writers: A Bibliography*. Santa Barbara, Cal.: ABC-CLIO, 1977, pp. 9, 19, 27, 37, 43, 55, 70, 90, 96, 108, 113, 118–19, 131, 133, 149, 150, 167, 186, 190–91, 200.

Seager, Joni. "As if It Mattered: A Resource Guide." *The American Review of Canadian Studies*, 15, No. 4 (Winter 1985), 505–08.

Seifert, Carol. "An Inventory of Articles Concerning Women in the *Canadian Magazine*, 1883–1919." *Resources for Feminist Research/Documentation sur la recherche féministe*, [Canadian Women's History: Teaching and Research/L'histoire de la femme au Canada: L'enseignement et la recherche], 8, No. 2 (July/juil. 1979), 67.

The Sense and Sensibility Collective, comp. *Women and Literature: An Annotated Bibliography of Women Writers*. 2nd rev. and enl. ed. Cambridge, Mass.: Sense & Sensibility, 1973, pp. 2, 14, 23, 29, 36, 42. Rpt. Comp. Iris Biblowitz, Liza Bingham, Frances M. Goodstein, Julia Homer, Jill

Janows, Ann Kautzmann, Peggy Kornegger, Virginia Rankin MacLean, Jane Tuchscherer, and Judy Wynn. 3rd ed. Cambridge, Mass.: Women and Literature, 1976, pp. 146–52, 187, 192, 373.

Teeple, Diane. See/voir Linden, Marjorie, and Diane Teeple.

Usmiani, Tina. See/voir Anthony, Geraldine, and Tina Usmiani.

Verthuy, Maïr. See/voir Maranda, Jeanne and Maïr Verthuy.

Wagner, Anton. "Bibliography." In *Women Pioneers*. Vol. II of *Canada's Lost Plays*. Ed. Anton Wagner. Toronto: Canadian Theatre Review, 1979, pp. 268–72.

Wickens, Marylynn. See/voir Bentley, D. M. R., and Marylynn Wickens.

Theses and Dissertations/Thèses

Frost, Wendy. See/voir Valiquette, Michèle, and Wendy Frost.

Miller, Judith A. "A Checklist of Women Authors." In her "The Canadian Short Story Database." Diss. York 1981, pp. 210–31.

Valiquette, Michèle, and Wendy Frost. "An Annotated Bibliography of Feminist Criticism." M.A. Thesis Simon Fraser 1983.

ॐ

Feminist Literary Theory/Théorie littéraire féministe (Books/Livres, Articles and Sections of Books/ Articles et sections de livres, Theses and Dissertations/Thèses, and/et Reviews/Comptes rendus)

Books/Livres

Brossard, Nicole. *La lettre aérienne*. Montréal: Remue-ménage, 1985. 154 pp.

Lamy, Suzanne. *d'elles*. Montréal: L'Hexagone, 1979. 110 pp.

———. *Quand je lis, je m'invente*. Montréal: L'Hexagone, 1984. 111 pp.

Ouellette-Michalska, Madeleine. *L'Echappée des discours de l'oeil*. Montréal: Nouvelle Optique, 1981. 327 pp.

Rule, Jane. *A Hot-Eyed Moderate*. Toronto: Lester & Orpen Dennys, 1986. 242 pp.

———. *Lesbian Images*. Garden City, N.Y.: Doubleday, 1975. 246 pp.

Articles and Sections of Books/ Articles et sections de livres

Allen, Lillian. "A Writing of Resistance: Black Women's Writing in Canada." In *In the Feminine: Women and Words/Les Femmes et les mots: Conference Proceedings 1983*. Ed. Ann Dybikowski, Victoria Freeman, Daphne Marlatt, Barbara Pulling, and Betsy Warland. Edmonton: Longspoon, 1985, pp. 63–67.

Andersen, Margret. "Feminism and the Literary Critic." *Atlantis: A Women's Studies Journal* [Acadia Univ.], 1, No. 1 (Fall 1975), 3–13.

———. "Feminist Criticism." In *Mother Was Not a Person*. Ed. Margret Andersen. Montreal: Black Rose, 1972, pp. 87–90.

Andersen, Marguerite. "Sacrée langue ou langue sacrée." *HERizons: The Manitoba Women's News Magazine*, Dec. 1984, pp. 30–32, 41.

Armstrong, Jeannette C. "Writing from a

Native Woman's Perspective." In *In the Feminine: Women and Words/Les Femmes et les mots: Conference Proceedings 1983*. Ed. Ann Dybikowski, Victoria Freeman, Daphne Marlatt, Barbara Pulling, and Betsy Warland. Edmonton: Longspoon, 1985, pp. 55–57.

Atwood, Margaret. "Sexual Bias in Reviewing." In *In the Feminine: Women and Words/Les Femmes et les mots: Conference Proceedings 1983*. Ed. Ann Dybiowski, Victoria Freeman, Daphne Marlatt, Barbara Pulling, and Betsy Warland. Edmonton: Longspoon, 1985, pp. 151–52.

Bayard, Caroline. "Diff-érance, dissémination et Subversion: Trois écrivaines féministes au Québec." 4th Conference of Interamerican Women Writers, Mexico. 6 June 1981. Emprunté dans *NDQ: North Dakota Quarterly* [Univ. of North Dakota], 52, no 3 (Summer 1984), 79–86.

———. "Le Forum des femmes: *la nouvelle barre du jour* en amant de la pensée théorique au Québec." *Lettres québécoises: Revue de l'actualité littéraire*, no 42 (été 1986), pp. 71–73.

———. "Qu'en est-il au fait de la théorie depuis que les dieux sont morts?". Dans *Féminité, subversion, écriture*. Ed. Suzanne Lamy et Irène Pagès. Montréal: Remue-ménage, 1983, pp. 185–93.

Bersianik, Louky [Lucile Durand]. "Comment naître femme sans le devenir." *la nouvelle barre du jour*, [Forum des femmes], no 172 (mars 1986), pp. 57–65.

———. "Le corps dans l'écriture." Breaking the Sequence, Wellesley College, Wellesley, Mass. May 1981.

———. "Le Corps de chanvre indien." *Signum*, [Numéro Special], [Actes XXIV Congrès Annuel de l'APFUCC, Univ. Dalhousie, 22–25 mai], 2 (mai 1981), 165–201.

———. "Women's Work." Trans. Erika Grundmann. In *In the Feminine: Women and Words/Les Femmes et les mots: Conference Proceedings 1983*. Ed. Ann Dybikowski, Victoria Freeman, Daphne Marlatt, Barbara Pulling, and Betsy Warland. Edmonton: Longspoon, 1985, pp. 155–65.

Bertrand, Claudine. "La maïeutique de l'écriture: une pratique." *MOEBIUS*, no 22 (été 1984), pp. 39–42.

Blackburn, Claire, et Lucie Goulet. "La perception de la femme dans les travaux scolaires." *études littéraires* [Univ. Laval], 14 (déc. 1981), 463–89.

Blais, Marie-Claire. Réponse à "Figurez-vous" de Louise Cotnoir. *la nouvelle barre du jour*, [Forum des femmes], no 172 (mars 1986), pp. 47–49.

Bouchard, Céline. Réponse à "Intercepter le réel" de Nicole Brossard. *la nouvelle barre du jour*, [Forum des femmes], no 172 (mars 1986), pp. 21–24.

Brant, Beth. "Coming Out as Indian Lesbian Writers." In *In the Feminine: Women and Words/Les Femmes et les mots: Conference Proceedings 1983*. Ed. Ann Dybikowski, Victoria Freeman, Daphne Marlatt, Barbara Pulling, and Betsy Warland. Edmonton: Longspoon, 1985, pp. 58–59.

Brossard, Nicole. "À la lumière des sens." *la nouvelle barre du jour*, no 112 (mars 1982), pp. 5–16.

———. "Champ d'action pour figures inédites. Cela s'explique qu'elle manque d'imagination." *la barre du jour*, no 29 (été 1971), pp. 45–53.

———. Collaboratrice. "Panel on The Woman Writer and Feminist Criticism/Table Ronde sur L'écrivaine et la critique féministe." Dialogue, York Univ., Downsview, Ont. 17 Oct./oct. 1981. Emprunté ("L'Appréciation critique") dans sa *La lettre aérienne*. Montréal: Remue-ménage, 1985, pp. 71–75. Repris ("Mouvements et stratégies de l'écriture de fiction") dans *Gynocritics/Gynocritiques: Feminist Approaches to Canadian and Quebec Women's Writing/Démarches féministes à l'écritures des Canadiennes et Québécoises*. Ed. Barbara Godard. Toronto: ECW, 1987, pp. 227–30.

———. "Le cortex exubérant." *la barre du jour*, no 44 (printemps 1974), pp. 2–22.

———. "Cuerpo y escritura." Traducción de Agueda Bazán. *Los Universitarios*, [Special Number on IV Congreso Interamericano de Escritoras], No. 187 (Julio 1981), p. 16.

———. "E muet mutant." *la barre du jour*, no 50 (hiver 1975), pp. 10–27. Rpt. trans. M. L. Taylor ["'E' muet mutant (Extrait)/Excerpt from 'E' muet mutant"] in *ellipse*, Nos. 23–24 (1979), pp. 45–63.

———. "L'Ecrivain." Dans sa *La Nef des Sorcières*. Montréal: Quinze, 1976, p. 80. Repris dans *Fireweed: A Feminist Literary & Cultural Journal*, [Women and Language], nos 5–6 (Winter–Spring 1979–80), pp. 107, 109, 111, 113, 115, 117. Rpt. trans. Linda Gaboriau ("The Writer") in *Fireweed: A Feminist Literary & Cultural Journal*, [Women and Language], Nos. 5–6 (Winter–Spring 1979–80), pp. 106, 108, 110, 112, 114, 116. Rpt. in *A Clash of Symbols*. Trans. Linda Gaboriau. Toronto: Coach House, 1979, n. pag.

———. "Enunciation (sic) Déformation ludique." *Stratégie: pratiques signifiantes*, nos 3–4 (hiver 1973), pp. 51–61.

———. "L'Épreuve de la modernité ou/et les preuves de modernité." *la nouvelle barre du jour*, nos 90–91 (mai 1980), pp. 55–63.

———. "La Femme et l'écriture: Actes de la Rencontre." *Liberté*, [Actes de la Rencontre Québécoise internationale des écrivains], 18, nos 4–5 [nos 106–107] (juil.–oct. 1976), 10–13.

———. "Fragments d'urgence." *Le Devoir* [Montréal], 19 avril 1980, pp. 21–22.

———. "L'identité comme science-fiction de soi." *Vlasta* [Paris], no 1 (printemps 1983), pp. 93–99.

———. "Intercepter le réel." *la nouvelle barre du jour*, [Forum des femmes], no 172 (mars 1986), pp. 15–19.

———. "Mais voici venir la fiction ou l'épreuve au féminin." *la nouvelle barre du jour*, nos 90–91 (mai 1980), pp. 64–68.

———. "Me couler douce l'échine-vulnérable." *la barre du jour*, no 38 (hiver 1973), pp. 24–33.

———. "Notes et fragments d'urgence." Dans *Femmes et politique*. Ed. Yolande Cohen. Montréal: Jour, 1981, pp. 10–19.

———. "Les stratégies du réel." Dans *les stratégies du réel/the story so far 6*. Ed. Nicole Brossard. Montréal/Toronto: La Nouvelle Barre du Jour/Coach House, 1979, p. 8. Rpt. trans. Barbara Godard ("Strategies of Reality") in *les stratégies du réel/the story so far 6*. Ed. Nicole Brossard. Montréal/Toronto: La Nouvelle Barre du Jour/Coach House, 1979, p. 9.

———. "Les surfaces." *la nouvelle barre du jour*, no 81 (sept. 1979), pp. 69–80.

———. "Tender Skin My Mind." In *In the Feminine: Women and Words/Les Femmes et les mots: Conference Proceedings 1983*. Ed. Ann Dybikowski, Victoria Freeman, Daphne Marlatt, Barbara Pulling, and Betsy Warland. Edmonton: Longspoon, 1985, pp. 180–83.

———. "La tête qu'elle fait." *la barre du jour*, nos 56–57 (mai–août 1977), pp. 83–92. Rpt. trans. Josée LeBlond ("The Face She Makes") in *Room of One's Own*, 4, Nos. 1–2 (1978), 39–43.

———. "Traversing Fiction." Trans. Barbara Godard. *Fireweed: A Feminist Literary & Cultural Journal*, No. 1 (Autumn 1978), pp. 20–21.

Chaske, Ivy, and Connie Fife. Editorial. *Fireweed: A Feminist Quarterly*, [Native Women], No. 22 (Winter 1986), pp. 5–6.

Chénard, Sylvie. Voir/see Un collectif de femmes.

Christopherson, Claudia. "Diary Keeping as a Feminine Art Form." *Branching Out: Canadian Magazine for Women*, 5, No. 2 (1978), pp. 30–33.

Un collectif de femmes [Chénard, Sylvie, Michèle Lévesque, Andrée Savard, et al.]. "Au coeur de nos censures." *Dérives*, [l'image, périphérie: le saguenay autrement], nos 24–25 (1980), p. 57–60.

Cotnoir, Louise. "Au dire des frontalières." *la nouvelle barre du jour*, no 78 (mai 1979), pp. 65–83.

———. "Figurez-vous." *la nouvelle barre du jour*, [Forum des femmes], no 172 (mars 1986), pp. 43–46.

———. "The Imaginary Body." Trans. Erika Grundmann. In *In the Feminine: Women and Words/Les Femmes et les mots: Conference Proceedings 1983*. Ed. Ann Dybikowski, Victoria Freeman, Daphne Marlatt, Barbara Pulling, and

Betsy Warland. Edmonton: Longspoon, 1985, pp. 166–70.

———. "The Marked Gender." Trans. Barbara Godard. In *In the Feminine: Women and Words/Les Femmes et les mots: Conference Proceedings 1983*. Ed. Ann Dybikowski, Victoria Freeman, Daphne Marlatt, Barbara Pulling, and Betsy Warland. Edmonton: Longspoon, 1985, pp. 99–104.

———. "S'écrire avec, dans et contre le langage." *Tessera*, no 1 [*Room of One's Own*, 8, no 4] (1983), 47–49. Rpt. trans. Barbara Godard ("Writing Ourselves with, in and against Language") in *Tessera*, No. 1 [*Room of One's Own*, 8, No. 4] (1983), 50–52.

Couillard, Marie. "La femme: d'objet mythique à sujet parlant." *Atlantis: A Women's Studies Journal/Journal d'études sur la femme* [Acadia Univ.], 5, no 1 (Fall/automne 1979), 40–50.

Crean, Susan. "Who's Afraid of Women's Culture?". In *In the Feminine: Women and Words/Les Femmes et les mots: Conference Proceedings 1983*. Ed. Ann Dybikowski, Victoria Freeman, Daphne Marlatt, Barbara Pulling, and Betsy Warland. Edmonton: Longspoon, 1985, pp. 37–39.

Cuthand, Beth. "Transmitting Our Identity as Indian Writers." In *In the Feminine: Women and Words/Les Femmes et les mots: Conference Proceedings 1983*. Ed. Ann Dybikowski, Victoria Freeman, Daphne Marlatt, Barbara Pulling, and Betsy Warland. Edmonton: Longspoon, 1985, pp. 53–54.

de Lotbinière-Harwood, Susanne. "Les Belles infidèles." *Resources for Feminist Research/Documentation sur la recherche féministe*, [Feminist Directions Féministes], 14, no 3 (Nov./nov. 1985), 20.

Diamond, Sara. "How Class Affects Women's Writing." In *In the Feminine: Women and Words/Les Femmes et les mots: Conference Proceedings 1983*. Ed. Ann Dybikowski, Victoria Freeman, Daphne Marlatt, Barbara Pulling, and

Betsy Warland. Edmonton: Longspoon, 1985, pp. 32–36.

di Cicco, Pier Giorgio. See/voir Smart, Carolyn, and Pier Giorgio di Cicco.

Downes, Gwladys. "Contrasts in Psychic Space." In *In the Feminine: Women and Words/Les Femmes et les mots: Conference Proceedings 1983*. Ed. Ann Dybikowski, Victoria Freeman, Daphne Marlatt, Barbara Pulling, and Betsy Warland. Edmonton: Longspoon, 1985, pp. 117–21.

Drapeau, Renée-Berthe. "L'écriture dont il pourrait être ici question." *la nouvelle barre du jour*, no 113 (avril 1982), pp. 65–77.

———. "Ecriture: l'Un/e et la différence (sexuelle)." *MOEBIUS*, no 22 (été 1984), pp. 75–82.

Drouin, Danielle. "Subversion et passion. Quelques réflections, errance." *MOEBIUS*, no 22 (été 1984), pp. 45–56.

Dumény-Miquel, Colette. "Du geste à l'écriture ou l'incarnation véritable l'être femme." Thèse de maîtrise Concordia 1978.

Dupré, Louise. "De la chair à la langue." *La vie en rose*, mai 1983, pp. 54–55.

———. "La Memoire Complice, Doublement." *Tessera*, no 1 [*Room of One's Own*, 8, no 4] (1983), 25–32. Rpt. trans. Kathy Mezei and Daphne Marlatt ("The Doubly Complicit Memory") in *Tessera*, No. 1 [*Room of One's Own*, 8, No. 4] (1983), 33–40.

———. "Star Words." *la nouvelle barre du jour*, [Forum des femmes], no 172 (mars 1986), pp. 79–84.

Engel, Marian. "Twins and a Typewriter." In *In the Feminine: Women and Words/Les Femmes et les mots: Conference Proceedings 1983*. Ed. Ann Dybikowski, Victoria Freeman, Daphne Marlatt, Barbara Pulling, and Betsy Warland. Edmonton: Longspoon, 1985, pp. 78–80.

Féral, Josette. "Antigone or *The Irony of the Tribe*." *Diacritics: a review of contemporary criticism* [Cornell Univ.], 8 (Fall 1978), 2–14.

———. "Du texte au sujet: Conditions pour une écriture et un discours au féminin."

Revue de l'Université d'Ottawa/University of Ottawa Quarterly, [Conférence des femmes-écrivains en Amérique], 50 (jan.–mars/Jan.–March 1980), 39–46.

Fife, Connie. See/voir Chaske, Ivy, and Connie Fife.

Finn, Geraldine. "Feminism and Fiction: In Praise of *Praxis*, Beyond *Bodily Harm*." *Socialist Studies/Etudes Socialistes: A Canadian Annual*, 1983, pp. 51–78.

Ford, Cathy. "Violence against the Feminine: Speaking the Unspeakable." In *In the Feminine: Women and Words/Les Femmes et les mots: Conference Proceedings 1983*. Ed. Ann Dybikowski, Victoria Freeman, Daphne Marlatt, Barbara Pulling, and Betsy Warland. Edmonton: Longspoon, 1985, p. 42.

Forsyth, Louise. "La critique au féminin: vers de nouveaux lieux communs." Parlons-en/Talking Together, Simone de Beauvoir Institute, Concordia Univ., Montréal. 2 juin 1980. Emprunté dans *Parlons-en/Talking Together: Conference Proceedings, First National Women's Studies Conference, Montreal, June 1 and 2, 1980*. Ed. S. E. Stewart. Montreal: Simone de Beauvoir Institute, 1980, pp. 95–102.

——— . "Emergence of a Culture in the Feminine: Sense and Nonsense." *Broadside: A Feminist Review* [Toronto], June 1982, p. 8.

——— . "Feminist Criticism as Creative Process." In *In the Feminine: Women and Words/Les Femmes et les mots: Conference Proceedings 1983*. Ed. Ann Dybikowski, Victoria Freeman, Daphne Marlatt, Barbara Pulling, and Betsy Warland. Edmonton: Longspoon, 1985, pp. 87–94.

Forsyth, Louise H., et Alain Goldschläger. "Femmes, nomination et pouvoir." *Resources for Feminist Research/Documentation sur la recherche féministe*, [Women and Language/Les Femmes et le langage], 13, no 3 (Nov./nov 1984), 27–29.

Fournier, Danielle. "Album double où les plages au rayon laser." *MOEBIUS*, no 22 (été 1984), pp. 9–22.

Franz, Advena. "A New Writing of Body." *HERizons: The Manitoba Women's News Magazine*, Aug. 1982, pp. 40–41.

Fraticelli, Rina. "The Invisibility Factor: Status of Women in Canadian Theatre." *Fuse: The Cultural News Magazine* [Toronto], Sept. 1982, pp. 112–24.

Frémont, Gabrielle. "Casse-texte." *études littéraires* [Univ. Laval], [Féminaire], 12 (déc. 1979), 315–30.

Frost, Wendy, and Michèle Valiquette. "Feminist Literary Criticism: The Cutting Edge of Our Vision." *The Radical Reviewer*, No. 5 (Winter 1981–82), p. 4–5.

Gagnon, Madeleine. "Ce que je veux s'écrire ne peut pas m'écrire autrement." *Les Nouvelles littéraires* [Paris], 26 mai 1976, p. 19.

——— . "Des mots plein la bouche." *la barre du jour*, nos 56–57 (mai–août 1977), pp. 139–47. Rpt. trans. Josée M. LeBlond ("Mouth Full of Words") in *Room of One's Own*, [Québécoises], 4, Nos. 1–2 (1978), 92–97.

——— . "dire ces femmes d'où je viens." *Magazine littéraire*, no 134 (mars 1978), pp. 94–96.

——— . "d'une nef à l'autre." *Chroniques*, no 16 (avril 1976), pp. 30–37.

——— . "Ecriture, sorcellerie, féminité." *études littéraires* [Univ. Laval], [Féminaire], 12 (déc. 1979), 357–61.

——— . "Elle est objet du sujet elle, ou l'histoire de l'Autre." *Le Devoir* [Montréal], 10 mai 1975, p. 19.

——— . "Elle m'a parlé de son sang . . . ." *Sorcières*, no 14 (sept. 1978), pp. 19–20.

——— . "La femme et le langage: sa fonction comme parole en son manque." *la barre du jour*, no 50 (hiver 1975), pp. 45–57.

——— . "La Femme et l'écriture: Actes de la Rencontre." *Liberté*, [Actes de la Rencontre Québécoise internationale des écrivains], 18, nos 4–5 [nos 106–107] (juil.–oct. 1976), 249–56.

——— . "Mon corps dans l'écriture: Corps I–Corps IV." Dans *La Venue à l'écriture*. Par Hélène Cixous, Madeleine Gagnon, et Annie Leclerc. Dirigée par Catherine B. Clément. Serie "féminin futur." Paris:

Union Générale, 1977, pp. 63–116. Rpt. trans. Isabelle de Courtivron (excerpt — ["Mon corps dans l'écriture: Corps 1"]) in *New French Feminisms*. Ed. Elaine Marks and Isabelle de Courtivron. Amherst, Mass.: Univ. of Massachusetts Press, 1980, pp. 179–80. Rpt. trans. Wendy Johnston (excerpt — "My Body in Writing") in *Feminism in Canada*. Ed. Angela Miles and Geraldine Finn. Montreal: Black Rose, 1982, pp. 269–82.

——— . "Pour les femmes et tous les autres." Dans *Souverain Québec*. Ed. Collectif Change (Michèle Lalonde, Gaston Miron, Hubert Aquin, Pierre Vadeboncoeur, André Beaudet, Nicole Bedard, et Jean Pierre Faye.) Change, nos 30–31. Paris: Seghers Laffont, 1977, pp. 136–39.

——— . "Si elle se mettait à parler . . . ." *Chroniques*, no 15 (mars 1976), pp. 33–38.

——— . "Une féminité textuelle? La geste poétique, peut-être dans sa coulée fictive et réflexive." Breaking the Sequence: Women, Literature, and the Future, Wellesley College, Wellesley, Mass. 30 April 1981.

Geirsson, Freya. "Does Sex Make a Difference? Some Propositions on Canadian Novelists." *Emergency Librarian*, 2, No. 1 (Oct. 1974), 5–8.

Godard, Barbara. "Epi(pro)logue: In Pursuit of the Long Poem." *Open Letter*, [Long-Liners Conference Issue], Ser. 6, Nos. 2–3 (Summer–Fall 1985), pp. 301–35.

——— . Introduction. In *Gynocritics/Gynocritiques: Feminist Approaches to Canadian and Quebec Women's Writing/Démarches féministes à l'écriture des Canadiennes et Québécoises*. Ed. Barbara Godard. Toronto: ECW, 1987, [English] pp. i–xi; [French] pp. xiii–xxiv.

——— . "Mapmaking: A Survey of Feminist Criticism." In *Gynocritics/Gynocritiques: Femininist Approaches to Canadian and Quebec Women's Writing/Démarches féministes à l'écriture des Canadiennes et Québécoises*. Ed. Barbara Godard. Toronto: ECW, 1987, pp. 1–30.

——— . "Meanderings around *une écriture*: Some Notes towards a Feminist Literary Criticism." Women's Studies Colloquium, York Univ./Univ. of Toronto, Ontario Institute for Studies in Education, Toronto. 21 Nov. 1980.

——— . "Redrawing the Circle." Femme, Simone de Beauvoir Institute, Concordia Univ., Montreal. Aug. 1982. Printed ("Redrawing the Circle: Power, Poetics, Language") in *Canadian Journal of Political and Social Theory* [Concordia Univ.], [Feminism Now], 9, Nos. 1–2 (hiver–printemps 1985), 165–81. Rpt. in *Feminism Now*. Ed. Marilouise Kroker, Arthur Kroker, Pamela McCallum, and Maïr Verthuy. Montreal: New World Perspectives/CJPST, 1985, pp. 165–81. Rpt. (abridged — "Redrawing the Circle") in *Femme: Proceedings of the 1982 Conference on Research and Teaching Related to Women*. Montreal: Simone de Beauvoir Institute, Concordia Univ., 1985, pp. 40–42.

——— . "Translating and Sexual Difference." *Resources for Feminist Research/Documentation sur la recherche féministe*, [Women and Language/Les Femmes et le langage], 13, No. 3 (Nov./nov. 1984), 13–15.

——— . "The Translator as She: The Relationship Between Writer and Translator." In *In the Feminine: Women and Words/Les Femmes et les mots: Conference Proceedings 1983*. Ed. Ann Dybikowski, Victoria Freeman, Daphne Marlatt, Barbara Pulling, and Betsy Warland. Edmonton: Longspoon, 1985, pp. 193–98.

——— . "Writing and Difference: Women Writers of Québec and English-Canada." In *In the Feminine: Women and Words/Les Femmes et les mots: Conference Proceedings 1983*. Ed. Ann Dybikowski, Victoria Freeman, Daphne Marlatt, Barbara Pulling, and Betsy Warland. Edmonton: Longspoon, 1985, pp. 122–26. Rpt. ("The Language of Difference") in *The Canadian Forum*, June–July 1985, pp. 44–46.

Godard, Barbara, Daphne Marlatt, Kathy Mezei, and Gail Scott. "SP/ELLE: Spelling Out the Reasons." *Tessera*, No. 1 [*Room of One's Own*, 8, No. 4] (1983), 4–18.

Goldschläger, Alain. Voir/see Forsyth, Louise H., et Alain Goldschläger.

Gould, Karen. "'Our Bodies in Writing': Quebec Women Writers on the Physicality of the Text." *Degré Second*, No. 4 (July 1983), pp. 133–50.

———. "Setting Words Free: Feminist Writing in Quebec." *Signs: Journal of Women in Culture and Society*, 6 (Summer 1981), 617–42.

———. "Spatial Poetics, Spatial Politics: Quebec Feminists on the City and the Countryside." *American Review of Canadian Studies*, 12, No. 1 (Spring 1982), 1–9.

Green, Mary Jean. "Structures of Liberation: Female Experience and Autobiographical Form in Quebec." *Yale French Studies*, No. 65 (1983), pp. 124–36.

Haggerty, Joan. "A Maze." In *In the Feminine: Women and Words/Les Femmes et les mots: Conference Proceedings 1983*. Ed. Ann Dybikowski, Victoria Freeman, Daphne Marlatt, Barbara Pulling, and Betsy Warland. Edmonton: Longspoon, 1983, pp. 81–83.

Houde, Christiane. "Essai critique au féminin." *la nouvelle barre du jour*, no 74 (jan. 1979), pp. 52–63.

Hutcheon, Linda. "Postmodernism, Poststructuralism and Feminism." *Canadian Women's Studies/les cahiers de la femme* [Centennial College], [Women's Studies/Conference: Les Etudes de la femme/Colloque], 6, No. 3 (Summer–Fall 1985), 36–39.

Jiles, Paulette. "Hustling at the New Poetics Colloquium." *Brick* [Toronto], No. 27 (Spring 1986), pp. 45–50.

———. "In Search of the Picara: Notes for Women's Literary Liberation." *This Magazine*, Dec. 1985, pp. 31–35.

Kamboureli, Smaro. "Dialogue with the Other: The Use of Myth in Canadian Women's Poetry." In *In the Feminine: Women and Words/Les Femmes et les mots: Conference Proceedings 1983*. Ed. Ann Dybikowski, Victoria Freeman, Daphne Marlatt, Barbara Pulling, and Betsy Warland. Edmonton: Longspoon, 1985, pp. 105–09.

Kanne, K. O. "When Is Art Subversive? When Does Politics Subvert Art?". In *In the Feminine: Women and Words/Les Femmes et les mots: Conference Proceedings 1983*. Ed. Ann Dybikowski, Victoria Freeman, Daphne Marlatt, Barbara Pulling, and Betsy Warland. Edmonton: Longspoon, 1985, pp. 46–49.

Kostash, Myrna. "Ethnicity and Feminism." In *In the Feminine: Women and Words/Les Femmes et les mots: Conference Proceedings 1983*. Ed. Ann Dybikowski, Victoria Freeman, Daphne Marlatt, Barbara Pulling, and Betsy Warland. Edmonton: Longspoon, 1985, pp. 60–62.

———. "Women's Culture: Myth or Reality." CRIAW Conference, Halifax, N.S. 13 Nov. 1981.

La Graf. "La jazzette ou le parler des negresses blanches d'Amérique." *Sorcières*, [La Jasette], no 14 (sept. 1978), pp. 4–6.

La Grenade, Carole. "On Governing categories. Négation du LANGAGE et femmes et Théories." *MOEBIUS*, no 22 (été 1984), pp. 57–72.

Lalonde, Michèle. "Prose intervenante: Parcours théorique: Anatomie du féminisme." Dans sa *Défense et illustration de la langue québécoise*. Paris: Seghers Laffont, 1979, pp. 212–39.

Lamothe, Jacqueline. Réponse à "Comment naître femme sans le devenir" de Louky Bersianik. *la nouvelle barre du jour*, [Forum des femmes], no 172 (mars 1986), pp. 67–70.

Lamy, Suzanne. "L'autre lecture." *Québec français*, no 47 (oct. 1982), pp. 34–35.

———. "Écritures de femmes et modernité ou Des enfants uniques, nés de père et de mère inconnus." Dialogue, York Univ., Downsview, Ont. 17 Oct./oct. 1981. Emprunté ("Des enfants uniques nés de père et de mère inconnus") dans *Gynocritics/Gynocritiques: Feminist Approaches to Canadian and Quebec Women's Writing/Démarches féministes à l'écriture des Canadiennes et Québécoises*. Ed. Barbara Godard. Toronto: ECW, 1987, pp. 199–210.

———. "Petite cantate à l'honnête voleuse."

la nouvelle barre du jour, [Forum des femmes], no 172 (mars 1986), pp. 85–89.

———. "Voyage autour d'une écriture." *Revue de l'Université d'Ottawa/University of Ottawa Quarterly*, [Conférence des femmes-écrivains en Amérique], 50 (jan.–mars/Jan.–March 1980), 34–38.

Lapointe, Jeanne. "La femme comme non-sujet dans les sciences dites humaines." Parlons-en/Talking Together, Simone de Beauvoir Institute, Concordia Univ., Montréal. 1–2 juin 1980. Emprunté dans *Parlons-en/Talking Together: Conference Proceedings, First National Women's Studies Conference, Montreal, June 1 and 2, 1980*. Ed. S. E. Stewart. Montreal: Simone de Beauvoir Institute, 1980, pp. 113–20. Rpt. trans. ("Woman as a Non-Subject in the So-Called Humanities") in *Parlons-en/Talking Together: Conference Proceedings, First National Women's Studies Conference, Montreal, June 1 and 2, 1980*. Ed. S. E. Stewart. Montreal: Simone de Beauvoir Institute, 1980, pp. 121–31.

LaRue, Monique. "Celles qui parlent." *Spirale*, no 9 (mai 1980), p. 7.

———. "Du discours de domination." *études littéraires* [Univ. Laval], [Féminaire], 12 (déc. 1979), 351–55.

Laurin, Danielle, et Élise Turcotte. "Fragments de mémoire." *MOEBIUS*, no 22 (été 1984), pp. 23–30.

Lebowitz, Andrea. "The Danger of Creating Another Literati." In *In the Feminine: Women and Words/Les Femmes et les mots: Conference Proceedings 1983*. Ed. Ann Dybikowski, Victoria Freeman, Daphne Marlatt, Barbara Pulling, and Betsy Warland. Edmonton: Longspoon, 1985, pp. 127–30.

———. "Hindsight Is 20/20: The Development, Achievements and Dilemmas of Feminist Criticism." In *Knowledge Reconsidered: A Feminist Overview/Le savoir en question: Vue d'ensemble féministe*. By Ursula Martins Franklin, Michèle Jean, Dorothy E. Smith, Susan Sherwin, Meg Luxton, and Sylvia Van Kirk. Ottawa: CRIAW/ICRAF, 1984, pp. 25–41.

———. "Is Feminist Literary Criticism Becoming Anti-Feminist?". *Tessera*, No. 1 [*Room of One's Own*, 8, No. 4] (1983), 97–108.

Lequin, Lucie. "Les Femmes québécoises ont inventé leurs paroles." *The American Review of Canadian Studies*, 9, no 2 (Autumn 1979), 113–24.

———. "La jasette dé-rangeante." *Des luttes et des rires de femmes*, 2, no 2 (déc.–jan. 1978–79), 64–66.

Lévesque, M.-Andrée. "L'Hystérie: écriture d'un ventre fantasmique." *la barre du jour*, nos 56–57 (mai–août 1977), pp. 174–95.

Lévesque, Michèle. Voir/see Un collectif de femmes.

Lister, Rota. "Some Principles of Feminist Criticism." CRIAW Conference, Halifax, N.S. Nov. 1976.

Livesay, Dorothy. "The Woman Writer and the Idea of Progress." *The Canadian Forum*, Nov. 1982, pp. 18–19, 35.

———. "Women Writers and Society." *Atlantis: A Women's Studies Journal/Journal d'Études sur la Femme* [Acadia Univ.], 4, No. 1 (Fall/automne 1978), 144–45.

Maertens, Jean-Thierry. "Ecrire le corps?". *études littéraires* [Univ. Laval], [Féminaire], 12 (déc. 1979), 339–50.

Major, Henriette. "Sexist Stereotypes in Children's Literature." In *In the Feminine: Women and Words/Les Femmes et les mots: Conference Proceedings 1983*. Ed. Ann Dybikowski, Victoria Freeman, Daphne Marlatt, Barbara Pulling, and Betsy Warland. Edmonton: Longspoon, 1985, pp. 143–50.

Marlatt, Daphne. Contributor. "Panel on The Woman Writer and Feminist Criticism/Table Ronde sur L'écrivaine et la critique féministe." Dialogue, York Univ., Downsview, Ont. 17 Oct./oct. 1981. Printed ("Musing with Mothertongue") in *Tessera*, No. 1 [*Room of One's Own*, 8, No. 4] (1983), 53–56. Rpt. ("musing with mothertongue") in *In the Feminine: Women and Words/Les Femmes et les mots:*

Conference Proceedings 1983. Ed. Ann Dybikowski, Victoria Freeman, Daphne Marlatt, Barbara Pulling, and Betsy Warland. Edmonton: Longspoon, 1985, pp. 171–74. Rpt. ("Musing with Mothertongue") in *Gynocritics/Gynocritiques: Feminist Approaches to Canadian and Quebec Women's Writing/Démarches féministes à l'écriture des Canadiennes et Québécoises*. Ed. Barbara Godard. Toronto: ECW, 1987, pp. 223–26.

———. See also/voir aussi Godard, Barbara, Daphne Marlatt, Kathy Mezei, and Gail Scott.

Mezei, Kathy. "Reading as Writing/Writing as Reading: the reader and the decline of the writer/the rise and fall of the slash." *Tessera*, [L'Écriture comme lecture], No. 2 [*la nouvelle barre du jour*, No. 157] (sept. 1985), pp. 22–25. Repris trad. Christine Dufresne ("La lecture comme écriture/L'écriture comme lecture: le lecteur et le déclin de l'auteur ou grandeur et décadence du trait oblique") dans *Tessera*, [L'Écriture comme lecteur], no 2 [*la nouvelle barre du jour*, no 157] (sept. 1985), pp. 26–30.

———. See also/voir aussi Godard, Barbara, Daphne Marlatt, Kathy Mezei, and Gail Scott.

Moisan, Lise. "Nicole Brossard et Adrienne Rich: conscience lesbienne et littérature." *La vie en rose*, sept. 1981, pp. 50–51.

Mouré, Erin. "I'll Start Out by Talking." *Poetry Canada Review*, 7, No. 2 (Winter 1985–86), 12–13, 16.

Namjoshi, Suniti. "Snow White and Rose Green or Some Notes on Sexism, Racism, and the Craft of Writing." *Canadian Women's Studies/les cahiers de la femme* [Centennial College], [Multiculture], 4, No. 2 (Winter 1982), 11–15.

Nelson, Sharon H. "Bemused, Branded and Belittled: Women and Writing in Canada." *Fireweed: A Feminist Quarterly*, [Feminist Aesthetics], No. 15 (Winter 1982), pp. 65–102.

———. "Canadian Women Writers: Some Issues and Problems." *The Radical Reviewer*, No. 6 (Spring 1982), pp. 1–2.

———. "Part Two: Canadian Women Writers: Biological Determinism as Literary Criticism." *The Radical Reviewer: A Feminist Journal of Creative & Critical Work*, Nos. 7–8 (1982), pp. 15–16.

———. "The Sexual Politics of Poetry." *League of Canadian Poets — Newsletter*, No. 32, (July–Aug. 1981), pp. 15–32.

———. "Women and Writing in Canada: A Report of Research Findings." Applebaum-Hébert Commission. Ottawa: Status of Women, 1982. 71 pp.

Neuman, Shirley. "Women, Words, and the Literary Canon." In *In the Feminine: Women and Words/Les Femmes et les mots: Conference Proceedings 1983*. Ed. Ann Dybikowski, Victoria Freeman, Daphne Marlatt, Barbara Pulling, and Betsy Warland. Edmonton: Longspoon, 1985, pp. 136–42.

Notar, Clea. "The Omnipresent Language of the Patriarchy and the Boys of the Avant Garde." *Hejira* [McGill Faculty of Nursing], 3, No. 2 (Spring 1986), 29–32.

Ouellette-Michalska, Madeleine. "La critique féminine ou la sortie du discours d'exclusion." Dialogue, York Univ., Downsview, Ont. 16 Oct./oct. 1981. Emprunté ("La critique littéraire, ou l'écriture de la transparence") dans *Gynocritics/Gynocritiques: Feminist Approaches to Canadian and Quebec Women's Writing/Démarches féministes à l'écriture des Canadiennes et Québécoises*. Ed. Barbara Godard. Toronto: ECW, 1987, pp. 41–49.

———. "Mythe et idéologie: de l'être de chair à l'être de parole." *Dérives*, [Idéologie, structuralisme & féminisme], no 27 (1981), pp. 3–21.

———. "Questions Pending." Trans. S. E. Stewart. In *In the Feminine: Women and Words/Les Femmes et les mots: Conference Proceedings 1983*. Ed. Ann Dybikowski, Victoria Freeman, Daphne Marlatt, Barbara Pulling, and Betsy Warland. Edmonton: Longspoon, 1985, pp. 27–31.

Ouvrard, Hélène. "La Femme et l'écriture: Actes de la Rencontre." *Liberté*, [Actes de la Rencontre Québécoise internationale des écrivains], 18, nos 4–5 [nos 106–107] (juil.–oct. 1976), 287–92.

Paradis, Suzanne. "La Femme et l'écriture: Actes de la Rencontre." *Liberté*, [Actes de la Rencontre Québécoise internationale des écrivains], 18, nos 4–5 [nos 106–107] juil.–oct. 1976), 183–89.

Patterson, Janet. "Consuming Passion." *Fireweed: A Feminist Quarterly*, [Popular Culture], No. 11 (1981), pp. 19–33.

Pedneault, Hélène. "La marquée." *Dérives*, [l'image, périphérie: le saguenay autrement], nos 24–25 (1980), pp. 61–63.

Pelletier, Francine. "L'art versus le féminisme (ou mon cul entre deux chaises)." *Trac Femmes*, déc. 1978, pp. 57–72.

———. Réponse à "Spaces Like Stairs" de Gail Scott. *la nouvelle barre du jour*, [Forum des femmes], no 172 (mars 1986), pp. 37–40.

Pelletier, Pol. "Myth and Women's Theatre." In *In the Feminine: Women and Words/ Les Femmes et les mots: Conference Proceedings 1983*. Ed. Ann Dybikowski, Victoria Freeman, Daphne Marlatt, Barbara Pulling, and Betsy Warland. Edmonton: Longspoon, 1985, pp. 110–13.

Roberge, Nicole. "Dans ce couloir, se creuse un chemin, l'institution." MOEBIUS, no 22 (été 1984), pp. 33–38.

Rooke, Constance. "Feminist Literary Criticism: A Brief Polemic." *Room of One's Own*, 2, No. 4 (1977), 40–43.

Rossov, Nanci. "Infiltrating the Mainstream: ACTRA Women's Caucus." In *In the Feminine: Women and Words/Les Femmes et les mots: Conference Proceedings 1983*. Ed. Ann Dybikowski, Victoria Freeman, Daphne Marlatt, Barbara Pulling, and Betsy Warland. Edmonton: Longspoon, 1985, pp. 224–26.

Rule, Jane. "The Practice of Writing." *Canadian Women's Studies/les cahiers de la femme* [Centennial College], 1, No. 3 (Spring/printemps 1979), 34–35.

Saillant, Francine. "Du poétique au féminin." *Dérives*, [Nationalismes et productions culturelles], nos 14–15 (1978), pp. 31–52.

———. "Un corps de l'autre . . . ." *études littéraires* [Univ. Laval], [Féminaire], 12 (déc. 1979), 331–37.

Sand, Cy-Thea. "The Feminist Art of Reading." *The Radical Reviewer*, No. 3 (Spring 1981), pp. 1, 10.

Savard, Andrée. Voir/see Un collectif de femmes.

Scheier, Libby. "Motherhood Is Not the End of Everything." In *In the Feminine: Women and Words/Les Femmes et les mots: Conference Proceedings 1983*. Ed. Ann Dybikowski, Victoria Freeman, Daphne Marlatt, Barbara Pulling, and Betsy Warland. Edmonton: Longspoon, 1985, pp. 75–77.

Scott, Gail. "Finding Her Voice." *The Canadian Forum*, June–July 1985, pp. 39–41, 44.

———. "Red Tin & White Tulle." *Tessera*, No. 1 [*Room of One's Own*, 8, No. 4] (1983), 123–29.

———. "Shaping a Vehicle for Her Use: Women and the Short Story." In *In the Feminine: Women and Words/Les Femmes et les mots: Conference Proceedings 1983*. Ed. Ann Dybikowski, Victoria Freeman, Daphne Marlatt, Barbara Pulling, and Betsy Warland. Edmonton: Longspoon, 1985, pp. 184–91.

———. "Spaces Like Stairs." *la nouvelle barre du jour*, [Forum des femmes], no 172 (mars 1986), pp. 25–30. Repris trad. Susanne de Lotbinière-Harwood ("Des espaces en escalier") *la nouvelle barre du jour*, [Forum des femmes], no 172 (mars 1986), pp. 31–36.

———. See also/voir aussi Godard, Barbara, Daphne Marlatt, Kathy Mezei, and Gail Scott.

Silvera, Makeda. "How Far Have We Come?". In *In the Feminine: Women and Words/Les Femmes et les mots: Conference Proceedings 1983*. Ed. Ann Dybikowski, Victoria Freeman, Daphne Marlatt, Barbara Pulling, and Betsy Warland. Edmonton: Longspoon, 1985, pp. 68–72.

Smart, Carolyn, and Pier Giorgio di Cicco. "Forum — On Craft: Carolyn Smart/Pier Giorgio di Cicco: Poetry and Feminism." *Poetry Canada Review*, 3, No. 3 (Spring

1982), p. 5.

Smyth, Donna E. "Feminist Aesthetics: Criticism as Process." Dialogue, York Univ., Downsview, Ont. 16 Oct./oct. 1981. Printed ("Dialogue: Self and Severed Head") in *Gynocritics/Gynocritiques: Feminist Approaches to Canadian and Quebec Women's Writing/Démarches féministes à l'écriture des Canadiennes et Québécoises*. Ed. Barbara Godard. Toronto: ECW, 1987, pp. 31–39.

———. "Violence against the Feminine: Using Our Anger." In *In the Feminine: Women and Words/Les Femmes et les mots: Conference Proceedings 1983*. Ed. Ann Dybikowski, Victoria Freeman, Daphne Marlatt, Barbara Pulling, and Betsy Warland. Edmonton: Longspoon, 1985, pp. 40–41.

Sun, Midnight. Editorial. *Fireweed: A Feminist Quarterly*, [Native Women], No. 22 (Winter 1986), pp. 6–7.

Théoret, France. "Au retour de refoulé, la fiction." *Chroniques*, 1, nos 6–7 (juin–juil. 1975), 109–12.

———. "La Femme et l'écriture: Actes de la Rencontre." *Liberté*, [Actes de la Rencontre Québécoise internationale des écrivains], 18, nos 4–5 [nos 106–107] (juil.–oct. 1976), 122–25.

———. "Pour une lecture critique des textes de femmes." *la nouvelle barre du jour*, no 66 (mai 1978), pp. 76–79.

———. "Prendre la parole quand on est femme." *Canadian Women's Studies/les cahiers de la femme* [Centennial College], [Belles lettres], 5, no 1 (Fall/automne 1983), 61–62.

———. "Territories of Criticism." Trans. Patricia Kealy. In *In the Feminine: Women and Words/Les Femmes et les mots: Conference Proceedings 1983*. Ed. Ann Dybikowski, Victoria Freeman, Daphne Marlatt, Barbara Pulling, and Betsy Warland. Edmonton: Longspoon, 1985, pp. 95–98.

———. "La Turbulence intèrieure." *la nouvelle barre du jour*, [Forum des femmes], no 172 (mars 1986), pp. 73–78.

Trofimenkoff, Susan Mann. "Nationalism, Feminism and Canadian Intellectual History." *Canadian Literature*, [Intellectual History], No. 83 (Winter 1979), pp. 7–20.

Turcotte, Élise. Voir/see Laurin, Danielle, et Élise Turcotte.

Valiquette, Michèle. See/voir Frost, Wendy, and Michèle Valiquette.

van Herk, Aritha. "Desire in Fiction: De-Siring Realism." *Dandelion*, 8, No. 2 (Fall–Winter 1981–82), 32–38.

Verduyn, Christl. "L'Ecriture féminine contemporaine: écriture de la folie." APFUCC, Univ. Dalhousie. 22–25 mai 1981. Emprunté dans *Signum*, [Numéro Special], [Actes 24ᵉ Congrès Annuel de l'APFUCC, Univ. Dalhousie, 22–25 mai], 2, Pt. III (mai 1981), 419–44. Repris ("L'écriture féminine contemporaine: une écriture de la folie?") das *Gynocritics/Gynocritiques: Feminist Approaches to Canadian and Quebec Women's Writing/Démarches féministes à l'écriture des Canadiennes et Québécoises*. Ed. Barbara Godard. Toronto: ECW, 1987, pp. 71–75.

———. "Les femmes et le langage." *Resources for Feminist Research/Documentation sur la recherche féministe*, [Women and Language/Les Femmes et le langage], 13, no 3 (Nov./nov. 1984), 16–17.

Verthuy, Maïr. "Discours féminin, discours subversif." MLA Conference, New York. Dec. 1976.

———. "Etudes de la femme." *Québec français*, no 47 (oct. 1982), p. 47.

———. "Langue et féminité." MLA Conference, Chicago. Dec. 1977.

———. "Y a-t-il une spécificité de l'écriture au féminin?". *Canadian Women's Studies/les cahiers de la femme* [Centennial College], 1, no 1 (automne/Fall 1978), 73–77.

Villemaire, Yolande. "Savez-vous parler en langue inventée?". *Tessera*, no 1 [*Room of One's Own*, 8, no 4] (1983), 41–43. Rpt. trans. Gail Scott ("Can You Speak the Language of Invention?") in *Tessera*, No. 1 [*Room of One's Own*, 8, No. 4] (1983), 44–46.

Voldeng, Evelyne. "L'intertextualité dans les écrits féminine d'inspiration féministe."

Dialogue, York Univ., Downsview, Ont. 17 Oct./oct. 1981. Emprunté dans *voix & images: littérature québécoise,* 7 (printemps 1982), 523–30. Repris dans *Gynocritics/Gynocritiques: Feminist Approaches to Canadian and Quebec Women's Writing/Démarches féministes à l'écriture des Canadiennes et Québécoises.* Ed. Barbara Godard. Toronto: ECW, 1987, pp. 51–58.

———. "Translata/Translatus." *Tessera,* no 1 [*Room of One's Own,* 8, no 4] (1983), 82–90. Rpt. trans. Frances Morgan in *Tessera,* No. 1 [*Room of One's Own,* 8, No. 4] (1983), 91–96.

Waddington, Miriam. "Women Writers Are More Innovative in Use of Language and Form." *The Globe and Mail* [Toronto]. "At the Mermaid Inn," 6 Jan. 1979, p. 6.

Warland, Betsy. "Emergence of a Culture in the Feminine: Presence and Absence." *Broadside: A Feminist Review* [Toronto], June 1982, p. 9.

———. "surrendering the english language: the lesbian writer as liberator." In *In the Feminine: Women and Words/Les Femmes et les mots: Conference Proceedings 1983.* Ed. Ann Dybikowski, Victoria Freeman, Daphne Marlatt, Barbara Pulling, and Betsy Warland. Edmonton: Longspoon, 1985, pp. 175–79.

Webb, Phyllis. "The Muse Figure." In *In the Feminine: Women and Words/Les Femmes et les mots: Conference Proceedings 1983.* Ed. Ann Dybikowski, Victoria Freeman, Daphne Marlatt, Barbara Pulling, and Betsy Warland. Edmonton: Longspoon, 1985, pp. 114–16.

Weir, Lorraine. "'Wholeness, Harmony, Radiance' and Women's Writing." *Tessera,* No. 1 [*Room of One's Own,* 8, No. 4] (1983), 19–24. Rpt. in *In the Feminine: Women and Words/Les Femmes et les mots: Conference Proceedings 1983.* Ed. Ann Dybikowski, Victoria Freeman, Daphne Marlatt, Barbara Pulling, and Betsy Warland. Edmonton: Longspoon, 1985, pp. 131–35.

———. "Women Reading." Dialogue, York Univ., Downsview, Ont. 16 Oct./oct.

1981. Printed ("Toward a Feminist Hermeneutics: Jay Macpherson's *Welcoming Disaster*") in *Gynocritics/Gynocritiques: Feminist Approaches to Canadian and Quebec Women's Writing/Démarches féministes à l'écriture des Canadiennes et Québécoises.* Ed. Barbara Godard. Toronto: ECW, 1987, pp. 59–70.

Wilson, Ann. "The Politics of the Script." *Canadian Theatre Review,* [Feminism: Canadian Theatre], No. 43 (Summer 1985), pp. 174–79.

Theses and Dissertations/Thèses

Dupré, Louise. "La nouvelle écriture québécoise au féminin: formes et significations." Thèse de doctorat Montréal 1984.

Galloway, Priscilla. "Sexism and the Senior English Curriculum in Ottawa Secondary Schools." Diss. Toronto 1977, esp. pp. 20–31.

Lanctôt, Mireille. "Questionnement sur l'écriture féminine." Mémoire de maîtrise Québec à Montréal 1977.

Ouellette-Michalska, Madeleine. "Le féminin comme lieu d'inscription scripturale." Mémoire de maîtrise Québec à Montréal 1977.

Reviews/Comptes rendus

Forsyth, Louise. Rev. of *Tessera,* No. 1 [*Room of One's Own,* 8, No. 4] (1983). *Resources for Feminist Research/Documentations sur la recherche féministe,* [Review Issue/Comptes rendus], 14, No. 2 (July/juil. 1985), 16–17.

Godard, Barbara. Rev. of *Possibles,* [Des femmes et des luttes], 4, no 1 (automne 1979); and *études littéraires,* [Féminaire], 12, no 3 (déc. 1979). *Resources for Feminist Research/Documentation sur la recherche féministe,* [Reviews Issue/Comptes rendus], 9, No. 3 (Nov./nov. 1980), 39–40.

Klein, Carroll. "Perpetual Emotion." Rev. of *The Ivory Swing,* by Janette Turner Hospital. *Broadside: A Feminist Review* [Toronto], May 1984, p. 13.

General Studies of Several Writers/ Vue globale de plusieures auteures (Books/Livres, Articles and Sections of Books/Articles et sections de livres, Theses and Dissertations/ Thèses, and/et Reviews/Comptes rendus)

Books/Livres

Allaire, Émilia B. *Profils féminins (trente figures de proue canadiennes).* Préface Jean-Charles Bonenfant. Introd. Émilia B. Allaire. Québec: Garneau, 1967. 9–10, 13–14, 284 pp.

———. *Têtes de femmes: essais biographiques.* Québec: L'Équinoxe, 1963. 239 pp.

Bellerive, Georges. *Brèves apologies de nos auteurs féminins.* Québec: Garneau, 1920. 137 pp.

Boynard-Frot, Janine. *Un matriarcat en procès: analyse systématique de romans canadiens-français 1860–1960.* Montréal: Les Presses de l'Univ. de Montréal, 1982. 231 pp.

Brown, Audrey Alexandra. "Poetry and Life." Canadian Authors' Association, Vancouver. 24 Aug. 1941. Printed in *Poetry and Life.* Toronto: Privately printed [Macmillan], 1941. 12 pp.

Conrad, Margaret. *Recording Angels: The Private Chronicles of Women from the Maritime Provinces of Canada, 1750–1950.* Ottawa: CRIAW/ICRAF, 1982. 36 pp.

Ducrocq-Poirier, Madeleine. *Les Femmes québécoises depuis 1960.* Paris: A. G. Nizet, 1978. 908 pp.

Fairbanks, Carol. *Prairie Women: Images in American and Canadian Fiction.* New Haven: Yale Univ. Press, 1986. 300 pp.

Fairbanks, Carol, and Sara Brooks Sunderg. *Farm Women on the Prairie Frontier: A Sourcebook for Canada and the United States.* Methuen, N.J.: Scarecrow, 1983.
237 pp.

Fowler, Marian. *The Embroidered Tent: Five Gentlewomen in Canada.* Toronto: House of Anansi, 1982. 239 pp.

Griffiths, N. E. S. *Penelope's Web: Some Perceptions of Women in European and Canadian Society.* Toronto: Oxford Univ. Press, 1976. 249 pp.

Hansen, Kéro. *Au fond des yeux: 25 québécoises qui écrivent.* Illus. Kéro Hansen. Montréal: Nouvelle Optique, 1981. 109 pp.

Hill, Barbara Rigney. *Lilith's Daughters: Women and Religion in Contemporary Fiction.* Madison, Wisc.: Univ. of Wisconsin Press, 1982. 120 pp.

Hughes, Terrance. *Gabrielle Roy et Margaret Laurence: deux chemins, une recherche.* Saint Boniface: Blé, 1983. 191 pp.

Irvine, Lorna. *Sub/version.* Toronto: ECW, 1986. 193 pp.

Lamy, Suzanne, et Irène Pagès, eds. *Féminité, subversion, écriture.* Montréal: Remue-ménage, 1983. 205 pp.
Voyez les inscriptions individuelles sous les titres suivants/see the individual entries under the following headings: Théorie littéraire féministe/Feminist Literary Theory (Carolyn *Bayard* et/and Barbara *Godard*); Vue globale de plusieures auteures: Articles/General Studies of Several Writers: Articles (Louise H. *Forsyth*); Ecrivaines individuelles/Individual Writers: Louky Bersianik (Evelyne *Voldeng*), France Théoret (Suzanne *Lamy*), Yolande Villemaire (Suzanne *Lamy*); et/and Journalistes/Journalists (Julia *Bettinotti*).

Lewis, Paula Gilbert, ed. *Traditionalism, Nationalism and Feminism: Women Writers of Quebec.* Westport, Conn.: Greenwood, 1984. 280 pp.
See the individual entries under the following headings/voir les inscriptions individuelles sous les titres suivants: General Studies of Several Writers: Articles/Vue globale de plusieurs auteurs: Articles (Micheline *Herz*, Paula Gilbert *Lewis*, Elaine *Marks*, Jane *Moss*, and/et Marthe

Rosenfeld); Individual Writers/Ecrivaines individuelles: Felicité Anger (François *Gallays*), Louky Bersianik (Maroussia *Hadjukowski-Ahmed*), Marie-Claire Blais (Mary Jean *Green*), Nicole Brossard (Louise *Forsyth*), Madeleine Gagnon (Karen *Gould*), Germaine Guèvremont (James J. *Herlan*), Anne Hébert (Susan L. *Rosenstreich* and/et Murray *Sacks*), Rina Lasnier (James P. *Gilroy*), Françoise Loranger (Carrol F. *Coates*), Louise Maheux-Forcier (Maurice *Cagnon*), Antonine Maillet (Marjorie A. *Fitzpatrick*), and/et Gabrielle Roy (Paula Gilbert *Lewis*).

Marchessault, Jovette. *La Saga des poules mouillées*. Montréal: Pleine lune, 1981. 178 pp. Rpt. trans. Linda Gaboriau (*Saga of the Wet Hens*). Vancouver: Talonbooks, 1983. 134 pp.

McClung, Molly G. *Women in Canadian Literature*. Gen. ed. Jean Cochrane and Pat Kincaid. Women in Canadian Life. Toronto: Fitzhenry and Whiteside, 1977. 96 pp.

Mercier, Lucie. *La femme dans la légende québécoise*. Québec: Centre d'étude sur la langue, les arts et les traditions, Univ. Laval, 1980. 48 pp.

Pagès, Irène. Voir/see Lamy, Suzanne, et Irène Pagès, eds.

Paradis, Suzanne. *Femme fictive, femme réelle: le personnage féminin dans le roman féminin canadien-français 1884–1966*. Québec: Garneau, 1966. 330 pp. Repris (extrait) dans *Le Soleil* [Québec], 22 oct. 1966, p. 7.

Sainte-Marie-Eleuthère, Soeur, C.N.D. *La mère dans le roman canadien-français contemporain, 1930–1960*. Montréal: Univ. de Montréal, 1961. 220 pp.

Sundberg, Sara Brooks. See/voir Fairbanks, Carol, and Sara Brooks Sundberg.

Waelti-Walters, Jennifer. *Fairy Tales and the Female Imagination*. Montreal: Eden, 1982. 161 pp.

Zaremba, Eve. *Privilege of Sex: A Century of Canadian Women*. Toronto: House of Anansi, 1974. 173 pp.

Articles and Sections of Books/ Articles et sections de livres

Andersen, Margret. "Autobiographie et Invention." Parlons-en/Talking Together, Simone de Beauvoir Institute, Concordia Univ., Montréal. 1980. Emprunté dans *Parlons-en/Talking Together: Conference Proceedings, First National Women's Studies Conference, Montreal, 1 and 2 June, 1980*. Ed. S.E. Stewart. Montréal: Simone de Beauvoir Institute, 1980, pp. 40–51.

———. "Innovatrice et conservatrice: Deux aspects de l'écriture canadienne au féminin." Canadian Research Institute for the Advancement of Women/Institut canadien de recherche pour l'avancement des femmes, Halifax, N.S. Nov. 1981. Emprunté dans *The CRIAW Papers/Les documents de l'ICRAF*, [Women's Culture: Selected Papers from the Halifax Conference/La Femme et la culture: recueil de textes choisis et présentés à la conférence à Halifax], no 3 (nov. 1982), pp. 12–21.

Anderson, D. "Women in Fiction, Where Are You?". *Chatelaine*, Sept. 1971, p. 1.

Aponiuk, Natalia. "Images of Ukrainian Women in Canadian Literature." Canadian Research Institute for the Advancement of Women/Institut canadien de recherche pour l'avancement des femmes, Halifax, N.S. Nov. 1981.

Arnapoulos, Sheila. "Women Writers Are Not Much in Evidence at Conference." *The Montreal Star*, 28 June 1967, p. 56.

Arnason, David. Editorial. *Journal of Canadian Fiction*, 4, No. 3 (1965), 6–8.

Atwood, Margaret. "The Curse of Eve — Or What I Learned in School." In *Women on Women*. Ed. Ann B. Shteir. Gerstein Lecture Series 1975–76. Toronto: York Univ., 1978, pp. 13–26. Rpt. in *Canadian Women's Studies/les cahiers de la femme* [Centennial College], 1, No. 3 (Spring/ printemps 1979), 30–33.

———. "Ice Women vs. Earth Mothers: The Stone Angel and the Absent Venus." In her *Survival: A Thematic Guide to Canadian Literature*. Toronto: House of

Anansi, 1972, pp. 195–212.

———. "Paradoxes and Dilemmas: The Women as Writer." In *Women in the Canadian Mosaic*. Ed. Gwen Matheson. Toronto: Peter Martin, 1976, pp. 257–73. Rpt. in *Woman as Writer*. Ed. Jeanette L. Webber and Joan Grunman. Boston: Houghton Mifflin, 1978, pp. 177–87.

Banting, Pamela. "Women and Words, 1983." *Prairie Fire*, 5, Nos. 2–3 (Spring 1984), 101–04.

Barbour, Sharon. "Applications." *The Dinosaur Review*, No. 7 (Fall 1985), pp. 56–58.

Barrette, Michèle. "dire aux éclats." *Jeu: cahiers de théâtre*, [Théâtre-femmes], no 16 (1980), pp. 79–94.

Barry, Mlle [Françoise]. "French Canadian Women in Literature." In *Women of Canada: Their Life and Work*. Ed. National Council of Women. 1900; rpt. Montréal: National Council of Women of Canada, 1975, pp. 190–97.

Basile, Jean. Voir/see Chéné, Yolande, Jean Basile, Gilles Marcotte et Gérard Bessette.

Batcher, Elaine. "Language and the New Woman." *Resources for Feminist Research/Documentation sur la recherche féministe*, [Women and Language/Les Femmes et le langage], 13, No. 3 (Nov./nov. 1984), 49–51.

Baum, Rosalie Murphy. "Artist and Woman: Young Lives in Laurence and Munro." *NDQ: North Dakota Quarterly* [Univ. of North Dakota], 52, No. 3 (Summer 1984), 196–211.

Bayard, Caroline. "The Ottawa Conference: A Setback for Feminism." *Canadian Women's Studies/les cahiers de la femme* [Centennial College], 1, No. 1 (automne/Fall 1978), 86–87.

Beaulne, Martine. Voir/see Chapdelaine-Desperrier, Hélène, et Martine Beaulne.

Belkin, Roslyn. "Changing Conventions in Fiction Written by Women." *Canadian Newsletter of Research on Women/Recherches sur la femme — Bulletin d'Information Canadien*, 7, No. 2 (July 1978), 18–20.

Belleau, Janick. "Les femmes et les mots." *HERizons: The Manitoba Women's News Magazine*, Aug. 1983, pp. 39–40.

Bersianik, Louky [Lucile Durand]. "Le monde de l'édition: Accoucheur ou marchand d'esclaves?". *Le Devoir* [Montréal], 21 nov. 1981, Supp. littéraire, pp. xvii, xix.

Bessai, Diane. "Fiddlehead Women Poets." *Branching Out: Canadian Magazine for Women*, 1, No. 1 [sic; 1, No. 4] (Aug. 1974), 36–38.

———. "A Survey Report: Women, Feminism and Prairie Theatre." *Canadian Theatre Review*, [Feminism: Canadian Theatre], No. 43 (Summer 1985), pp. 28–43.

Bessette, Gérard. Voir/see Chéné, Yolande, Jean Basile, Gilles Marcotte et Gérard Bessette.

Black, Florence Deacon. "The Library Table." *The Canadian Magazine of Politics, Science, Art and Literature* [Toronto], Nov. 1924, pp. 78–81.

Boivin, Aurélien. "Des proses et des femmes au Québec des origines à 1970." *Québec français*, no 47 (oct. 1982), pp. 22–25.

Bosco, Monique. "La femme de l'écriture." *Liberté*, [Actes de la Rencontre Québécoise internationale des écrivains], 18, nos 4–5 [nos 106–107] (juil.–oct. 1976), pp. 74–80.

Boucher, Yvon. "Femme et écriture: une problématique rose bonbonne?". Rev. of *Liberté*, [Actes de la Rencontre Québécoise internationale des écrivains], 18, nos 4–5 [nos 106–107] (juil.–oct. 1976). *Le Devoir* [Montréal], 13 nov. 1976, pp. 19–20.

Boynard-Frot, Janine. "L'émergence d'une production littéraire féminine, 1925–1935." Dans *A l'ombre de Desrochers: L'effervescence culturelle d'une region: le mouvement littéraire des cantons de l'est 1925–1950*. Par Joseph Bonenfant, Janine Boynard-Frot, Richard Giguère et Antoine Sirois. Sherbrooke: La Tribune et Les Presses de l'Univ. de Sherbrooke, 1985, pp. 107–17.

———. "Une lecture féministe des romans du terroir canadien-français de 1860 à

1960." *Possibles*, [Des femmes et des luttes], 4, no 1 (automne 1979), 41–53.

———. Voir aussi/see also Frot, Janine; et/and Frot-Boynard, Janine.

Bradshaw, Leah. "Portraits in Women's Literature." *Queen's Quarterly*, 87 (Autumn 1980), 458–64.

Brady, Elizabeth. "Towards a Happier History: Women and Domination." In *Domination*. Ed. Alkis Kontos. Toronto: Univ. Leage for Social Reform, Univ. of Toronto Press, 1975, pp. 17–31.

———. "Voices from the Periphery: First-Generation Lesbian Fiction in Canada." *Resources for Feminist Research/Documentation sur la recherche féministe*, [The Lesbian Issue/Être Lesbienne], 12, No. 1 (March/mars 1983), 22–26.

Brodie, Allan Douglas. "Canadian Short Story Writers." *The Canadian Magazine of Politics, Science, Art and Literature* [Toronto], Feb. 1895, pp. 332–38, 341–42.

Buchanan, Roberta. "Newfoundland: Outport Reminders." *Canadian Theatre Review*, [Feminism: Canadian Theatre], No. 43 (Summer 1985), pp. 111–18.

C. [William Wilfred Campbell.] *The Globe* [Toronto]. "At the Mermaid Inn," 22 Oct. 1892, p. 8. Rpt. in *At the Mermaid Inn*. Ed. Barrie Davies. Toronto: Univ. of Toronto Press, 1979, p. 177.

Camerlain, Lorraine. "En/de multiples scènes." *Canadian Theatre Review*, [Feminism: Canadian Theatre], No. 43 (Summer 1985), pp. 73–90.

Camerlain, Lorraine, et Carole Fréchette. "Le théâtre expérimentale des femmes: essai en trois mouvements." *Jeu: cahiers de théâtre*, no 36 (1985), pp. 59–66.

Campbell, Mary L. "Verse Writers." In *Women of Canada: Their Life and Work*. Ed. National Council of Women. 1900; rpt. Montreal: National Council of Women of Canada, 1975, pp. 185–89.

Chapdelaine-Desperrier, Hélène, et Martine Beaulne. "unir le féminin et le masculin, vivre enfin au pluriel." *Jeu: cahiers de théâtre*, [Théâtre-femmes], no 16 (1980), pp. 188–90.

Charasson, Henriette. "La femme dans la vie littéraire." *Le Devoir* [Montréal], 13 déc. 1937, p. 5.

Charlesworth, Hector W. "The Canadian Girl: An Appreciative Medley." *The Canadian Magazine of Politics, Science, Art and Literature* [Toronto], May 1893, pp. 186–93.

Chauvin, Solange. "La femme: sujet littéraire choyé en 64." *Le Devoir* [Montréal], 8 avril 1965, Supp. littéraire, p. 42.

Chéné, Yolande, Jean Basile, Gilles Marcotte et Gérard Bessette. "Les grands thèmes du roman canadien: la femme." *Liberté*, 7, no 6 [no 42] (nov. 1965), 536–39.

Claube, Annette. "Newfoundland: Downtown View." *Canadian Theatre Review*, [Feminism: Canadian Theatre], No. 43 (Summer 1985), pp. 119–26.

Cloutier, Cécile. "L'homme dans les romans écrits par des femmes." *Incidences* [Univ. d'Ottawa], no 5 (avril 1964), pp. 9–12.

Collet, Paulette. "Les romancières québécoises des années 60 face à la maternité." *Atlantis: A Women's Studies Journal/Journal d'études sur la femme* [Acadia Univ.], 5, no 2 (Spring/printemps 1980), 131–41.

Collin, Solange. "An Alternative to the Traditional Theatre in Québec." In *In the Feminine: Women and Words/Les Femmes et les mots: Conference Proceedings 1983*. Ed. Ann Dybikowski, Victoria Freeman, Daphne Marlatt, Barbara Pulling, and Betsy Warland. Edmonton: Longspoon, 1985, pp. 219–23.

Corbeil, Carol. "Six Women Asked for a Work of Passion." *The Globe and Mail* [Toronto], 13 Jan. 1986, p. C12.

Cotnoir, Diane. "la l.n.i., comme dans la 'vraie' vie." *Jeu: cahiers de théâtre*, [Théâtre-femmes], no 16 (1980), pp. 15–22.

Cotnoir, Louise. "A portée de voix." *Arcade*, [femmes d'écritures], no 8 (oct. 1984), pp. 44–47.

———. "Contribution des femmes-écrivains du continent américain à la littérature." *Revue de l'Université d'Ottawa/University of Ottawa Quarterly*, [Conférence des femmes-écrivains en Amérique], 50 (jan.–mars/Jan.–March 1980), 30–33.

Couillard, Marie. "Écrire et vivre au Québec des femmes: Impression et expression d'une culture." *NDQ: North Dakota Quarterly* [Univ. of North Dakota], 52, No. 3 (Summer 1984), 87–99.

——— . "La femme-écrivain canadienne-française et québécoise face aux idéologies de son temps." *Canadian Ethnic Studies/études ethnique au Canada,* 13, no 1 (1981), 43–51.

——— . "La femme et le sacré dans le roman québécoise contemporain." Dans *La femme et la réligion au Canada français: Un fait socioculturel; perspectives et prospectives.* Ed. Elisabeth Lacelle. Montréal: Bellarmin, 1979, p. 232.

——— . "*Rue Deschambault* de Gabrielle Roy et *Lives of Girls and Women* d'Alice Munro." ACQL/ALCQ, Univ. de Guelph, Guelph, Ont. 5 juin 1984.

——— . "La voie/voix a/venir." Dialogue, York Univ., Downsview, Ont. 17 Oct./oct. 1981. Emprunté [écrit par Marie Couillard et Francine Dumouchel] ("Symphonie féministe") dans *Gynocritics/ Gynocritiques: Feminist Approaches to Canadian and Quebec Women's Writing/ Démarches féministes à l'écriture des Canadiennes et Québécoises.* Ed. Barbara Godard. Toronto: ECW, 1987, pp. 77–83.

——— . Voir aussi/see also Couillard-Goodenough Marie.

Couillard-Goodenough, Marie. "La Femme et le sacré dans quelques romans québécois contemporains." *Revue de l'Université d'Ottawa/University of Ottawa Quarterly,* [Conférence des femmes-écrivains en Amérique], 50 (jan.–mars/ Jan.–March 1980), 74–81.

——— . Voir aussi/see also Couillard, Marie.

Cowan, Cindy. "Nova Scotia and New Brunswick: Messages in the Wilderness." *Canadian Theatre Review* [York Univ.], [Feminism: Canadian Theatre], No. 43 (Summer 1985), pp. 100–10.

Creighton, Ellen. "Women and Words: Phallocentric Language and Silence." *Resources for Feminist Research/Docu-mentation sur la recherche féministe,* [Women and Language/Les Femmes et le langage], 13, No. 3 (Nov./nov. 1984), 44–45.

Crosland, Margaret. *Beyond the Lighthouse: English Women Novelists in the Twentieth Century.* London: Constable, 1981, pp. 81, 94, 137–41, 164.

Dandurand, Anne. "mon long chemin." *Jeu: cahiers de théâtre,* [Théâtre-femmes], no 16 (1980), pp. 184–85.

Dandurand, Mme [Vieuxtemps, Marie]. "Celles qui écrivent." *Le Coin de feu,* avril 1893, pp. 105–07.

——— . "Les clubs littéraires." *Le Coin du feu,* mai 1894, pp. 132–34.

"Dans la vie de sept femmes que d'heures passées à écrire." *Métro express* [Montréal], 6 avril 1966, p. 18.

"Dans nos roman féminins: la femme par elle-même?". *L'Action* [Québec], 30 déc. 1966, p. 10.

D'Auteuil, Georges-Henri. "Visages de femmes." *Relations,* avril 1976, pp. 124–25.

Davidson, Cathy N. "Canadian Wry: Comic Vision in Atwood's *Lady Oracle* and Laurence's *The Diviners.*" *Regionalism and the Female Imagination* [Pennsylvania State Univ.], 3, Nos. 2–3 (Autumn–Winter 1977–78), 50–55.

——— . "A Literature of Survivors: On Teaching Canada's Women Writers." *Women's Studies Newsletter,* 6, No. 3 (Fall 1978), 12–15.

——— . Foreword. *Journal of Popular Culture,* [Canadian Women Writers], 15, No. 3 (Winter 1981), 1–3.

Davies, Gwendolyn. "Belles and the Backwoods: A Study of Fiction in Nineteenth-Century Maritime Periodicals." In *Atlantic Provinces Literature Colloquium Papers.* Marco Polo Papers 1. Ed. Kenneth MacKinnon. Saint John: Atlantic Institute, 1977, pp. 40–55.

——— . "Nineteenth Century Women Writers." Dialogue, York Univ., Downsview, Ont. 16 Oct./oct. 1981. Printed ("'Dearer Than His Dog': Literary Women in Pre-Confederation Nova Scotia") in *Gyno-*

critics/Gynocritiques: Feminist Approaches to Canadian and Quebec Women's Writing/Démarches féministes à l'écriture des Canadiennes et Québécoises. Ed. Barbara Godard. Toronto: ECW, 1987, pp. 111–29.

Dé, Claire, et Renée Noiseux. "avant de passer à l'annonymat." *Jeu: cahiers de théâtre*, [Théâtre-femmes], no 16 (1980), pp. 200–02.

de Santana, Hubert. "Wonder Women." *Today Magazine,* 13 Dec. 1980, pp. 14, 16.

Delbaere-Garant, Jeanne. "Decolonizing the Self in *Surfacing, Bear* and *A Fringe of Leaves.*" In *Colonisations.* Ed. Xavier Pons and Marcienne Rocard. Traveaux de l'Université de Toulouse-Le Mirail. Série B, Tome 07. Toulouse: Univ. de Toulouse-Le Mirail, 1985, 67–78.

Delisle, Jeanne-Mance. "as-tu lu jean-paul sartre?". *Jeu: cahiers de théâtre*, [Théâtre-femmes], no 16 (1980), pp. 202–04.

Demers, Anne-Marie. "La Conférence des femmes écrivains du continent américain." *Canadian Women's Studies/les cahiers de la femme* [Centennial College], 1, no 1 (automne/Fall 1978), 84–86.

Demers, France. "Vos femmes écrivains sont plus évoluées que leurs confrères." *La Patrie* [Montréal], 8 oct. 1967, p. 55.

Deslongchamps, Ginette. "Le rôle de la femme dans les téléromans." *Relations*, juil.–août 1973, pp. 203–05.

Dewar, Elaine. "Femcanlit." *City Woman,* March–April 1979, pp. 44–48, 50.

———. "Thoroughly Modern Orphans." *City Woman*, [The Modern Woman in Canadian Fiction], Spring 1982, pp. 23–32.

Downes, Gladys V. "Women Poets in Quebec Society." *The Malahat Review* [Univ. of Victoria], No. 63 (Oct. 1982), pp. 100–10.

Ducrocq-Poirier, Madeleine. "Les romancières québécoises contemporaines et la condition féminine." *L'Esprit créateur,* 23, no 3 (Fall 1983), 40–47.

Dumais, Monique. "Les femmes et la religion dans les écrits de langue française." *Atlantis: A Women's Studies Journal/ Journal d'Études sur la Femme* [Acadia Univ.], 4, no 2 (Spring/printemps 1979), 152–62.

Dumouchel, Francine. Voir/see Couillard, Marie. "La voix/voix a/venir."

Dupré, Louise. "L'écriture féminine dans *Les Herbes rouges.*" *Revue de l'Université d'Ottawa/University of Ottawa Quarterly,* [Conférence des femmes-écrivains en Amérique], 50 (jan.–mars/Jan.–March 1980), 89–94.

———. "Questions de maîtrise." *Arcade*, [femmes d'écritures], no 8 (oct. 1984), pp. 48–51.

Eichler, Margaret. "Sociology of Feminist Research in Canada." *Signs: Journal of Women in Culture and Society,* 3 (Winter 1977), 413–14.

Emerson, Mary. "Women Writers." *The Canadian Magazine of Politics, Science, Art and Literature* [Toronto], Feb. 1905, pp. 379–80.

Engel, Marian. "The Woman as Storyteller." *Communiqué,* [Women in Arts in Canada], No. 8 (May/mai 1975), pp. 6–7, 44–45.

Fairbanks, Carol. "Lives of Girls and Women on the Canadian and American Prairies." *International Journal of Women's Studies,* 2 (Sept.–Oct. 1979), 452–72.

"La Femme dans le théâtre canadien." Editoriale. *Canadian Drama/L'Art dramatique canadien* [Univ. de Waterloo], 5 (Fall/automne 1979), 80–81.

Fidelis [Agnes Machar]. "The New Ideal of Womanhood." *Rose Belford's Canadian Monthly and National Review*, June 1879, pp. 650–76.

Fitzgibbon, Agnes. "English Speaking Prose Writers of Canada." In *Women of Canada: Their Life and Work.* Ed. National Council of Women. 1900; rpt. Montreal: National Council of Women of Canada, 1975, pp. 178–84.

Forsyth, Louise H. "L'écriture au féminin: *L'Euguélionne* de Louky Bersianik, *l'Absent aigu* de Geneviève Amyot, *l'Amèr* de Nicole Brossard." *Journal of Canadian Fiction*, [Les romanciers Québécois et leurs oeuvres], nos 25–26 (1979),

pp. 199–211.

———. "First Person Feminine Singular: Monologues by Women in Several Modern Quebec Plays." *Canadian Drama/ L'Art dramatique canadien* [Univ. of Waterloo], 5 (Fall/automne 1979), 189–203.

———. "The Mother-Daughter Relationship in Recent Quebec Literature." Conference of National Women's Studies Association, Indiana. May 1980.

———. "Les Numéros spéciaux de *La (Nouvelle) Barre du jour*: Lieux communs, lieux en recherche, lieu de rencontre." Dans *Féminité, subversion, écriture*. Ed. Suzanne Lamy et Irène Pagès. Montréal: Remue-ménage, 1983, pp. 175–84.

———. "The Radical Transformation of the Mother-Daughter Relationship in Some Women Writers of Quebec." *Frontiers: A Journal of Women's Studies* [Univ. of Colorado], 6, Nos. 1–2 (Spring–Summer 1981), 44–49.

Fournier, Danielle. "Laissons un peu de féminin dans le sujet." *Arcade*, [femmes d'écritures], no 8 (oct. 1984), pp. 52–55.

Fraticelli, Rina. "'Any Black Crippled Woman Can!' or A feminist's notes from outside the sheltered workshop." *Room of One's Own*, 8, No. 2 (1983), 7–18.

Fréchette, Carol. Voir/see Camerlain, Lorraine, et Carole Fréchette.

Frémont, Gabrielle. "Le féminisme de la *NBJ*: un second souffle." *voix & images: littérature québécoise*, 10, no 2 (hiver 1985), 133–37.

———. "Traces d'elles: essai de filiation." Dialogue, York Univ., Downsview, Ont. 16 Oct./oct. 1981. Emprunté dans *Gynocritics/Gynocritiques: Feminist Approaches to Canadian and Quebec Women's Writing/Démarches féministes à l'écriture des Canadiennes et Québécoises*. Ed. Barbara Godard. Toronto: ECW, 1987, pp. 85–95.

French, William. "The Women in Our Literary Life." *Imperial Oil Review*, No. 1 (1975), pp. 2–7. Rpt. in *Canadian Author & Bookman*, 51, No. 3 (Spring 1976), 1–6.

Frot, Janine. "La Femme et le nationalisme dans le roman du terroir de l'entre-deux-guerres." *voix et images: études québécoises*, 3 (sept. 1977), 54–70.

———. Voir aussi/see also Boynard-Frot, Janine; et/and Frot-Boynard, Janine.

Frot-Boynard, Janine. "Les écrivaines dans l'histoire littéraires québécoise." *voix et images: études québécoises*, 7 (automne 1981), 147–68. Repris dans *A l'ombre de Desrochers: L'effervescence culturelle d'une region: le mouvement littéraire des cantons de l'est 1925–1950*. Par Joseph Bonenfant, Janine Boynard-Frot, Richard Giguère et Antoine Sirois. Sherbrooke: La Tribune et Les Presses de l'Univ. de Sherbrooke, 1985, pp. 119–48.

———. Voir aussi/see also Boynard-Frot, Janine; et/and Frot, Janine.

Frum, Barbara. "Great Dames." *Maclean's*, April 1973, pp. 32–38.

Fulton, E. Margaret. "Out of Our Past: A New Future." *Laurentian University Review/Revue de l'Université Laurentienne*, [The Social and Political Novel in English Canada/Le roman engagé au Canada français], 9, No. 1 (Nov. 1976), 87–102.

Gagnon, Madeleine, et Mireille Lanctôt. "femmes du québéc: un mouvement et des écritures." *Magazine littéraire*, no 134 (mars 1978), pp. 97–99.

Gauvin, Lise. "Les possibles présents des écritures femmes." *Arcade*, [femmes d'écritures], no 8 (oct. 1984), pp. 56–60.

Gayla with Eleanor [Wachtel]. "*Room* Explores Quebec Feminism." *Kinesis*, Dec.–Jan. 1978–79, p. 23.

Gerson, Carole. "Three Writers of Victorian Canada: Rosanna Leprohon, James De Mille, Agnes Maule Machar." In *Canadian Writers and Their Works*. Ed. Robert Lecker, Jack David, and Ellen Quigley. Fiction Series. Vol. 1. Downsview, Ont.: ECW, 1983, 195–256; esp. 195–99, 203–08, 212–50, 251–53, 254–56.

Gerstenberger, Donna. "Conceptions Literary and Otherwise: Women Writers and the Modern Imagination." *Novel: A*

Forum on Fiction, 9, No. 2 (Winter 1976), 141–50.

Giguère, Richard. "La Tentation de l'éros: la libération du discours amoreux et le 'mouvement féminin.'" Dans son *Exil, révolt et dissidence*. Vie des Lettres québécoises, no 23. Québec: Les Presses de l'Univ. Laval, 1984, pp. 127–61.

Gionet, Lise, et Louise Lahaye. "le théâtre pour enfants, une affaire de femmes?". *Jeu: cahiers de théâtre*, [Théâtre-femmes], no 16 (1980), pp. 193–96.

Godard, Barbara. "*La barre du jour*: vers une poétique féministe." Dans *Féminité, subversion, écriture*. Ed. Suzanne Lamy et Irène Pagès. Montréal: Remue-Ménage, 1983, pp. 195–205.

———. "Ex-centriques, Eccentric, Avant-Garde: Women and Modernism in the Literatures of Canada." Conference of Interamerican Women Writers, Mexico. 4 June 1981. Printed in *Tessera*, No. 1 [*Room of One's Own*, 8, No. 4] (1983), 57–75.

———. "My (m)Other, My Self: Strategies for Subversion in Atwood and Hébert." ACQL Learned Societies, Halifax, N.S. 23 May 1980. Printed in *Essays on Canadian Writing*, No. 26 (Summer 1983), pp. 13–44.

———. "A Portrait with Three Faces: The New Woman in Fiction by Canadian Women, 1880–1920." *The Literary Criterion* [Mysore, India], [Special Canadian Issue], 19, Nos. 3–4, Pt. 1 (July–Oct. 1984), 72–92.

———. "Talking about Ourselves: The Literary Productions of Native Women." CRIAW Conference, Vancouver. Nov. 1983. Printed (*Talking about Ourselves: The Literary Productions of Native Women*). CRIAW, No. 1. Ottawa: CRIAW, 1985. 44 pp.

———. "Transgressions." *Fireweed: A Feminist Literary & Cultural Journal*, [Women and Language], Nos. 5–6 (Winter–Spring 1979–80), pp. 120–29.

———. "The View from Below: The Female Novel of the Land." Intersections, Lincoln, Neb. 19 March 1982.

———. "The Women Who Did: Women Writers 1890–1920." Canadian Literature Discussion Group. MLA Conference, New York. 28 Dec. 1983.

Gottlieb, Lois. "The Spirit of Canadian Women Playwrights: A Review Essay on Women Writers for Theatre." *Canadian Drama/L'Art dramatique canadien* [Univ. of Waterloo], 5 (Fall/automne 1979), 213–20.

———. See also/voir aussi Gottlieb, Lois C., and Wendy Keitner.

Gottlieb, Lois C., and Wendy Keitner. "Demeter's Daughters, The Mother-Daughter Motif in Fiction by Canadian Women." *Atlantis: A Women's Studies Journal/Journal d'Études sur la Femme* [Acadia Univ.], 3, No. 1 (Fall/automne 1977), 130–42.

———. "Images of Canadian Women in Literature and Society in the 1970's." *International Journal of Women's Studies*, 2 (Nov.–Dec. 1979), 513–27.

———. "Mothers and Daughters in Four Recent Canadian Novels." *The Sphinx: A Magazine of Literature and Society*, 1, No. 4 (Summer 1975), 21–34.

———. "Reflections on Canadian Women's Writing of the 1970's: Preliminary Results of 'An Annotated Bibliography of Canadian Women Writers (in English): A Feasibility Study, 1970–75.'" *Canadian Newsletter of Research on Women/Recherches sur la Femme – Bulletin d'Information Canadien*, 7, No. 2 (July 1978), 21–22.

Gould, Karen. "Female Tracings: Writing as Re-Vision in Recent Works of Louky Bersianik, Madeleine Gagnon, and Nicole Brossard." *The American Review of Canadian Studies*, 13, No. 2 (Summer 1983), 74–89.

———. "Quebec Feminists Look Back: Inventing the Text through History." *Québec Studies*, 1, No. 1 (Spring 1983), 298–306.

———. See also/voir aussi Green, Mary Jane, Paula Gilbert Lewis, and Karen Gould.

Grace, Sherrill. "Quest for the Peaceable Kingdom: Urban/Rural Codes in Roy, Laurence, and Atwood." In *Women*

Writers in the City: Essays in Feminist Literary Criticism. Ed. Susan Merrill Squier. Knoxville, Tenn.: Univ. of Tennessee Press, 1984, pp. 193–209.

Grant, Cynthia. "Tipping the Balance: Is Toronto Theatre a 'club'?". *Toronto Free Press,* 2, No. 2 (Jan. 1986), 2.

Grayson, J. Paul. "Male Hegemony and the English Canadian Novel." *Canadian Review of Sociology and Anthropology,* 20, No. 1 (Feb. 1983), 1–21.

Green, Mary Jean. "Gabrielle Roy and Germaine Guèvremont: Quebec's Daughters Face a Changing World." *Journal of Women's Studies in Literature,* 1 (Summer 1979), 243–57.

Green, Mary Jean, Paula Gilbert Lewis, and Karen Gould. "Inscriptions of the Feminine: A Century of Women Writing in Quebec." *The American Review of Canadian Studies,* 15, No. 4 (Winter 1985), 363–88.

Gros-Louis, Dolores. "Pens and Needles: Daughters and Mothers in Recent Canadian Literature." *Kate Chopin Newsletter* [Pennsylvania State Univ.], 2, No. 3 (1976–77), 8–13.

Guèvremont, Germaine. "Les prix Nobel et les femmes: Mme Germaine Guèvremont à la société d'étude." *Le Devoir* [Montréal], 1 mars 1950, p. 5.

Gwyn, Sandra. "The Literary Arts." In her *Women in the Arts in Canada.* Vol. VII of *Report of the Royal Commission on the Status of Women in Canada.* Ottawa: Gov't. of Canada, Queen's Printer, 1971, pp. 60–96.

——— . "Women in the Arts in Canada." *Communiqué,* [Women in Arts in Canada], No. 8 (May/mai 1975), pp. 3–5, 43–44.

Hale, Amanda. "Afterthoughts on 4-Play." *Broadside: A Feminist Review* [Toronto], Feb. 1986, p. 11.

Halmberg-Schwartz, Debbie. "Giving Birth to Creativity." HERizons: *The Manitoba Women's News Magazine,* Aug. 1983, p. 41.

Hamilton, Roberta. "Sexual Politics." *The Canadian Forum,* Feb. 1980, pp. 27–29.

Harvor, Beth. "The Special World of the ww's Through Female Reality with Alice, Jennifer, Edna, Nadine, Doris, and All Those Other Girls." *Saturday Night,* Aug. 1969, pp. 33–35.

Hauser, Gwen. "The Women's Writing Collective Comes to Town." *Intrinsic,* [Special Women's Issue], No. 1 (Summer 1977), pp. 6–9.

Hébert, Lorraine. "réquisitoires." *Jeu: cahiers de théâtre,* [Théâtre-femmes], no 16 (1980), pp. 57–78.

Hedenstrom, Joanne. "Puzzled Patriarchs and Free Women: Patterns in the Canadian Novel." *Atlantis: A Women's Studies Journal/Journal d'études sur la femme* [Acadia Univ.], 4, No. 1 (Fall/automne 1978), 2–9.

Herz, Micheline. "A Québécois and an Acadian Novel Compared: The Use of Myth in Jovette Marchessault's *Comme une enfant de la terre* and Antonine Maillet's *Pélagie-la-charette.*" In *Traditionalism, Nationalism and Feminism: Women Writers of Quebec.* Ed. Paula Gilbert Lewis. Contributions in Women's Studies, No. 53. Westport, Conn.: Greenwood, 1985, pp. 173–83.

Hesse, M. G. Introduction. In *Women in Canadian Literature.* Ed. M. G. Hesse. Ottawa: Borealis, 1976, pp. xi–xv.

Hollingsworth, Margaret. "Why We Don't Write." *Canadian Theatre Review,* [Feminism: Canadian Theatre], No. 43 (Summer 1985), pp. 21–27.

Howells, Coral Ann. "Some International Perspectives on Canadian Women's Fiction: Margaret Laurence: *The Diviners* and Audrey Thomas: *Latakia.*" *Canadian Women's Studies/les cahiers de la femme* [Centennial College], [International], 6, No. 1 (Fall 1984), 98–100.

Irvine, Lorna. Foreword. *The American Review of Canadian Studies,* 15, No. 4 (Winter 1985), i–ii.

——— . "Hostility and Reconciliation: The Mother in English Canadian Fiction." *The American Review of Canadian Studies,* 8, No. 1 (Spring 1978), 56–64.

——— . "A Psychological Journey: Mothers

and Daughters in English-Canadian Fiction." In *The Lost Tradition: Mothers and Daughters in Literature*. Ed. Cathy N. Davidson and E. M. Broner. New York: Frederick Ungar, 1980, pp. 242–51.

———. "Surfacing, Surviving, Surpassing: Canada's Women Writers." *Journal of Popular Culture*, 15, No. 3 (Winter 1981), 70–79.

Jackel, Susan. "The House on the Prairies." *Canadian Literature*, [The Living Mosaic], No. 42 (Autumn 1969), pp. 46–55. Rpt. in *Writers of the Prairies*. Ed. Donald Stephens. Vancouver: Univ. of British Columbia Press, 1973, pp. 165–74.

———. "Self Portraits." Dialogue, York Univ., Downsview, Ont. 16 Oct./oct. 1981. Printed ("Canadian Women's Autobiography: A Problem in Criticism") in *Gynocritics/Gynocritiques: Feminist Approaches to Canadian and Quebec Women's Writing/Démarches féministes à l'écriture des Canadiennes et Québécoises*. Ed. Barbara Godard. Toronto: ECW, 1987, pp. 97–110.

Jensen, Maggie. "Between Dinner, Dishes and Diapers: A Woman Writer's Plight." *Room of One's Own*, 2, Nos. 2–3 (1976), 66–79.

Keitner, Wendy. "All Eve's Inquire: Marian Engel and Audrey Thomas." Canadian Literature Discussion Group, MLA Conference, New York. 28 Dec. 1983.

———. "Canadian Women Poets and the Syndrome of the Female Man: A Note on the Poetry of Audrey Alexandra Brown and Anne Wilkinson." *Tessera*, No. 1 [*Room of One's Own*, 8, No. 4] (1983), 76–81.

———. "Mother Tongue? A Study of Language and Personae in Contemporary Poetry by Canadian Women." Commonwealth in Canada Conference, Univ. of Manitoba, Winnipeg, Man. Oct. 1981.

———. "Real Mothers Don't Write Books: The Penelope-Calypso Motif in the Fiction of Audrey Thomas and Marian Engel." MLA Conference, New York. 27 Dec. 1984. Printed ("Real Mothers Don't Write Books: A Study of the Penelope-Calypso Motif in the Fiction of Audrey Thomas and Marian Engel") in *Present Tense: A Critical Anthology*. Vol. IV of *The Canadian Novel*. Ed. John Moss. Toronto: NC, 1985, pp. 185–204.

———. See also/voir aussi Gottlieb, Lois C., and Wendy Keitner.

King, Adele. "Images of Women, Children and Family Life in some French Canadian and New Zealand Novels Written by Women." *Australian Canadian Studies* [Australian Association of Canadian Studies], 2 (1984), 64–69.

Kostash, Myrna. "Rating the Chauvinists on a Richler Scale." *Maclean's*, Jan. 1974, p. 75.

Kröller, Eva-Marie. "La Lampe dans la fenêtre: The Visualization of Quebec Fiction." *Canadian Literature*, [Contemporary Quebec Fiction], No. 88 (Spring 1981), pp. 74–82.

———. "Resurrections: Susanna Moodie, Catherine Parr Traill and Emily Carr in Contemporary Canadian Literature." *Journal of Popular Culture*, 15, No. 3 (Winter 1981), 39–46.

Kushner, Joanne. "Raising Profiles." *Quill & Quire*, May 1976, p. 29.

Laberge, Marie. "Ecrire pour le théâtre." *Études littéraires*, 18, no 3 (hiver 1985), 213–22.

Labrèche, Julianne. "Bad News for Good Books: Mrs. Grundy Rides Again." *Maclean's*, 2 Oct. 1978, pp. 52b–52c.

Lafon, Dominique. "L'image de la femme dans le théâtre québécois." *Revue de l'Université d'Ottawa/University of Ottawa Quarterly*, [Conférences des femmes-écrivains en Amérique], 50 (jan.–mars/Jan.–March 1980), 148–52.

Lahaye, Louise. Voir/see Gionet, Lise, et Louise Lahaye.

Lamy, Suzanne. "Des parcours irréversibles: Littérature québécoise et féminisme." *Le Devoir* [Montréal], 5 nov. 1983, Cahier special: Salon du livre de Montréal, p. xiii.

———. "L'émergence du féminin: la lumière diffuse et la subversion sourde." *Le Devoir* [Montréal], 21 nov. 1981, Supp.

littéraire, p. xiii.

———. "Pas de souvenirs justes, juste des souvenirs." Conference of Interamerican Women Writers, Mexico City. 3 June 1981.

Lancôt, Mireille. Voir/see Gagnon, Madeleine, et Mireille Lanctôt.

Landry, Kenneth. Voir/see Boivin, Aurelien, et Kenneth Landry.

Langer, Beryl Donaldson. "Women and Literary Production: Canada and Australia." *Australian Canadian Studies* [Australian Association of Canadian Studies], 2 (1984), 70–83.

Lapointe, Monique. "alors que les femmes entre elles . . . ." *Jeu: cahiers de théâtre*, [Théâtre-femmes], no 16 (1980), p. 185.

Lautredoux, Florence. "Littérature féminine, littérature féministe dans le québec contemporain. Ruptures et continuité." *Études Canadiennes/Canadian Studies* [Univ. de Bordeaux III], no 18 (juin/June 1984), pp. 45–50.

Lejeune, Claire. "Lettre aux Québécoises." *Dérives*, no 12 (1978), pp. 5–16.

Lemieux, Denise. "Les femmes, la forêt et le Nord en littérature québécoise: un exemple de rédéfinition des modèles feminine." Canadian Research Institute for the Advancement of Women/Institut canadien de recherche pour l'avancement des femmes, Montréal. Nov. 1984. Emprunté dans *Femmes: images, modèles/Women: images, role-models: Actes du Colloque 1984/Proceedings of the 1984 Conference*. Ed. Evelyne Tardy. Ottawa: CRIAW/ICRAF, 1985, pp. 99–105.

Le Moyne, Jean. "La Littérature canadienne-française et la femme." Dans son *Convergences*. Montréal: HMH, 1961, pp. 101–08. Rpt. ("Woman and French-Canadian Literature") in his *Convergence: Essays from Quebec*. Trans. Philip Stratford. Toronto: Ryerson, 1966, pp. 91–98.

Lerek, Anita. "Head Way: When I Met the Lady Poets." *Branching Out: Canadian Magazine for Women*, 3, No. 1 (Feb.–March 1976), 44–45.

Lewis, Paula Gilbert. Introduction. In *Traditionalism, Nationalism and Feminism: Women Writers of Quebec*. Ed. Paula Gilbert Lewis. Contributions in Women's Studies, No. 53. Westport, Conn.: Greenwood, 1985, pp. 3–10.

———. "Literary Relationships between Quebec and the United States: A Meagre Reciprocity." *Essays on Canadian Writing*, [Canadian-American Literary Relations], No. 22 (Summer 1981), pp. 86–110; esp. pp. 90–93.

———. See also/voir aussi Green, Mary Jane, Paula Gilbert Lewis, and Karen Gould.

Livesay, Dorothy. Foreword. *Air*, [Woman's Eye], Nos. 19–21 (1974), p. v.

———. "Livesay's Choice." *Canadian Dimension*, [Women: A Special Issue], 10, No. 8 (June 1975), 15–16.

———. "Two Women Novelists of Canada's West." *Review of National Literatures*, 7 (1976), 127–32.

———. "Women as Poets." *Room of One's Own*, 1, No. 1 (Spring 1975), 12–13.

Machar, Agnes. See/voir Fidelis.

MacMillan, Carrie. "Images of Women in English Canadian Literature." *Chautauqua* [Council of Teachers of English of New Brunswick Teachers' Association, Fredericton], 9, No. 2 (April 1980), 9–10.

Magny, Michèle. "de la mise à vie, à la mise au jeu." *Jeu: cahiers de théâtre*, [Théâtre-femmes], no 16 (1980), pp. 177–79.

Makward, Christiane. "Quebec Women Writers." *Women and Literature*, 7, No. 1 (Winter 1979), 3–11.

Manathorne, Jacquie. "Le Colloque sur les périodiques féministes: un succès." *Communiqu'Elles*, 11, no 5 (sept. 1985), 17–18.

Maranda, Jeanne, and Mair Verthuy. "Quebec Feminist Writing." *Emergency Librarian*, [Quebec Feminist Writing], 5, No. 1 (Sept.–Oct. 1977), 2–11. Repris trad. ("Les Ecrits Féministes au Québec") dans *Emergency Librarian*, 5, no 1 (sept.–oct. 1977), 12–20.

Marchak, Patricia. "Given a Certain Latitude: A (Hinterland) Sociologist's View of Anglo-Canadian Literature." In *In Our Own House: Social Perspectives on Canadian Literature*. Ed. Paul Cappon. Toronto: McClelland and Stewart, 1978,

p. 193.

Marchessault, Jovette. "Les Femmes du Québec écrivent encore." *Bulletin de la société des professeurs français en Amérique,* 1978, pp. 25–36.

Marcotte, Gilles. Voir/see Chéné, Yolande, Jean Basile, Gilles Marcotte et Gérard Bessette.

Marigny. "La jeune fille dans la poésie." *La revue moderne,* 9, no 5 (mars 1928), 2.

Marks, Elaine. Foreword. In *Traditionalism, Nationalism and Feminism: Women Writers of Quebec.* Ed. Paula Gilbert Lewis. Contributions in Women's Studies, No. 53. Westport, Conn.: Greenwood, 1985, pp. xi–xii.

Marlatt, Daphne. "Listening In." *Contemporary Verse 2,* 9, No. 2 (Fall 1985), 36–39.

Marlatt, Daphne, Barbara Pulling, Victoria Freeman, and Betsy Warland. "In the Feminine." In *In the Feminine: Women and Words/Les Femmes et les mots: Conference Proceedings 1983.* Ed. Ann Dybikowski, Victoria Freeman, Daphne Marlatt, Barbara Pulling, and Betsy Warland. Edmonton: Longspoon, 1985, pp. 11–17.

Martin, Claire. "L'homme dans le roman canadien-français." *Incidences* [Univ. d'Ottawa], no 5 (avril 1964), pp. 5–8.

Mathews-Klein, Yvonne, and Ann Pearson. "A Stage of Seven Women: Feminist Theatre in Quebec." *Branching Out: Canadian Magazine for Women,* 3, No. 4 (Sept.–Oct. 1976), 17–19.

McCullough, Elizabeth. Introduction. In *The Role of Woman in Canadian Literature.* Ed. Elizabeth McCullough. Themes in Canadian Literature. Toronto: Macmillan, 1975.

McKenna, Isobel. "Women in Canadian Literature." *Canadian Literature,* [Canadians — Conscious or Self-Conscious?], No. 62 (Autumn 1974), pp. 69–78.

McMullen, Lorraine. "The Divided Self." *Atlantis: A Women's Studies Journal/ Journal d'études sur la femme* [Acadia Univ.], 5, No. 2 (Spring/printemps 1980), 52–67.

———. "Ethnicity and Femininity: Double Jeopardy." *Canadian Ethnic Studies/ études ethnique au Canada,* 13, No. 1 (1981), 52–62.

———. "Images of Women in Canadian Literature: The Movement toward Androgyny in Modern Canadian Fiction." *Etudes Canadiennes/Canadian Studies* [Univ. de Bordeaux III], No. 6 (juin 1979), pp. 125–36.

———. "Images of Women in Canadian Literature: Woman as Hero." CRIAW Conference, Halifax, N.S. 1976. Printed in *Atlantis: A Women's Studies Journal/ Journal d'Études sur la Femme* [Acadia Univ.], 2, No. 2, Pt. II (Spring/printemps 1977), 134–42.

———. "She's My Best Friend, My Best Woman Friend, I've Known Her Two Months: Women's Friendship in Canadian Literature." CRIAW Conference, Halifax, N.S. 13–15 Nov. 1981.

———. "Woman Divided." Interamerican Women Writers Conference, Mexico. 3–6 June 1981.

"Les meilleurs poètes féminins." *Châtelaine,* déc. 1972, pp. 21–25.

Mercier, Lucie. "La Représentation du personnage féminin dans la légende québécoise." Canadian Research Institute for the Advancement of Women/Institut canadien de recherche pour l'avancement des femmes, Montréal. Nov. 1984. Emprunté dans *Femmes: images, modèles/Women: images, role-models: Actes du colloque 1984/Proceedings of the 1984 Conference.* Ed. Evelyne Tardy. Ottawa: CRIAW/ICRAF, 1985, pp. 234–39.

Milot, Louise. "Margaret Atwood et Nicole Brossard: la question de la représentation." *voix & images: littérature québécoise,* 11, no 1 (automne 1985), 56–62.

Mitcham, Alison. "Women in Revolt: Anne Hébert's Marie-Claire Blais' and Claire Martin's Nightmare Visions of an Unjust Society." *Alive* [Guelph, Ont.], June 1973, pp. 13–14.

Mitcham, Elizabeth Allison. "The Canadian Matriarch: A Study in Contemporary French and English-Canadian Fiction." *La Revue de l'Université de Moncton,* 7,

No. 1 (jan. 1974), 37–42.

Morley, Patricia. "Engel, Wiseman, Laurence: Women Writers, Women's Lives." *World Literature Written in English* [Univ. of Texas at Arlington], [Women Writers of the Commonwealth], 17 (April 1978), 154–64.

———. "Literature engagé." *Branching Out: Canadian Magazine for Women*, 1, No. 1 (March–April 1974), 30, 43.

———. "No Mean Feat." *Canadian Newsletter of Research on Women/Recherches sur la Femme — Bulletin d'Information Canadien*, 7, No. 2 (July 1978), 26.

Moss, Jane. "Creation Reenacted: The Woman Artist as Dramatic Figure." *The American Review of Canadian Studies*, 15, No. 3 (Autumn 1985), 263–77.

———. "Women's Theatre in Québec: Choruses, Monologues and Dialogues." *Québec Studies*, 1, No. 1 (Spring 1983), 276–85. Rpt. ("Women's Theatre in Quebec") in *Traditionalism, Nationalism and Feminism: Women Writers of Quebec*. Ed. Paula Gilbert Lewis. Contributions in Women's Studies, No. 53. Westport, Conn.: Greenwood, 1985, pp. 241–54.

Moss, John. *Sex and Violence in the Canadian Novel: The Ancestral Present*. Toronto: McClelland and Stewart, 1977, pp. 69–76.

Munk, Linda. "Four Women Poets." *The Globe and Mail* [Toronto], 28 Jan. 1965, Sec. W, p. 1.

Nantel, Louise. "à nous de jouer." *Jeu: cahiers de théâtre*, [Théâtre-femmes], no 16 (1980), pp. 205–06.

Noël, Francine. "plaidoyer pour mon image." *Jeu: cahiers de théâtre*, [Théâtre-femmes], no 16 (1980), pp. 23–56.

Noiseux, Renée. Voir/see Dé, Claire, et Renée Noiseux.

O'Donnell, Kathleen. "Dorothy Livesay and Simone Routier: A Parallel Study." *Humanities Association Bulletin*, 23, No. 4 (Fall 1972), 28–37.

O'Hagan, Thomas. "Canadian Women Writers." In *Canada: An Encyclopedia of the Country*. Ed. J. Castelle Hopkins. Vol. v. Toronto: Linscott, 1899, 171.

———. "Some Canadian Women Writers." *The Catholic World* [Paulist Fathers, Paramus, N.J.], Sept. 1896, pp. 779–95.

"On Women Writers." *The Canadian Author*, 11, No. 1 (Sept. 1933), 9–10.

Orenstein, Gloria Feman. "Onstage in Montreal: Quebecoise Heritage." *Ms.* [New York], Aug. 1981, p. 79.

Ouellette-Michalska, Madeleine. "La femme et l'écriture: Actes de la rencontre." *Liberté*, [Actes de la Rencontre Québécoise internationale des écrivains], 18, nos 4–5 [nos 106–107] (juil.– oct. 1976), 81–92.

———. "Vous avez dit femme, féminine ou féministe?". *Le Devoir* [Montréal], 21 nov. 1981, Supp. littéraire, p. iii.

"Our Women Writers." *The Canadian Magazine of Politics, Science, Art and Literature* [Toronto], Oct. 1905, pp. 583–86.

Ouvrard, Hélène. "La littérature féminine québécoise — une double libération." *Culture française*, no 4 (Winter 1977), 11–24.

Parizeau, Alice. "L'érotisme à la canadienne." *Liberté*, [de l'Erotisme], 9, no 6 [no 54] (nov. 1967), 94–100.

Pascal, Gabrielle. "Problématique de la liberté chez trois écrivains québécoises de 1945 à 1970." Congrès des femmes écrivaines des Amériques, Mexico. 3 juin 1981.

Pearson, Ann. See/voir Mathews-Klein, Yvonne, and Ann Pearson.

Pellerin, Johanne. "autopsie." *Jeu: cahiers de théâtre*, [Théâtre-femmes], no 16 (1980), pp. 186–87.

Pelletier, Francine. "cinq pieces de femmes." *Jeu: cahiers de théâtre*, [Théâtre-femmes], no 16 (1980), pp. 219–24.

Pelletier, Pol. "Petite Histoire . . . ." *Possibles*, [Des femmes et des luttes], 4, no 1 (automne 1979), 175–87.

Piccione, Marie-Lyne. "De Michel Tremblay à Elizabeth Bourget: images de la femme dans le théâtre québécois contemporain." *Études Canadiennes/Canadian Studies* [Univ. de Bordeaux III], no 15 (déc. 1983), pp. 47–52.

Plantos, Ted. "Mothering Poetry: Forging a

Language and a Sensibility." *Cross-Canada Writers' Quarterly,* 8, No. 2 (1986), 2.

Poulin, Gabrielle. "Romans québécois de 1975: Des femmes racontent et se racontent." *Relations,* avril 1976, pp. 125–27.

———. "Romans québécois féminins des années '70: la femme et le pays toujours futurs." *Relations,* déc. 1976, pp. 347–50.

Pratt, Annis. "Affairs with Bears." Dialogue, York Univ., Downsview, Ont. 17 Oct./oct. 1981. Printed ("Affairs with Bears: Some Notes for Feminist Archetypal Hypotheses for Canadian Literature") in *Gynocritics/Gynocritiques: Feminist Approaches to Canadian and Quebec Women's Writing/Démarches féministes à l'écriture des Canadiennes et Québécoises.* Ed. Barbara Godard. Toronto: ECW, 1987, pp. 157–78.

Prégent, Sylvie. "le théâtre au féminin." *Jeu: cahiers de théâtre,* [Théâtre-femmes], no 16 (1980), pp. 206–07.

Proulx, Danielle. "un jeu qui fait mal." *Jeu: cahiers de théâtre,* [Théâtre-femmes], no 16 (1980), pp. 180–83.

Provencher, Anne Marie. "Octobre 78." *Trac Femmes,* déc. 1978, pp. 41–47.

Regan, Nancy. "A Home of One's Own: Women's Bodies in Recent Women's Fiction." *Journal of Popular Culture,* 11 (Spring 1978), 772–88.

Renaud, André. "L'héroïne du roman canadien-français et l'expérience de l'amour." Dans *Le Roman canadien-français.* Tome III de *Archives des lettres canadiennes.* Ed. Paul Wyczynski, Bernard Julien, Jean Menard, et Rejean Robidoux. Montréal: Fides, 1964, pp. 184–96. Repris ("Les personnages féminins dans quelques romans québécois") dans *Le Roman canadien-français.* Tome III de *Archives des lettres canadiennes.* Ed. Paul Wyczynski, Bernard Julien, Jean Menard, et Rejean Robidoux. Rev. ed. Montréal: Fides, 1977, 183–96.

Ricard, François. "Littérature québécoise: romancière." *Liberté,* 18, no 3 [no 105] (mai–juin 1976), 91–99.

Rièse, Laure. "Femmes écrivaines : Le printemps de l'écriture." *L'Express* [Toronto], 8–14 avril 1986, p. 6.

Ringwood, Gwen Pharis. "Women and the Theatrical Tradition." *Atlantis: A Women's Studies Journal/Journal d'Études sur la Femme* [Acadia Univ.], 4, No. 1 (Fall/automne 1978), 154–58.

Ritter, Erika. "The Woman Playwright in English Canada." *Etudes Canadiennes/Canadian Studies* [Univ. de Bordeaux III], No. 15 (déc. 1983), pp. 65–70.

Robert, Francine. "Le Salon du livre de Québec 1965: les auteurs féminins viendront rencontrer leurs lectrices." *Le Soleil* [Québec], 5 nov. 1965, p. 23.

Roberts, Kevin. "Poetry and Politics: The Battle for Peace and Equality at Home and Abroad." *Books in Canada,* Aug.–Sept. 1982, pp. 3–4.

Rogat, Ellen Hawkes. "Form of One's Own." *MOSAIC: A Journal for the Comparative Study of Literature and Ideas* [Univ. of Manitoba], [Literature and Ideas: The Creative Element in Literature and the Arts], 8, No. 1 (Fall 1974), 77–90.

Rosenfeld, Marthe. "The Development of a Lesbian Sensibility in the Work of Jovette Marchessault and Nicole Brossard." In *Traditionalism, Nationalism and Feminism: Women Writers of Quebec.* Ed. Paula Gilbert Lewis. Contributions in Women's Studies, No. 53. Westport, Conn.: Greenwood, 1985, pp. 227–39.

Ross, Catherine Sheldrick. "Calling Back the Ghost of the Old-Time Heroine: Duncan, Montgomery, Atwood, Laurence and Munro." *Studies in Canadian Literature,* 4 (Winter 1979), 43–58.

———. "'A Singing Spirit': Female Rites of Passage in *Klee Wyck, Surfacing* and *The Diviners.*" *Atlantis: A Women's Studies Journal/Journal d'Études sur la Femme* [Acadia Univ.], 4, No. 1 (Fall/automne 1978), 86–94.

Roy, Lise. "Le CEAD a vingt ans: *Les belles soeurs du théâtre.*" *La vie en rose,* mars 1986, p. 40.

———. "histoires d'amour, . . . histoires de théâtre!". *Jeu: cahiers de théâtre,*

[Théâtre-femmes], no 16 (1980), pp. 190–92.

Royer, Jean. "1966: il y a loin de Laure Conan à Marie-Claire Blais." *L'Action* [Québec], 30 déc. 1966, p. 9.

Rubinger, Catherine. "Actualité de deux contes-témoins: *Le torrent* d'Anne Hébert et *Un jardin au bout du monde* de Gabrielle Roy." *Présence francophone: Revue littéraire* [Univ. de Sherbrooke], no 20 (printemps 1980), pp. 121–26.

———. "Some Pioneer Women Writers of French Canada." *Canadian Women's Studies/les cahiers de la femme* [Centennial College], 3, No. 1 (1981), 37–39.

Rule, Jane. "Seventh Wave." *Branching Out: Canadian Magazine for Women*, 6, No. 1 (1979), 16–17.

———. "Sexuality in Literature." *Fireweed: A Feminist Literary & Cultural Journal*, [Women and Language], Nos. 5–6 (Winter–Spring 1979–80), pp. 22–27.

Saddlemyer, Ann. "Circus Feminus: 100 Plays by English-Canadian Women." *Room of One's Own*, 8, No. 2 (1983), 78–91.

Saint-Martin, Fernande. "La femme et l'écriture: Actes de la rencontre." *Liberté*, [Actes de la Rencontre Québécoise internationale des écrivains], 18, nos 4–5 [nos 106–107] (juil.–oct. 1976), 299–304.

St. Pierre, Françoise. "La Femme littéraire." *Le 5316* [Montréal], 1, no 1 (juin 1964), p. 42.

Sainte-Marie-Eleuthère, Soeur. "Mythes et symboles de la mère dans le roman canadien-français." Dans *Le Roman canadien-français*. Tome III de *Archives des lettres canadiennes*. Ed. Paul Wyczynski, Bernard Julien, Jean Ménard, et Réjean Robidoux. Montréal: Fides, 1964, pp. 197–205.

Sand, Cy-Thea. "Reading Working Class." *Kinesis*, Sept. 1985, p. 25.

Scheier, Libby. "Creativity and Motherhood: Having the Baby and the Book." *This Magazine*, Nov. 1984, pp. 9–12.

Shain, Merle. "Some of our Best Poets Are . . . Women." *Chatelaine*, Oct. 1972, pp. 48–50, 103–07.

Sheard, Charlene. "The Women's Writing Collective." *Canadian Women's Studies/les cahiers de la femme* [Centennial College], 1, No. 1 (automne/Fall 1978), 108–09.

Shields, Carol. "Three Canadian Women: Fiction or Autobiography?". *Atlantis: A Women's Studies Journal/Journal d'Études sur la Femme* [Acadia Univ.], 4, No. 1 (Fall/automne 1978), 49–54.

Simon, Sherry. "Feminist Writing in Quebec." *The Canadian Forum*, Aug. 1980, pp. 5–8.

Skelton, Robin. "A Response to 'The Sexual Politics of Poetry.'" *League of Canadian Poetry — Newsletter*, No. 34 (Dec. 1981), pp. 31–33.

Response to Sharon H. Nelson's article in the same journal. See Nelson's article in Feminist Literary Theory/Théorie littéraire féministe.

Smart, Patricia. "Un Cadavre sous les fondations de l'édifice: la violence fait à la femme dans le roman québécois contemporain." Dans *Violence in the Canadian Novel since 1960/dans le roman canadien depuis 1960*. Ed. Virginia Harger-Grinling and Terry Goldie. St. John's: Memorial Univ., 1981, pp. 25–32.

———. "L'Ecriture autre: le féminisme dans la littérature québécoise récent." Nordic Association for Canadian Studies/Association Nordic d'études canadiennes, Univ. of Aarhus, Denmark. 1984. Emprunté dans *Canadiana: Studies in Canadian Literature/Etudes de Littérature Canadienne*. Ed. Jørn Carlsen and Knud Larsen. Aarhus, Den.: Dept. of English, Univ. of Aarhus, 1985, pp. 74–80.

———. "Our Two Cultures." *The Canadian Forum*, Dec. 1984, pp. 14–19; esp. pp. 17, 19.

———. "Voices of Commitment and Discovery: Women Writers in Quebec." *Room of One's Own*, [Québécoises], 4, Nos. 1–2 (1978), 7–18.

Smith, André. "Théâtre au féminin: *Encore 5 minutes*; et *Les Fées ont soif*." *voix & images: littérature québécoise*, 7 (hiver 1982), 351–65.

Smith, Rebecca. "The Only Flying Turtle Under the Sun: The *Bildungsroman* in Contemporary Women's Fiction." *Atlantis: A Women's Studies Journal/Journal d'Études sur la Femme* [Acadia Univ.], 2, No. 2, Pt. II (Spring/printemps 1977), 124–32.

Smyth, Donna. "A Sense of Community: Women's Studies in Canada." *Emergent Literature Act.* Guest ed. James Carley. [*Book Forum* (New York), 4 (1978)], pp. 135–38.

Sonthoff, Helen. "The Stories of Wilson & Engel." *Canadian Literature*, [The Structure of Fiction], No. 86 (Autumn 1980), pp. 148–52.

Stanton, Julie. "L'écriture des femmes, un ghetto?". *La Gazette des femmes*, 2, no 7 (fév. 1981), 6–7.

Strong-Boag, Veronica. "'You be sure to tell it like it is': The Recovery of Canada's Past." *Journal of Canadian Studies/Revue d'études candiennes* [Trent Univ.], 16, Nos. 3–4 (Fall–Winter 1981), 217–21.

Surguy, Phil. "Initiation Writes." *Books in Canada*, April 1978, pp. 7–9.

Swan, Susan. "Why Women Write the Most Interesting Books: The Astonishing Matriarchy in Canadian Letters." *Saturday Night*, Nov. 1978, pp. 21–23.

Thacker, Robert. "'twisting toward insanity': Landscape and Female Entrapment in Plains Fiction." *NDQ: North Dakota Quarterly* [Univ. of North Dakota], 52, No. 3 (Summer 1984), 181–94.

Thério, Adrien. "Présentation Littérature Féministe, Littérature au féminin." *Lettres québécoises: Revue de l'actualité littéraire*, [Littérature féministe, Littérature au féminin], no 27 (automne 1982), p. 11.

Thomas, Clara. "Aging in the Works of Canadian Women Writers." *Canadian Women's Studies/les cahiers de la femme* [Centennial College], [Aging/Le 3ᵉᵐᵉ âge], 5, No. 3 (Spring/printemps 1984), 45–48.

——— . "Divided Selves: Anna Jameson and Sara Jeannette Duncan." Canadian Literature Discussion Group, MLA Conference, New York. 28 Dec. 1983.

——— . "Happily Ever After: Canadian Women in Fiction and Fact." *Canadian Literature*, [Views of Leonard Cohen], No. 34 (Autumn 1967), pp. 43–53.

——— . "Heroinism, Feminism and Humanism: Anna Jameson to Margaret Laurence." *Atlantis: A Women's Studies Journal/Journal d'Études sur la Femme* [Acadia Univ.], 4, No. 1 (Fall/automne 1978), 19–29.

——— . *Our Nature — Our Voices: A Guidebook to English Canadian Literature.* Vol. 1 of *Our Nature — Our Voices.* Toronto: new, 1972, pp. 6–7, 10–12, 27–32, 42–45, 60–61, 64–69, 76–78, 89–91, 101–06, 109–10, 142–43, 150–51, 156–61.

——— . "Women Writers and the New Land." In *The New Land: Studies in a Literary Theme.* Ed. Richard Chadbourne and Hallvard Dahlie. Waterloo, Ont.: Wilfrid Laurier Univ. Press for Calgary Institute for the Humanities, 1978, pp. 45–59.

Tisdale, Suzanne. "femme dans l'métier ou l'métier d'être femme." *Jeu: cahiers de théâtre*, [Théâtre-femmes], no 16 (1980), pp. 192–93.

Twigg, Alan. "Writers Union Gears Up for Action at AGM." *Quill & Quire*, Aug. 1986, pp. 14–15.

Urbas, Jeannette. "Equations and Flutes." *Journal of Canadian Fiction*, 1, No. 2 (Spring 1972), 69–73.

——— . "La femme d'aucun homme." Conference of Interamerican Women Writers, Ottawa, Ont. June 1978.

Vaillancourt, Lise. "Montrer l'ensemble d'un monde vu et réalisé par des femmes." *Jeu: cahiers de théâtre*, no 36 (1985), pp. 67–69.

Vallée, Manon. "mais ça, c'est une autre histoire." *Jeu: cahiers de théâtre*, [Théâtre-femmes], no 16 (1980), pp. 187–88.

van Herk, Aritha. "Women Writers and the Prairie: Spies in an Indifferent Landscape." Nordic Association for Canadian Studies/Association Nordic d'études canadiennes, Univ. of Aarhus, Denmark.

1984. Printed in *Canadiana: Studies in Canadian Literature/Etudes de Littérature Canadienne.* Ed. Jo̸rn Carlsen and Knud Larsen. Aarhus, Den.: Dept. of English, Univ. of Aarhus, 1985, pp. 120–30.

Verduyn, Christl. "Ecrire le moi au féminin." *Journal of Canadian Studies/Revue d'études canadiennes* [Trent Univ.], 20, no 2 (Summer/été 1985), 18–28.

———. "La femme dans la littérature féminine et féministe du Canada anglais et français depuis 1960." Canadian Research Institute for the Advancement of Women/Institut canadien de recherche pour l'avancement des femmes, Montréal. Nov. 1984. Emprunté dans *Femmes: images, modèles/Women: images, role-models: Actes du Colloque 1984/Proceedings of the 1984 Conference.* Ed. Evelyne Tardy. Ottawa: CRIAW/ICRAF, 1985, pp. 93–99.

———. "From the 'Word on Flesh' to the 'Flesh Made Word': Women's Fiction in Canada." *The American Review of Canadian Studies,* 15, No. 4 (Winter 1985), 449–64.

Verthuy, Maïr. "La Culture québécoise au féminin." Festival on Women in the Arts/Festival des femmes dans les arts, Centennial College, Toronto. Oct. 1978.

———. "Les Ecrits féministes au Québec et l'influence sur ceux-ci des presses féministes, des modes intellectuelles et du contexte socio-politique." Women's Worlds International Conference on Women's Studies, Haifa, Israel. Dec. 1981.

———. See also/voir aussi Maranda, Jeanne, and Maïr Verthuy.

Vézina, France. "les étiquettes . . . ." *Jeu: cahiers de théâtre,* [Théâtre-femmes], no 16 (1980), p. 204.

Villeneuve, Lucie. "Go, c'est parti!". *La vie en rose,* mars 1986, p. 41.

Voldeng, Evelyne. *Femme plurielle.* Ottawa: Dépt. d'études françaises, Carleton Univ., 1980, pp. 5–6, 8–9, 10, 14, 18, 21, 25, 28, 32, 37, 40, 43, 45, 49–51, 55, 58, 60, 63, 69, 71, 74–76, 83, 86, 88–95.

———. "La poésie contemporaine d'inspir-

ation féministe." APFUCC, Univ. du Québec à Montréal. May 1980. Emprunté dans *Dérives,* [Littérature/Erotisme/Prostitution], no 22 (1980), pp. 3–14.

———. "La production poétique comme duplication ou dérivation textuelle d'une langue à une autre." APFUCC, Univ. de Québec à Montréal. May 1980. Emprunté dans *La Traduction: l'universitaire et le praticien.* Ed. Arlette Thomas et Jacques Flammand. Cahiers de la traductologie, no 5. Ottawa: Les Presses de l'Univ. d'Ottawa, 1984, pp. 150–59.

Wachtel, Eleanor. "British Columbia: Two Steps Backward from the One Step Forward." *Canadian Theatre Review* [York Univ.], [Feminism: Canadian Theatre], No. 43 (Summer 1985), pp. 12–20.

———. "Introduction; or Affront/A Front of Language." *Room of One's Own,* [Québécoises], 4, Nos. 1–2 (1978), 2–6.

———. See also/voir aussi Gayla with Eleanor [Wachtel].

Wagner, Anton. "Women Pioneers: An Introduction." In *Women Pioneers.* Vol. II of *Canada's Lost Plays.* Ed. Anton Wagner and Richard Plant. Toronto: Canadian Theatre Review, 1979, pp. 4–21.

Warland, Betsy. "The Heart of the Matter: Organizing *West Word.*" *Contemporary Verse 2,* 9, No. 2 (Fall 1985), 8–10.

Waterston, Elizabeth. *Survey: A Short History of Canadian Literature.* Methuen Canadian Literature Series. Toronto: Methuen, 1973, pp. 65–78, 88, 140, 150, 167, 207, 208.

———. "Women in Canadian Fiction." Nordic Association for Canadian Studies/Association Nordic d'études canadiennes, Univ. of Aarhus, Denmark. 1984. Printed in *Canadiana: Studies in Canadian Literature/Etudes de Littérature Canadienne.* Ed. Jo̸rn Carlsen and Knud Larsen. Aarhus, Den.: Dept. of English, Univ. of Aarhus, 1985, pp. 100–08.

Weir, Lorraine. "'Fauna of Mirrors': The Poetry of Hébert and Atwood." *Ariel,* 10, No. 3 (July 1979), 99–113.

Whitridge, Margaret Coulby. "The Distaff

Side of the Confederation Group: Women's Contribution to Early Nationalist Canadian Literature." *Atlantis: A Women's Studies Journal/Journal d'Études sur la Femme* [Acadia Univ.], 4, No. 1 (Fall/automne 1978), 30–39.

Williamson, Janice. "West Word: Transforming Text." *Broadside: A Feminist Review* [Toronto], Oct. 1985, p. 5.

Wiseman, Adele. "Word Power: Women and Prose in Canada Today." *Journal of Canadian Studies/Revue d'études canadiennes* [Trent Univ.], 20, No. 2 (Summer/été 1985), 5–17.

"Woman Poet Speaks about Women in the Arts." *Scarborough News,* 31 March 1966, p. 4.

"Women in Canadian Drama." Editorial. *Canadian Drama/L'Art dramatique canadien* [Univ. of Waterloo], 5 (Fall/automne 1979), 79–80.

"Women Write!". *Hysteria* [Kitchener, Ont.], 1, No. 1 (March 1980), 19–20.

"Women Writers Top Prize List." *The Montreal Star,* 23 March 1967, p. 61.

Wood, Susan. "God's Doormats: Women in Canadian Prairie Fiction." *Journal of Popular Culture,* 14 (Fall 1980), 350–59.

Yvonne. "La femme et la littérature." *Le Coin du Feu,* mai 1893, pp. 136–37.

Theses and Dissertations/Thèses

Barret, Caroline. "La femme et la société dans la littérature sentimentale populaire québécoise, 1940–1960." Thèse de maîtrise Laval 1980.

Breen, Loretto Helen. "Les écrivains féminins du Canada français de 1900 à 1940." Thèse de maîtrise Laval 1947.

Chawla, Saroj. "Canadian Fiction: Literature as Role Exploration, an Analysis of Novels Written by Women, 1920–1974." Diss. York 1981.

Coderre, Annette-Eglantine. "The Evolving Role of Women in Canadian Fiction in English and French." M.A. Thesis Sherbrooke 1968.

Coderre, Annette. "Le nouveau visage de la femme dans le roman contemporain en littérature québécoise et canadienne-anglaise." Diss. Sherbrooke 1984.

Cossette, Nicole. "L'image de la femme dans le téléroman québécois." Thèse de maîtrise Montréal 1980.

De Sève-Bergeron, Suzanne. "Les systèmes de personnages dans le roman féminin québécois de 1950 à 1960." Thèse de doctorat Sherbrooke 1973.

Dinnick, Sarah. "The Varied Roles of Women in Contemporary Canadian Fiction (1967–1972)." M.A. Thesis Sherbrooke 1974.

Eleanor, M. (Soeur). "Les écrivains féminins du Canada français de 1900 à 1940." Thèse de maîtrise Laval 1947.

Elder, Jo-Ann. "Fiction by Women Since 1975." M.A. Thesis Sherbrooke 1980.

Ethier, Pauline. "Monographie du conte-type 590A: l'épouse traîtresse dans la tradition canadienne-française." Thèse de maîtrise Laval 1976.

Fairbanks, Carol. "Garmented with Space: American and Canadian Prairie Women's Fiction." Diss. Minnesota 1982.

Fraser, Ann K. "Sexuality and Guilt in the Novels of Anne Hébert and Margaret Laurence." M.A. Thesis Sherbrooke 1978.

Freeman, Audrey. "Portrait de la femme canadienne-française d'après la littérature du pays, 1840–1945." Thèse de maîtrise Queen's 1946.

Frot-Boynard, Janine. "Fonctions et qualifications d'un objet de valeur: la femme québécoise dans le roman du terroir." Thèse de doctorat Sherbrooke 1975.

Geminder, Kathleen. "Callisto: The Recurrence and Variation on Her Myth from Ovid to Atwood." Diss. Manitoba 1984.

Girard, Jocelyn-Ann. "A Quarter Century of Love and Sex in the Canadian Novel (1945–70)." M.A. Thesis Sherbrooke 1974.

Hamel, Reginald. "Génèse, évolution et influence de l'écriture féminin au Canada français de 1764 à 1961." Thèse doctorat d'état Paris IV 1978.

Hogan, Lesley Sylvia. "A Study of the Male-Female Relationship as Exemplified in the

Canadian Novel." M.A. Thesis Victoria 1979.

Hoy, Helen Elizabeth. "The Portrayal of Women in Recent Canadian Fiction." Diss. Toronto 1977.

Irvine, Lorna Marie. "Hostility and Reconciliation: The Mother in English Canadian Fiction." Diss. American 1977.

Jackel, Susan. "Prairie Wife: Female Characterization in Canadian Prairie Fiction, 1908–1964." M.A. Thesis Toronto 1967.

Kargut, Susan. "Concepts of Character in the Novels and Short Stories of Laurence, Roy, and Wilson." M.A. Thesis Saskatchewan 1973.

Kowalewski, Jean. "A Sociolinguistic Analysis of Sex Differences in Language as Represented in a Selection of Canadian Novels." M.A. Thesis York 1981.

Laforest, Marie-Thérèse [Soeur Sainte-Marie-Eleuthère]. "La Mère dans le roman canadien-français contemporain: 1930–1960." Thèse de doctorat Montréal 1964.

Levine-Keating, Hélane. "Myth and Archetype from a Female Perspective: An Exploration of Twentieth Century North and South American Women Poets." Diss. New York 1980.

Limin, Gloria Hope. "Teaching the Theme of Women in Canadian Prairie Fiction." M.A. Thesis Calgary 1977.

Mallinson, Anna Jean. "Versions and Subversions: Formal Strategies in the Poetry of Contemporary Women." Diss. Simon Fraser 1982.

Masterson, Kathleen Elizabeth. "Women in Contemporary Canadian Fiction." M.A. Thesis Bishop's 1974.

McQuaid, Catherine. "Women's Changing Roles in the Novels of Anne Hébert and Margaret Laurence." M.A. Thesis Sherbrooke 1978.

Miners, Marion Frances. "Women in Selected English-Canadian Novels, 1954 to 1972." M.A. Thesis Calgary 1977.

Ouellet-Samuelson, Aline. "La fortune des auteurs féminins du Canada français dans les histoires littéraires." Doctorat ès lettres Sherbrooke 1977.

Packer, Miriam. "Beyond the Garrison: Approaching the Wilderness in Margaret Laurence, Alice Munro, and Margaret Atwood." Diss. Montreal 1977.

Rackowski, Cheryl Stokes. "Women by Women: Five Contemporary English and French Canadian Novelists." Diss. Connecticut 1978.

Rosenthal, Helene. "The Poet as Woman, Shapes of Experience: A Study of Poetic Motivation and Craft in Twentieth Century Women Poets, Incorporating a Select Anthology." M.A. Thesis British Columbia 1974.

Scott, Donna Lynn. "Block-and-Tackle: Multiple Roles of Women in Canadian and Australian Pioneer Fiction." M.A. Thesis Queen's 1974.

Scott, Howard. "Problems of Translating New Quebec Feminist Writing." M.A. Thesis Concordia 1982.

Trehel, Lucienne. "La jeune fille dans le roman canadien-français de 1900 à 1970." Thèse de doctorat Sherbrooke 1969.

Urbas, Jeannette. "Le personnage féminin dans le roman canadien-français de 1940 à 1967." Thèse de doctorat Toronto 1971.

Verduyn, Christl. "L'idée de la découverte de soi dans le roman féminin canadien depuis 1960: étude d'oeuvres québécois et canadiennes-anglaises." Thèse de doctorat Ottawa 1979.

Zelmer, Lois Anne Walford. "Ethnicity, Nationalism and Sex Roles in Children's Books in Southern Ontario." M.A. Thesis York 1979. Esp. pp. 26–30, 87–115, 170–80.

Interviews/Entretiens

Beaudin, Pauline, Marie-José des Rivières, et Chantal Hébert. "rare au féminin: à partir d'entretiens avec des femmes metteurs en scène de québec." *Jeu: cahiers de théâtre*, [Théâtre-femmes], no 16 (1980), pp. 115–25.

des Rivières, Marie-José. Voir/see Beaudin, Pauline, Marie-José des Rivières, et Chantal Hébert; et/and des Rivières,

Marie-José, et Chantal Hébert.

des Rivières, Marie-José, et Chantal Hébert. "des femmes en coulisses: à partir d'entretiens avec des femmes du trident et du grand théâtre du québec." *Jeu: cahiers de théâtre*, [Théâtre-femmes], no 16, (1980), pp. 126–43.

Dumas, Hélène, et Colette Tougas. "sous forme d'entretien . . . ." *Jeu: cahiers de théâtre*, [Théâtre-femmes], no 16 (1980), pp. 196–97.

Gould, Karen. "Ecrire au féminin: Interview avec Denise Boucher, Madeleine Gagnon et Louky Bersianik." *Québec Studies*, 1, no 2 (1984), 125–42.

Hébert, Chantal. Voir/see Beaudin, Pauline, Marie-José des Rivières, et Chantal Hébert; et/and des Rivières, Marie-José, et Chantal Hébert.

Lasnier, Michèlle. "Les quatre romancières de l'année." Entretien avec Suzanne Paradis, Diane Giguère, Marie-Claire Blais et Monique Bosco. *Châtelaine*, juin 1962, pp. 30–32, 94–96, 98, 101, 102.

O'Neill, Patrick. "The Playwright's Studio Group Toronto: An Interview with Two Women Playwrights of the 1930's." *Atlantis: A Women's Studies Journal/Journal d'études sur la femme* [Mt. St. Vincent Univ.], 8, No. 1 (Autumn 1982), 89–96.

Tougas, Colette. Voir/see Dumas, Hélène et Colette Tougas.

Williamson, Janice. "Speaking in and of Each Other." Interview with Daphne Marlatt and Betsy Warland. *Fuse*, Feb.–March 1985, pp. 25–29.

Wright, Ellea. "Text and Tissue: Body Language." Interview with Daphne Marlatt and Betsy Warland. *Broadside: A Feminist Review* [Toronto], Dec.–Jan. 1984–85, pp. 4–5.

Reviews/Comptes rendus

Alonzo, Anne-Marie. "La vague de mars." Compte rendu d'*Arcade*, nos 8–9; *Vlasta*, no 3; et *Possibles*, 9, no 2. *La vie en rose*, juin 1985, p. 55.

Amiel, Barbara. "Sweet Ms-teries of Life." Rev. of *Two Women*, by Doris Anderson; and *A Casual Affair*, by Sylvia Fraser. *Maclean's*, 20 March 1978, p. 70.

Atwood, Margaret. "Why Annie Got Her Gun." Rev. of *A Harvest Yet to Reap: A History of Prairie Women*, ed. Linda Rasmussen, Lorna Rasmussen, Candace Savage, and Anne Wheeler. Introd. Candace Savage. *Books in Canada*, Feb. 1977, pp. 9–10.

Batt, Sharon. Rev. of *West of Fiction*, ed. Leah Flater, Aritha van Herk, and Rudy Wiebe. *Room of One's Own*, 9, No. 1 (Feb. 1984), 69–73.

Bayard, Caroline. "Letters in Canada: 1981. Poésie." Compte rendu d'*Au coeur de la lettre*, par Madeleine Gagnon; *Entre le souffle et l'aine*, par Madeleine Ouellette-Michalska; et *Femmes fragmentée*, par Célyne Fortin. *University of Toronto Quarterly*, 51 (Summer 1982), 362–64, 369–70.

Beauchamp, Colette. "Les québécoises écrivent une parole autre puisée dans leur corps et leur sensualité." Compte rendu de *Retailles: complaintes politiques*, par Madeleine Gagnon et Denise Boucher. *Le Jour* [Montréal], 22 juil. 1977, p. 5.

Bennett, Donna. "Their Own Tongue." Rev. of *Touch to My Tongue*, by Daphne Marlatt; *open is broken*, by Betsy Warland; *Banff/Breaking*, by Charles Noble; and *Animus*, by Penny Kemp. *Canadian Literature*, [The Times Between], No. 107 (Winter 1985), pp. 152–55.

Bilan, R.P. "Letters in Canada: 1978. Fiction." Rev. of *At Peace*, by Ann Copeland; *Judith*, by Aritha van Herk; and *Abra*, by Joan Barfoot. *University of Toronto Quarterly*, 48 (Summer 1979), 311–18.

Brown, Russell. "New Poets and Old Stories." Rev. of *Artemis Hates Romance*, by Sharon Thesen; *Settlement Poems*, by Kristjana Gunnars; *Bread and Chocolate*, by Mary di Michele; and *Marrying into the Family*, by Bronwen Wallace. *The Canadian Forum*, Feb. 1982, pp. 37–39.

C[olin]., Fr[ançoise]. "Denise Boucher et Madeleine Gagnon, *Retailles*." *Les Cahiers du GRIF* [Brussels], nos 17–18 *(sept.* 1977), p. 114.

Collins, Anne. "On the Racks." Rev. of *The Tent Peg*, by Aritha van Herk; and *Lunatic Villas*, by Marian Engel. *Books in Canada*, March 1982, pp. 27–28.

Cooper-Clark, Diana. "Thin Poems." Rev. of *The Ordinary Invisible Woman*, by Gwen Hauser; *the loneliness of the poet/ housewife*, by Mary Baldridge; *The Ultimate Contact*, by Kathy Tyler; and *When a Girl Looks Down*, by Kay Smith. *Canadian Literature*, [The Structure of Fiction], No. 86 (Autumn 1980), pp. 108–10.

Creighton, Ellen. Rev. of *Women and Words: The Anthology/Les Femmes et les Mots: Une Anthologie*, ed. West Coast Editorial Collective. *Canadian Women's Studies/les cahiers de la femme* [Centennial College], [The Future/le futur], 6, No. 2 (Spring 1985), 91–92.

David, Carole. "La séduction du romanesque." Compte rendu d'*Estuaire*, no 37 (automne 1985). *Le Devoir* [Montréal], 21 déc. 1985, p. 24.

de Grandpré, Chantal. "Le Québec au féminin vu des Etats-Unis." Compte rendu de *Traditionalism, Nationalism and Feminism: Women Writers of Québec*, ed. Paula Gilbert Lewis. *voix & images: littérature québécoise*, no 32 (hiver 1986), pp. 328–29.

DeGrass, Jan. Rev. of *Baker's Dozen: Stories by Women*, ed. The Fictive Collective. *Kinesis*, Dec.–Jan. 1984–85, p. 30.

de Lotbinière-Harwood, Susanne. "L'ambiguité d'un concept." Compte rendu de *Mauve*, par Nicole Brossard et Daphne Marlatt. *Spirale*, no 62 (été 1986), p. 13.

De Wiel, Alexa. "Mothers, Moons and Mafiosi." Rev. of *A Sleep Full of Dreams*, by Edna Alford; *Real Mothers*, by Audrey Thomas; and *The Moons of Jupiter*, by Alice Munro. *Broadside: A Feminist Review* [Toronto], May 1983, pp. 11, 13.

Djwa, Sandra. "Letters in Canada: 1981. Poetry." Rev. of *Poems Twice Told: The Boatman & Welcoming Disaster*, by Jay Macpherson; *True Stories*, by Margaret Atwood; *Evening Dance of the Grey Flies*, by P. K. Page; *The Visitants*, by Miriam Waddington; *The Circular Coast: Poems New and Selected*, by Anne Marriott; *Queens of the Next Hot Star*, by Linda Rogers; *The Womb Rattles Its Pod*, by Cathy Ford; *Wake-Pick Poems*, by Kristjana Gunnars; and *What Matters: Writing 1968–70*, by Daphne Marlatt. *University of Toronto Quarterly,* 51 (Summer 1982), 344–49, 354–55.

Dretzsky, George. "The New 'Woman's Novel.'" Rev. of *Abra*, by Joan Barfoot; *Judith*, by Aritha van Herk; and *The Glassy Sea*, by Marian Engel. *The Fiddlehead*, No. 120 (Winter 1979), pp. 142–45.

Duffy, Dennis. "Critical Sympathies." Rev. of *The Road Past Altamont*, by Gabrielle Roy; and *A Jest of God*, by Margaret Laurence. *The Tamarack Review*, No. 42 (Winter 1967), pp. 78–81.

Engel, Marian. "Two Ladies Not for Burning." Rev. of *The Malahat Review*, [Margaret Atwood: A Symposium], No. 41 (Jan. 1977); and *Canadian Fiction Magazine*, [A Special Issue on Jane Rule], No. 23 (Autumn 1976). *Books in Canada*, May 1977, pp. 14, 16.

Feral, Josette. Rev. of *Room of One's Own*, [Québécoises], 4, Nos. 1–2 (1978). Trans. Michèlle Lacombe. *Fireweed: A Feminist Literary & Cultural Journal*, [Women and Language], Nos. 5–6 (Winter–Spring 1979–80), pp. 194–95.

Gagnon, Madeleine. Compte rendu d'*Une mémoire déchirée*, par Thérèse Renaud; et d'*Une voix pour Odile*, par France Théoret. *voix et images: études québécoises*, 4 (sept. 1978), 143–45.

Giguère, Richard. "La Poésie 1. Les écritures de femmes en 1982: interiorisation et transformation." Compte rendu de *La Nomade*, par Julie Stanton; *Femme fragmentée*, par Célyne Fortin; *Orpailleuse*, par Jocelyn Felx; et *Au coeur de la lettre*, par Madeleine Gagnon. *Lettres québécoises: Revue de l'actualité littéraire*, [Littérature féministe, Littérature au féminin], no 27 (automne 1982), pp. 35–38.

Gingell, Susan. "Women's Bonds." Rev. of *Double Bond: An Anthology of Prairie Women's Fiction*, ed. Caroline Heath.

Canadian Literature, [Mothers and Daughters], No. 109 (Summer 1986), pp. 111–12.

Godard, Barbara. "Crazy Quilt." Rev. of Junction, by Elizabeth Brewster; Héloïse, by Anne Hébert; and Quilt, by Donna Smyth. The Fiddlehead, No. 141 (Autumn 1984), pp. 83–89.

———. "Mothering Redoubled." Rev. of Journal intime, by Nicole Brossard; and L'autrement pareille, by Marguerite Andersen. Canadian Literature, [Italian-Canadian Connections], No. 106 (Fall 1985), pp. 101–04.

———. Rev. of Lunatic Villas, by Marian Engel; The Charcoal Burners, by Susan Musgrave; and The Tent Peg, by Aritha van Herk. The Fiddlehead, No. 132 (April 1982), pp. 90–95.

———. Rev. of The Body Labyrinth, by Sharon Berg; and Water and Light: Ghazals and Anti-Ghazals, by Phillis Webb. Poetry Canada Review, 7, No. 2 (Winter 1985–86), 34.

———. "Three New Anthologies Celebrate Short Fiction by Women." Rev. of Baker's Dozen: Stories by Women, ed. The Fictive Collective; Double Bond: An Anthology of Prairie Women's Fiction, ed. Caroline Heath; and Stories by Canadian Women, ed. Rosemary Sullivan. Quill & Quire, Oct. 1984, p. 31.

Gottlieb, Lois C. See/voyez Keitner, Wendy, with Lois C. Gottlieb.

Haeck, Philippe. "Brossard et Massé, deux écritures désirantes." Compte rendu de Reject, par Carole Massé; et La partie pour le tout, par Nicole Brossard. Le Devoir [Montréal], 21 juin 1975, p. 13.

———. "Noir sur blanc." Compte rendu de Féminité, subversion, écriture, ed. Suzanne Lamy et Irène Pagès. Dérives, no 46 (automne 1984), pp. 99–106.

Hale, Amanda. "Jessica's Journey." Rev. of Jessica: A Transformation, by Linda Griffiths and Maria Campbell, Theatre Passe Muraille, Toronto, 25 March–13 April 1986. Broadside: A Feminist Review [Toronto], May 1986, p. 11.

Halliday, Brenda. Rev. of In Praise of Older Women, by Marya Fiamengo; Pomegranite: A Selected Anthology of Vancouver Poetry, ed. Nellie McClung; and Two Women: The Poetry of Jeanette Foster and Valerie Taylor, by Jeanette Foster and Valerie Taylor. Emergency Librarian, 4, No. 5 (May–June 1977), 15–16.

Hamelin, Carole. Compte rendu de De ce nom de l'amour, par Louise Cocteau et Danielle Fournier. Arcade, [désirs et passions], no 10 (oct. 1985), pp. 54–56.

Hlus, Carolyn. Rev. of No Memory of a Move, by Anne Campbell; Split Levels, by Judith Fitzgerald; and Mad Women & Crazy Ladies, by Sharon H. Nelson. CV/II, 8, No. 1 (May 1984), 17–19.

———. Rev. of Remembering History, by Rhea Tregebov; Traditions, by Heather Cadsby; Mimosa and Other Poems, by Mary di Michele; and These Are the Women, by Joni Miller. CV/II, 7, No. 3 (Sept. 1983), 18–21.

Hosek, Chaviva. Rev. of The Killing Room, by Marilyn Bowering; Two Kinds of Honey, by Rosemary Aubert; and A Stone Diary, by Pat Lowther. The Fiddlehead, No. 118 (Summer 1978), pp. 162–65.

Irvine, Lorna. "Separate Space." Rev. of Censored Letters, by Betsy Struthers; and Margaret Atwood: A Feminist Poetics, by Frank Davey. Canadian Literature, [The Times Between], No. 107 (Winter 1985), pp. 120–23.

———. "Women's Voices." Rev. of Out on the Plain, by Frankie Finn; and Penumbra, by Susan Kerslake. Canadian Literature, [Popular Culture], No. 108 (Spring 1986), pp. 170–73.

Kadar, Marlene. Rev. of Double Bond: An Anthology of Prairie Women's Fiction, ed. Caroline Heath; and Country of the Heart, by Sharon Butala. Canadian Women's Studies/les cahiers de la femme [Centennial College], [Affirmative Action/Action positive], 6, No. 4 (Winter/hiver 1985), 124–25.

Kamboureli, Smaro. Rev. of D'Sonoqua: An Anthology of Women Poets of British Columbia, ed. Ingrid Klassen. Branching Out: Canadian Feminist Quarterly, 7,

No. 2 (1980), 57–58.

Keefer, Janice Kulyk. "Wonderbread, Schmaltz, & Food for Thought." Rev. of *Baker's Dozen: Stories by Women*, ed. The Fictive Collective; *Blood Ties*, by Robin Matthews; and *The Mikveh Man*, by Sharon Drache. *The Fiddlehead*, No. 146 (Winter 1985), pp. 95–99.

Kinesis Staff Writers. "Finding *Common Ground* and Enjoying the Discoveries." Rev. of *Common Ground*, ed. Marilyn Berge, Linda Field, Cynthia Flood, Penny Goldsmith, and Lark. *Kinesis*, Nov. 1980, p. 23.

Klein, Carroll. "Baker's Bounty." Rev. of *Baker's Dozen: Stories by Women*, ed. The Fictive Collective. *Broadside: A Feminist Review* [Toronto], Nov. 1984, p. 15.

———. "The Personal Is Historical." Rev. of *Remembering History*, by Rhea Tregebov; *Power Source*, by Carolyn Smart; and *A Game of Angels*, by Anne Szumigalski. *Broadside: A Feminist Review* [Toronto], May 1983, p. 12.

Kostash, Myrna. "IWY One: Too Little from on High." Rev. of *To See Ourselves: Five Views on Canadian Women*, by Sheila Arnopoulous, Sharon Brown, Dian Cohen, Margaret Daly, and Katherine Govier; *All Work and No Play*, ed. Wendy Edmond and Suzie Fleming; *Every Woman's Almanac 1976*, ed. The Women's Press Collective; *Herstory 1976: A Canadian Women's Almanac*, by Saskatoon Women's Calendar Collective; and *Once More with Love*, by Joan Sutton. *Books in Canada*, Feb. 1976, pp. 12–13.

Kroetsch, Robert. Rev. of *Women and Words: The Anthology/Les Femmes et les Mots: Une Anthologie*, ed. West Coast Editorial Collective. *Contemporary Verse 2*, 9, No. 2 (Fall 1985), 58–60.

Lamy, Susanne. "Sans lieu mais avec feu: *Tessera*." Compte rendu de *Tessera*, no 2 [*la nouvelle barre du jour*, no 157] (sept. 1985). *Canadian Women's Studies/les Cahiers de la femme* [Centennial College], [post Nairobi], 7, nos 1–2 (Spring– Summer 1986), 231–32.

Lawrence, Karen. "Getting Where?". Rev. of *Getting Here*, ed. Rudy Wiebe. *Branching Out: Canadian Magazine for Women*, 4, No. 3 (July–Aug. 1977), 42–43.

Lequin, Lucie. Compte rendu de *Manitoba des femmes/Questionnaire Gabrielle Roy*, par Janick Belleau; *Encore une partie pour Berri*, par Pauline Harvey; *Anaïs, dans la queue de la comète*, par Jovette Marchessault. *Canadian Women's Studies/les cahiers de la femme* [Centennial College], [post Nairobi], 7, nos 1–2 (Spring–Summer 1986), 233–34.

MacMillan, Carrie. "Women in Canadian Literature." Rev. of *Women in Canadian Literature*, by Molly G. McClung; and *Women in Canadian Literature*, ed. M. G. Hesse. *Atlantis: A Women's Studies Journal/Journal d'Études sur la Femme* [Acadia Univ.], 3, No. 2 (Spring/ printemps 1978), 156–69.

Mailhot, Michèle A. "Châtelaine a lu pour vous: quatre excellentes femmes écrivains." Compte rendu de *Doux-amer*, par Claire Martin; *La Spiritualité de la voix*, par Lucie de Vienne; et *Des Cavernes à César*, par Lise Nantass et Madeleine Lemieux. *Châtelaine*, jan. 1961, p. 7.

Maika, Pat. Rev. of *Women and Words: The Anthology/Les Femmes et les Mots: Une Anthologie*, ed. West Coast Editorial Collective. *Kinesis*, Dec.–Jan. 1984–85, p. 24.

Mallinson, Jean. "Subversive Gestures: The Poems of Beth Jankola and Nellie McClung." Rev. of *The Way I See It*, *Girl of the Golden West*, *Jody Said*, and *Mirror/Mirror*, by Beth Jankola; and *BARAKA: The Poems of Nellie McClung*, by Nellie McClung. *CV/II*, 5, No. 2 (Winter 1980–81), 57–59.

Mandel, Ann. Rev. of *True Stories*, by Margaret Atwood; and *Wilson's Bowl*, by Phyllis Webb. *The Fiddlehead*, No. 131 (Jan. 1982), pp. 63–70.

Marchessault, Jovette. "*Retraite* par Soeur Madeleine Gagnon et Soeur Denise Boucher." Compte rendu de *Retailles: complaintes politiques*, par Madeleine Gagnon et Denise Boucher. *Les têtes du pioche*, 2, no 6 (oct. 1977), 6.

Martens, Debra. Rev. of *Stories by Canadian*

Women, ed. Rosemary Sullivan. *Room of One's Own*, 10, No. 2 (Dec. 1985), 98–101.

Martin, Agathe. Compte rendu de *Retailles: complaintes politiques*, par Madeleine Gagnon et Denise Boucher. *Livres et auteurs québécois 1977*. Ed. Marcel Bélanger. Québec: Les Presses de l'Univ. Laval, 1978, pp. 75–78.

Martin, Sandra. "Bucolically Speaking, One Woman's Pits Can Be Another's Liberation." Rev. of *Abra*, by Joan Barfoot; and *Where the Cherries End Up*, by Gail Henley. *Books in Canada*, Nov. 1978, pp. 38–39.

Martin, Simone. "Feminism in French Canadian Literature." Rev. of *Windflower*, by Gabrielle Roy, trans. Joyce Marshall; *La Sagouine*, by Antonine Maillet; *Les Enfants du sabbat*, by Anne Hébert; and *Le Corps étranger*, by Hélène Ouvrard. *Branching Out: Canadian Magazine for Women*, 4, No. 4 (Sept.–Oct. 1977), 43–44.

McDougall, Anne. "The Trouble with Her Parties." Rev. of *40 Women Poets of Canada*, ed. Dorothy Livesay and Seymour Mayne. *Times* [Victoria], 11 March 1972, p. 14.

Millen, Judy. "Intense Interplay." Rev. of *Women and Words: The Anthology/Les Femmes et les Mots: Une Anthologie*, ed. West Coast Editorial Collective. *Broadside: A Feminist Review* [Toronto], March 1985, p. 11.

Mitcham, Alison. "Women in Revolt: (Anne Hébert's, Marie-Claire Blais' and Claire Martin's Nightmare Visions of an Unjust Society)." Rev. of *Dans un gant de fer*, by Claire Martin; *La Belle Bête* and *Une Saison dans la vie d'Emmanuel*, by Marie-Claire Blais; and *Le Torrent* and *Kamouraska*, by Anne Hébert. *Alive* [Guelph, Ont.], June 1973, pp. 13–14.

Mitchell, Penni. Rev. of *Baker's Dozen: Stories by Women*, ed. The Fictive Collective. *HERizons: The Manitoba Women's News Magazine*, Oct. 1984, p. 41.

Morris, Roberta. "Domestic Affairs." Rev. of *In Search of April Raintree*, by Beatrice Culleton; *A Bolt of White Cloth*, by Leon Rooke; and *Intertidal Life*, by Audrey Thomas. *Waves*, 14, Nos. 1–2 (Fall 1985), 112–13.

Novak, Barbara. "After Anger, Change?". Rev. of *The Country of Mapmakers*, by Kim Maltman; *Landfall*, by Roo Borson; and *Time and Untime*, by Kathleen Forsythe. *Branching Out: Canadian Magazine for Women*, 5, No. 2 (1978), 46.

———. "Grit and Gold." Rev. of *Ice Age*, by Dorothy Livesay; *Living Together*, by Joan Finnegan; *The Price of Gold*, by Miriam Waddington; *Landscape of Kin*, by Jane Berland; *The Sun in Winter*, by Anne Scott; and *Some Wild Gypsy*, by Brenda Fleet. *Branching Out: Canadian Magazine for Women*, 4, No. 1 (March–April, 1977), 45–46.

———. "Lunar Distractions." Rev. of *Real Mothers*, by Audrey Thomas; and *The Man Who Sold Prayers*, by Margaret Creal. *Books in Canada*, Feb. 1982, pp. 18–20. Rpt. (excerpt) in *Contemporary Literary Criticism: Excerpts from Criticism of the Works of Today's Novelists, Poets, Playwrights, Short Story Writers, Filmmakers, and Other Creative Writers*. Ed. Daniel G. Marowski. Vol. XXXVII. Detroit: Gale, 1986, 418–19.

Nuse, Betsy. "In Our Mother Tongue." Rev. of *open is broken*, by Betsy Warland; and *Touch to My Tongue*, by Daphne Marlatt. *Broadside: A Feminist Review* [Toronto], Dec.–Jan. 1984–85, p. 16.

———. "Personal Journeys." Rev. of *What Place Is This?*, by Rosalind McPhee; *Diana Lucifera*, by Marilyn Krysl; and *Binding Twine*, by Penny Kemp. *Broadside: A Feminist Review* [Toronto], Nov. 1984, p. 14.

———. "Vital Illumination." Rev. of *Full Moon: An Anthology of Canadian Women Poets*, ed. Janice LaDuke and Steve Luxton; and *Anything Is Possible: A Selection of Eleven Women Poets*, ed. Mary di Michele. *Broadside: A Feminist Review* [Toronto], April 1985, p. 12.

O'Neill, Patrick B. Rev. *Women Pioneers*, vol. II of *Canada's Lost Plays*, ed. Anton

Wagner. *Atlantis: A Women's Studies Journal/Journal d'études sur la femme* [Mt. St. Vincent Univ.], 7, No. 1 (Fall/automne 1981), 141–44.

Orenstein, Gloria Feman. "Ecstacy and Tenderness: A Feminist Reclaiming of Love." Rev. of *Retailles: complaintes politiques*, by Madeleine Gagnon and Denise Boucher; and *Femmes de paroles*, by Pauline Julien. *Book Forum* [New York], March 1978, pp. 92–98.

Ouellette-Michalska, Madeleine. "Les Intelligentes . . . ." Compte rendu de *La Venue à l'écriture*, par Hélène Cixous, Madeleine Gagnon, et Annie Leclerc, dirigée par Catherine B. Clément et Hélène Cixous. *Châtelaine*, oct. 1977, p. 8.

Parks, Joy. "Poetry, Passion and Politics." Rev. of *Interlunar*, by Margaret Atwood; *Golden Earrings*, by Sharon Stevenson; and *Falling from Grace*, by E. Van de Walle. HERizons: *The Manitoba Women's News Magazine*, Oct. 1984, p. 44.

———. Rev. of *Room of One's Own*, [Special Issue on Marian Engel], 9, No. 2 (June 1984). *Kinesis*, Dec.–Jan. 1984–85, p. 34.

———. Rev. of *Stories by Canadian Women*, ed. Rosemary Sullivan. HERizons: *The Manitoba Women's News Magazine*, Oct.–Nov. 1985, p. 42.

———. Rev. of *The Inanna Poems*, by Karen Lawrence; and *Where Have You Been*, by Miriam Mandel. *Hysteria* [Kitchener, Ont.], 1, No. 4 (Spring 1982), 17.

———. Rev. of *The Murdered Dreams Awake*, by Cathy Ford; *Mouth for Music*, by Mona Fertig; and *Split Rock*, by Carolyn Zonailo. *Branching Out: Canadian Feminist Quarterly*, 7, No. 1 (1980), 49–50.

———. Rev. of *Women and Words: The Anthology/Les Femmes et les Mots: Une Anthologie*, ed. West Coast Editorial Collective. HERizons: *The Manitoba Women's News Magazine*, March 1985, p. 44.

Parthun, Mary Lassance. "Examining Feminist Thoughts on Women's Literature."

Rev. of *In the Feminine: Women and Words/Les Femmes et les mots: Conference Proceedings 1983*, ed. Ann Dybikowski, Victoria Freeman, Daphne Marlatt, Barbara Pulling, and Betsy Warland. *The Globe and Mail* [Toronto], 8 March 1986, p. D18.

Pedneault, Hélène, et Francine Pelletier. "*Mademoiselle Autobody*: la porno frappe encore." Compte rendu de *Mademoiselle Autobody*, par Les Folles Alliées [Hélène Bernier, Jocelyne Corbeil, Agnès Maltais, Lucie Godbout et Pascale Gagnon]. *La vie en rose*, nov. 1985, pp. 52–53.

Pelletier, Francine. Voir/see Pedneault, Hélène, et Francine Pelletier.

Poissant, Louise. "Des femmes et des textes." Compte rendu de *Féminité, subversion, écriture*, ed. Suzanne Lamy et Irène Pagès. *Possibles*, 8, no 3 (printemps 1984), 73–81.

Posesorski, Sherie. "Wanting Too Much." Rev. of *The Day Is Dark* and *Three Travellers*, by Marie-Claire Blais; and *Baker's Dozen: Stories by Women*, ed. The Fictive Collective. *Canadian Literature*, [Mothers and Daughters], No. 109 (Summer 1986), pp. 110–11.

Poulin, Gabrielle. "La femme et l'écriture." Compte rendu de *Liberté*, [Actes de la Rencontre Québécoise internationale des écrivains], 18, nos 4–5 [nos 106–107] (juil.–oct. 1976). *Le Droit* [Ottawa], 4 déc. 1976, p. 18.

Rev. of *Baker's Dozen: Stories by Women*, ed. The Fictive Collective. *Communiqu'Elles* [Montreal], 10, No. 5 (Sept. 1984), 26.

R[icou]., L[aurie]. "Notes." Rev. of *Mrs. Blood*, by Audrey Thomas; *Magic Animals*, by Gwendolyn MacEwen; and *Anything Is Possible: A Selection of Eleven Women Poets*, ed. Mary di Michele. *Canadian Literature*, [Italian-Canadian Connections], No. 106 (Fall 1985), p. 187.

Roy, Monique. Compte rendu des *Nuits de l'Underground*, par Marie-Claire Blais; *Te prends-tu pour une folle, Madame Chose?*, par Collectif; et *Une voix pour*

Odile, par France Théoret. *Canadian Women's Studies/les cahiers de la femme* [Centennial College], 1, no 1 (automne/Fall 1978), 110–12.

———. "Pour les femmes et les autres." Compte rendu de *La venue à l'écriture*, par Hélène Cixous, Madeleine Gagnon, et Annie Leclerc, dirigée par Catherine Clément et Hélène Cixous. *Le Devoir* [Montréal], 28 mai 1977, p. 13.

Royer, Jean. "Sur la table des écritures." Compte rendu de *Autobiographie: 1. Fictions*, par Madeleine Gagnon; les articles sur Madeleine Gagnon dans *voix et images: littérature québécoise*, 8, par Madeleine Boulanger, Louise Desjardins, Gabrielle Frémont, et Lucie Robert et Ruth Major; *La Table*, par Francis Ponge; et *études françaises* [Univ. de Montréal], [Francis Ponge], 17, nos 1–2. *Le Devoir* [Montréal], 9 avril 1983, p. 19.

Runte, Hans R. "Of Women, Men, & Muses." Rev. of *Gravité: Poèmes 1967–1973*, by Guy Gervais; *Aux Mouvances du temps: Poésie*, by Marie Laberge; and *La Nomade*, by Julie Stanton. *Canadian Literature*, [Poetic Form], No. 97 (Summer 1983), pp. 114–15.

Saint-Martin, Lori. "La critique au féminin." Compte rendu de *Féminité, subversion, écriture*, ed. Suzanne Lamy et Irène Pagès. *Spirale*, no 43 (mai 1984), p. 12.

———. "Le regard de l'autre." Compte rendu de *Traditionalism, Nationalism and Feminism: Women Writers of Quebec*, ed. Paula Gilbert Lewis. *Spirale*, no 57 (déc. 1985), p. 5.

———. "Tales of Misogyny." Rev. of *In the Shadow of the Wind*, by Anne Hébert; and *Pierre, la guerre du printemps 1981*, by Marie-Claire Blais. *The Women's Review of Books* [Wellesley, Mass.], Nov. 1984, pp. 15–16.

Sand, Cy-Thea. "A Little Night Reading." Rev. of *Saga of the Wet Hens*, by Jovette Marchessault, trans. Linda Gaboriau; *Gold Earrings*, by Sharon Stevenson; *The Promise*, by Wanda Blynn Campbell; *Work and Madness: The Rise of Community Psychiatry*, by Diana Ralph; *Tessera*,

No. 1 [*Room of One's Own*, 8, No. 4] (1983); and *Fireweed: A Feminist Quarterly*, [Atlantic Women], No. 18 (Winter–Spring 1984). *Kinesis*, June 1984, p. 24.

Sanders, Leslie. "Poetic Presence." Rev. of *Women Poets of the World*, ed. Joanna Bankier and Deidre Lashgari; *Personal Luggage*, by Marleen Cookshaw; *Feeling the World/New Poems*, by Dorothy Livesay; *Domestic Fuel*, by Erin Mouré; and *Jonestown & Other Madness*, by Pat Parker. *Broadside: A Feminist Review* [Toronto], Feb. 1986, p. 11.

Savona, Jeannette Laillou. Compte rendu de *Féminité, subversion, écriture*, ed. Suzanne Lamy et Irène Pagès. *Resources for Feminist Research/Documentation sur la recherche féministe*, [Women and Language/Les Femmes et le langage], 13, no 3 (Nov./nov. 1984), 57.

Scheier, Libby. "Women and Words." Rev. of *Primitive Offensive*, by Dionne Brand; *A Gathering Instinct*, by Betsy Warland; and *Life Still*, by Gay Allison. *Books in Canada*, Dec. 1983, pp. 31–32.

Schendlinger, Mary. Rev. of *Women and Words: The Anthology/Les Femmes et les Mots: Une Anthologie*, ed. West Coast Editorial Collective. *Room of One's Own*, 10, No. 1 (1985), 94–96.

Sefrioui, Anne. "Québécoises deboutte." Compte rendu de *Retailles: complaintes politiques*, par Madeleine Gagnon et Denise Boucher. *Les Nouvelles littéraires* [Paris], 1–8 déc. 1977, p. 20.

Simon, Sherry. "Comment choisir?". Compte rendu de *Women and Words: The Anthology/Les Femmes et les Mots: Une Anthologie*, ed. West Coast Editorial Collective; et *Stories by Canadian Women*, ed. Rosemary Sullivan. *Spirale*, no 52 (mai 1985), p. 5.

Sirois, Denise. Compte rendu de *Femme plurielle*, par Evelyne Voldeng. *Des luttes et des rires de femmes*, 4, no 2 (déc.–jan. 1980–81), 53.

Smart, Patricia. "Letters in Canada. 1984. Humanities." Compte rendu de *Un Parti pris révolutionnaire*, par Pierre Maheur;

Féminité, subversion, écriture, ed. Suzanne Lamy et Irène Pagès; *Quand je lis je m'invente*, par Suzanne Lamy; et *Ecrire l'amour*, Communications de la onzième Rencontre québécoise internationale des écrivains. *University of Toronto Quarterly*, 54 (Summer 1985), 494–98.

Smyth, Donna E. Rev. of *Flux*, by Elizabeth Jones; and *Two Kinds of Honey*, by Rosemary Aubert. *Atlantis: A Women's Studies Journal/Journal d'Études sur la Femme* [Acadia Univ.], 4, No. 2 (Spring/printemps 1979), 221–24.

Sowton, Ian. "Pastoral Lines." Rev. of *Castle Mountain*, by Luanne Armstrong; *Daughters*, by Jane Munro; and *The Authentic Lie*, by Suniti Namjoshi. *Canadian Literature*, [Poetic Form], No. 97 (Summer 1983), pp. 124–26.

Stephens, Donald. "Apparent & Real." Rev. of *84 Best Canadian Stories* and *Coming Attractions*, ed. David Helwig and Sandra Martin. *Canadian Literature*, [Italian-Canadian Connections], No. 106 (Fall 1985), pp. 160–61.

Théoret, France. "Une littérature de bon ton." Compte rendu de *Mélano*, par Marie Lafleur; et *Les cloisons*, par Solange Levesque. *Spirale*, no 4 (déc. 1979), p. 5.

Théry, Chantal. "*Féminité, subversion, écriture*: L'aube-scène sextuelle et les motmificateurs." Compte rendu de *Féminité, subversion, écriture*, ed. Suzanne Lamy et Irène Pagès. *Lettres québécoises: Revue de l'actualité littéraire*, no 34 (été 1984), pp. 68–69.

Thesen, Sharon. "Finding the Words." Rev. of *Colour of Her Speech*, by Lola Lemire Tostevin; *Split Levels*, by Judith Fitzgerald; *Matinee Light*, by Diane Hartog; and *Lost Language: Selected Poems by Maxine Gadd*, by Maxine Gadd, ed. Daphne Marlatt and Ingrid Klassen. *line*, No. 3 (Spring 1984), pp. 82–87.

Thomas, Deb. "Small Press Poetry." Rev. of *Digging In*, by Elizabeth Brewster; and *The Women Who Hate Me*, by Dorothy Allison. *Kinesis*, Dec.–Jan. 1984–85, p. 23.

Vaisius, Andrew. ". . . And the Women Get Better." Rev. of *Domestic Fuel*, by Erin Mouré; *Censored Letters*, by Betsy Struthers; *Common Magic*, by Bronwen Wallace; and *Grasshopper*, by Helen Hawley. *Waves*, 14, Nos. 1–2 (Fall 1985), 116–20.

Van Daele, Christa. "Musgrave, Fiamengo and Yeo: Three Poets, Three Voices." Rev. of *The Impstone*, by Susan Musgrave; *In Praise of Older Women*, by Marya Fiamengo; and *The Custodian of Chaos*, by Mary Yeo. *Branching Out: Canadian Magazine for Women*, 3, No. 4 (Sept.–Oct. 1976), 42–43.

——— . "Psyche Meets Daydream Daughter." Rev. of *One Who Became Lost*, by Marilyn Bowering; and *Daydream Daughter*, by Catherine Firestone. *Branching Out: Canadian Magazine for Women*, 4, No. 2 (May–June 1977), 42–44.

Van Gorder, Julia. "West Coast Fiction Comes of Age." Rev. of *West of Fiction*, ed. Leah Flater, Aritha van Herk, and Rudy Wiebe. HERizons: *The Manitoba Women's News Magazine*, Oct. 1984, p. 44.

Van Varseveld, Gail. Rev. of *Women in Canadian Literature*, ed. M. G. Hesse. *Room of One's Own*, 3, No. 4 (1978), 64–65.

——— . "Snakes and Irises." Rev. of *Room of One's Own*, [Special Issue on Marian Engel], 9, No. 2 (June 1984). *Broadside: A Feminist Review* [Toronto], Dec.–Jan. 1984–85, p. 15.

Waddington, Miriam. "The New Woman." Rev. of *Abra*, by Joan Barfoot; and *Judith*, by Aritha van Herk. *Canadian Literature*, [Psychological Fictions: Myth, Carr, Lowry], No. 84 (Spring 1980), pp. 101–05.

Whiteman, Bruce. "Seven Women." Rev. of *Where Have You Been*, by Miriam Mandel; *Lying in Bed*, by Mary Howes; *The Inanna Poems*, by Karen Lawrence; *Songs & Dances*, by Elizabeth Gourlay; *the wide arable land*, by Carolyn Zonailo; *In Search of Living Things*, by Gail Fox; and *This Series Has Been Discontinued*, by Joan Finnegan. *The Fiddlehead*, No. 132

(April 1982), pp. 112–15.

Wilson, Jean. "Common Ground, Common Stories." Rev. of *Common Ground: Stories by Women*, ed. Marilyn Berge, Linda Field, Cynthia Flood, Penny Goldsmith, and Lark. *Broadside: A Feminist Review* [Toronto], Oct. 1980, p. 21.

—————. "Creating Erotic Language." Rev. of *Touch to My Tongue*, by Daphne Marlatt; and *open is broken*, by Betsy Warland. *Kinesis*, Dec.–Jan. 1984–85, p. 33.

—————. Rev. of *Mad Women & Crazy Ladies*, by Sharon H. Nelson; and *The Larger Life*, by Libby Scheier. *Room of One's Own*, 9, No. 1 (Feb. 1984), 76–81.

—————. "'Screams Should Be Heard and Not Seen.'" Rev. of *True Stories*, by Margaret Atwood; and *Wilson's Bowl*, by Phyllis Webb. *Broadside: A Feminist Review* [Toronto], May 1981, p. 14.

Young, D. Rev. of *Women and Words: The Anthology/Les Femmes et les Mots: Une Anthologie*, ed. West Coast Editorial Collective. *Hejira* [McGill Faculty of Nursing], 2, No. 4 (Spring 1985), 34–36.

❧

Individual Writers/Écrivains individuelles (Books/Livres, Articles and Sections of Books/Articles et sections de livres, Theses and Dissertations/Thèses, Interviews/ Entretiens, Reviews/Comptes rendus, and/et Miscellaneous/ Matière diverse

Allen, Charlotte Vale

Reviews/Comptes rendus

Marie, G. "Incest: A Very Personal Response to a Very Personal Memoir." Rev. of *Daddy's Girl: A Very Personal Memoir*. *Kinesis*, [vsw: Celebrating Our First Ten Years], Feb. 1981, p. 18.

Allen, Lillian

Interviews/Entretiens

Kerr, Kandance. "Lillian Allen Considers Community, Culture and Criticism." *Kinesis*, July–Aug. 1986, pp. 16–17.

Reviews/Comptes rendus

Guzman, Roevel. "Review of Dub Poet Lillian Allen's Performance." *Hejira* [McGill Faculty of Nursing], 3, No. 2 (Spring 1986), 45–46.

Allison, Gay

Interviews/Entretiens

Fitzgerald, Judith. "Gay Allison." *Cross-Canada Writers' Quarterly*, 8, No. 2 (1986), 16–17.

Alonzo, Anne-Marie

Interviews/Entretiens

"'Je n'ai pas écrit pour, j'ai écrit point': une entrevue avec Anne-Marie Alonzo." *La Gazette des femmes,* 3, no 1 (juin 1981), 14–15.

Reviews/Comptes rendus

Cotnoir, Louise. "La geste, la parole." Compte rendu de *Geste. Spirale,* no 9 (mai 1980), p. 7.

Kern, Anne Brigitte. "Lectures de *Geste.*" *des femmes en mouvements hebdo* [Paris], 16–23 nov. 1979, p. 25.

La Palme Reyes, Marie. Compte rendu de *Geste. Canadian Women's Studies/les cahiers de la femme* [Centennial College], 3, no 2 (1981), 116.

Orenstein, Gloria Feman. Rev. of *Geste. 13th Moon* [Cathedral Station, N.Y.], 5, Nos. 1–2 (1981), 145–46.

Amyot, Geneviève

Reviews/Comptes rendus

Bougé, Réjane. Compte rendu de *Journal de l'année passée. Canadian Women's Studies/les cahiers de la femme* [Centennial College], 2, no 1 (1980), 91–92.

Andersen, Marguerite

Reviews/Comptes rendus

Beauchamp, Colette. Compte rendu de *De Mémoire de femme. Resources for Feminist Research/Documentation sur la recherche féministe,* [Reviews Issue/Comptes rendus], 12, no 4 [sic; 2] (July 1983), 19–20.

Bersianik, Louky [Lucile Durand]. Compte rendu de *L'autrement pareille. Arcade,* [désirs et passions], no 10 (oct. 1985), pp. 52–53.

Hornosty, Cornelia C. Rev. of *L'autrement pareille. Hysteria* [Kitchener, Ont.], 4, No. 2 (Fall 1985), 26–27.

Anderson, Doris

Articles and Sections of Books/ Articles et sections de livres

Stoffman, Judy. "The Importance of Being Doris." *Weekend Magazine* [*The Globe and Mail*] [Toronto], 4 March 1978, pp. 8–10.

Reviews/Comptes rendus

Bagnall, Janet. "'Rough' Separates Image from Reality." Rev. of *Rough Layout. The Gazette* [Montreal], 14 Nov. 1981, p. 26.

Batt, Sharon. "Oh Julia! Oh Hilary! Oh Doris . . . ." Rev. of *Two Women. Branching Out: Canadian Magazine for Women,* 5, No. 3 (1978), 42.

Cheda, Sherrill. Rev. of *Rough Layout. Canadian Women's Studies/les cahiers de la femme* [York Univ./Centennial College], 3, No. 4 (Summer 1982), 63.

French, William. "Doris Doesn't Go Far Enough for Libel Suits." Rev. of *Rough Layout. The Globe and Mail* [Toronto], 29 Oct. 1981, p. E1.

Hosek, Chaviva. "Women's Fiction Lives." Rev. of *Two Women. Status of Women News/Statut de la femme,* 4, No. 4 (June 1978), 18.

Wachtel, Eleanor. "Chatelaine as Fiction." Rev. of *Rough Layout. The Vancouver Sun,* 27 Nov. 1981, p. L39.

Anger, Felicité (pseud. Laure Conan)

Articles and Sections of Books/ Articles et sections de livres

Belle-Isle, Francine. "La voix-séduction: A propos de Laure Conan." *études littéraires* [Univ. Laval], 11 (déc. 1978),

459–72.

Brunelle, Yves. "Bibliographical Note." In *Angeline de Montbrun*. By Laure Conan. Trans. and introd. Yves Brunelle. Toronto: Univ. of Toronto Press, 1974, pp. xxviii–xxxiii.

Dumont, Micheline. "Laure Conan, 1845–1925." Dans *The Clear Spirit: Twenty Canadian Women and Their Times*. Ed. Mary Quayle Innis. Toronto: Canadian Federation of University Women/Univ. of Toronto Press, 1966, pp. 91–102.

Gallays, François. "Reflections in the Pool: The Subtext of Laure Conan's *Angéline de Montbrun*." In *Traditionalism, Nationalism and Feminism: Women Writers of Quebec*. Ed. Paula Gilbert Lewis. Contributions in Women's Studies, No. 53. Westport, Conn.: Greenwood, 1985, pp. 11–26.

Theses and Dissertations/Thèses

Belle-Isle-Letourneau, F. "Laure Conan ou l'anonymat sexuel. Essai d'étude psychoérotique." Thèse de maîtrise Laval 1978.

Roden, Lethem Sutcliffe. "Laure Conan the First French-Canadian Woman Novelist." Diss. Toronto 1956.

Atwood, Margaret

Books/Livres

Davey, Frank. *Margaret Atwood: A Feminist Poetics*. New Canadian Criticism. Vancouver: Talonbooks, 1984. 178 pp.

Grace, Sherrill. *Violent Duality: A Study of Margaret Atwood*. Montreal: Véhicule, 1980. 154 pp; esp. pp. 117–23.

Articles and Sections of Books/
Articles et sections de livres

Allen, Carolyn. "Failures of Word, Uses of Silence, Djuna Barnes, Adrienne Rich, and Margaret Atwood." *Regionalism and the Female Imagination* [Pennsylvania State Univ.], 4, No. 1 (Spring 1978), 1–8.

——— . "Margaret Atwood: Power of Transformation, Power of Knowledge." *Essays on Canadian Writing*, No. 6 (Spring 1977), pp. 5–17.

Atwood, Margaret. "'My Craft and Sullen Art': The Writers Speak. Margaret Atwood." *Atlantis: A Women's Studies Journal/Journal d'Études sur la Femme* [Acadia Univ.], 4, No. 1 (Fall/automne 1978), 161–63.

——— . "A Reply." *Signs: Journal of Women in Culture and Society*, 2 (Winter 1976), 340–41.

Bjerring, Nancy E. "The Problem of Language in Atwood's 'Surfacing.'" *Queen's Quarterly*, 83 (Winter 1976), 597–612.

Blakely, Barbara. "The Pronunciations of Flesh: A Feminist Reading of Atwood's Poetry." In *Margaret Atwood: Language, Text and System*. Ed. Sherrill Grace and Lorraine Weir. Vancouver: Univ. of British Columbia Press, 1983, pp. 33–52.

Brownstein, Rachel M. *Becoming a Heroine: Reading about Women in Novels*. New York: Viking, 1982, p. xvii. Rpt. Harmondsworth, Eng.: Penguin, 1984, p. xvii.

Cameron, Elspeth. "Femininity or Parody of Autonomy: Anorexia Nervosa and *The Edible Woman*." *Journal of Canadian Studies/Revue d'études canadiennes* [Trent Univ.], 20, No. 2 (Summer/été 1985), 45–69.

——— . "Margaret Atwood: A Patchwork Self." *Book Forum* [New York], 4 (1978), 33–45.

Campbell, Josie P. "The Woman as Hero in Margaret Atwood's *Surfacing*." *MOSAIC: A Journal for the Comparative Study of Literature and Ideas* [Univ. of Manitoba], [Post-War Canadian Fiction], 11, No. 3 (Spring 1978), 17–28.

Christ, Carol P. "Margaret Atwood: The Surfacing of Women's Spiritual Quest and Vision." *Signs: Journal of Women in Culture and Society*, 2 (Winter 1976), 316–30.

——— . "Refusing to Be Victim: Margaret Atwood." In her *Diving Deep and Surfacing: Women Writers on Spiritual Quest*.

Boston: Beacon, 1980, pp. 41–54.

Collison, Robert. "Margaret Atwood Takes N.Y.C." *Chatelaine*, June 1986, pp. 64–65, 99–100, 102–04.

Edgington, Kay. "Victims, Survivors, and Modern Literature." *Women: A Journal of Liberation*, [With or Without Men], 7, No. 1 ([1980]), 44–46.

Frankel, Vivian. "Margaret Atwood: A Personal View." *Branching Out: Canadian Magazine for Women*, 2, No. 1 (Jan.–Feb. 1975), 24–26.

Friebert, Lucy M. "The Artist as Picaro: The Revelation of Margaret Atwood's *Lady Oracle*." *Canadian Literature*, [Fiction in the Seventies], No. 92 (Spring 1982), pp. 23–33.

Gerstenberger, Donna. "Conceptions Literary and Otherwise: Women Writers and the Modern Imagination." *Novel: A Forum on Fiction*, 9, No. 2 (Winter 1976), 141–50.

Goddard, John. "Lady Oracle." *Books in Canada*, Nov. 1985, pp. 6–10.

Gottlieb, Lois C., and Wendy Keitner. "Colonialism as Metaphor and Experience in *The Grass Is Singing* and *Surfacing*." ACLALS Conference, Delhi. Jan. 1977.

Grace, Sherrill E. Introduction. In *The Circle Game*. By Margaret Atwood. Toronto: House of Anansi, 1978, pp. 9–15.

Homans, Margaret. "'Her Very Own Howl': The Ambiguities of Representation in Recent Women's Fiction." *Signs: Journal of Women in Culture and Society*, 9 (Winter 1983), 186–205.

Horne, Alan J. "Margaret Atwood: An Annotated Bibliography (Poetry)." In *The Annotated Bibliography of Canada's Major Authors*. Ed. Robert Lecker and Jack David. Vol. II. Downsview, Ont.: ECW, 1980, 13–53.

———. "Margaret Atwood: An Annotated Bibliography (Prose)." In *The Annotated Bibliography of Canada's Major Authors*. Ed. Robert Lecker and Jack David. Vol. I. Downsview, Ont.: ECW, 1979, 13–46.

Hulley, Kathleen. "Margaret Atwood and Leonard Cohen: The Feminine Voice."

Etudes Canadiennes/Canadian Studies [Univ. de Bordeaux III], No. 1 (déc. 1975), pp. 73–78.

Irvine, Lorna. "One Woman Leads to Another." In *The Art of Margaret Atwood: Essays in Criticism*. Ed. Arnold E. Davidson and Cathy N. Davidson. Toronto: House of Anansi, 1981, pp. 95–106.

———. "The Red and Silver Heroes Have Collapsed." *Concerning Poetry* [Western Washington Univ.], 12, No. 2 (Fall 1979), 59–68.

Johnston, Sue Ann. "The Daughter as Escape Artist." *Atlantis: A Women's Studies Journal/Journal d'études sur la femme* [Mt. St. Vincent Univ.], 9, No. 2 (Spring/printemps 1984), 23–34.

Kostash, Myrna. "Margaret Atwood No Flash in the Pan." *The Edmonton Journal*, 5 April 1980, p. I4.

Lauter, Estelle. "Margaret Atwood: Remythologizing Circe." In her *Women as Mythmakers: Poetry and Visual Art by Twentieth-Century Women*. Bloomington: Univ. of Indianna Press, 1984, pp. 62–78.

Leclaire, Jacques. "*Life Before Man*, critique d'un mode de vie: les problèmes nés du féminisme et le désenchantement de la liberté." *Etudes Canadiennes/Canadian Studies* [Univ. de Bordeaux III], no 15 (déc. 1983), pp. 129–36.

Lyons, Bonnie. "'Neither Victims nor Executioners' in Margaret Atwood's Fiction." *World Literature Written in English* [Univ. of Texas at Arlinton], [Women Writers of the Commonwealth], 17 (April 1978), 181–87.

MacLeod, Hilary. "Margaret Atwood — Art and Motherhood." *Canadian Author & Bookman*, 61, No. 4 (July 1986), 2–3.

McCombs, Judith. "Atwood's Haunted Sequences: *The Circle Game*, *The Journals of Susanna Moodie*, and *Power Politics*." In *The Art of Margaret Atwood: Essays in Criticism*. Ed. Arnold E. Davidson and Cathy N. Davidson. Toronto: House of Anansi, 1981, pp. 35–54.

———. "Atwood's Nature Concepts: An Overview." *Waves*, 7, No. 1 (Fall 1978), 68–77.

Meigs, Mary. "Atwood's Perfect Pitch." *Broadside: A Feminist Review* [Toronto], May 1983, p. 8.

Onley, Gloria. "Power Politics in Bluebeard's Castle." *Canadian Literature*, [Contemporary Canadian Poets], No. 60 (Spring 1974), pp. 21–42.

Piercy, Marge. "Margaret Atwood: Beyond Victimhood." *The American Poetry Review*, 2, No. 6 (Nov.–Dec. 1973), 41–44. Rpt. in *Parti-Colored Blocks for a Quilt*. By Marge Piercy. Poets on Poetry. Ann Arbor: Univ. of Michigan Press, 1982, pp. 281–99.

Plaskow, Judith. "On Carol Christ on Margaret Atwood: Some Reflections." *Signs: Journal of Women in Culture and Society*, 2 (Winter 1976), 331–39.

Pratt, Annis. "Margaret Atwood and the Elixir of Maternity." In her *Archetypal Patterns in Women's Fiction*. Bloomington: Indiana Univ. Press, 1981, pp. 157–61.

———. "*Surfacing* and the Rebirth Journey." In *The Art of Margaret Atwood: Essays in Criticism*. Ed. Arnold E. Davidson and Cathy N. Davidson. Toronto: House of Anansi, 1981, pp. 139–58.

Pyke, S. W. "Children's Literature: Conceptions of Sex Roles." In *Socialization, Social Stratification and Ethnicity*. Vol. II of *Socialization and Values in Canadian Society*. Ed. Robert M. Pike and Elia Zureik. Toronto: McClelland and Stewart, 1975, pp. 51–73.

Rich, Adrienne. "Motherhood: Daughterhood. 6." In her *Of Woman Born: Motherhood as Experience and Institution*. New York: Norton, 1976, pp. 243–45. Rpt. New York: Bantam, 1977, pp. 243–45.

Rigney, Barbara Hill. "After the Failure of Logic: Descent and Return in *Surfacing*." In *Madness and Sexual Politics in the Feminist Novel: Studies in Brontë, Woolf, Lessing and Atwood*. Ed. B. H. Rigney. Madison: Univ. of Wisconsin Press, 1978, pp. 91–115.

Rocard, Marcienne. "La femme objet de consommation dans *The Edible Woman* de Margaret Atwood." *Caliban*, 17 (1980), 111–20.

Slopen, Beverley. "Paperclips: Sisterhood Celebrated in Poetry and Politics . . . the Ghost of Quotations Past . . . and Women Against Virginity." *Quill & Quire*, April 1980, p. 26.

Stewart, Grace. *A New Mythos: The Novel of the Artist as Heroine, 1877–1977*. Montreal: Eden, 1979, pp. 170–74.

Sweetapple, Rosemary. "Margaret Atwood: Victims and Survivors." *Southern Review: Literary and Interdisciplinary Essays* [Univ. of Adelaide], 9 (March 1976), 50–69.

Texmo, Dell. "The Other Side of the Looking Glass: Image and Identity in Margaret Atwood's *The Edible Woman*." *Atlantis: A Women's Studies Journal/ Journal d'Études sur la Femme* [Acadia Univ.], 2, No. 2, Pt. 1 (Spring/printemps 1977), 64–76.

Vincent Sibyl Korf. "The Mirror and the Cameo: Margaret Atwood's Comic/ Gothic Novel *Lady Oracle*." In *The Female Gothic*. Ed. Juliann E. Fleenor. Montreal: Eden, 1983, pp. 153–63.

Waters, Katherine E. "Margaret Atwood: Love on the Dark Side of the Moon." In *Mother was Not a Person*. Ed. Margret Andersen. Montreal: Black Rose, 1972, pp. 102–19.

Yalom, Marilyn. "Margaret Atwood: *Surfacing*." In *Maternity, Mortality and the Literature of Madness*. Ed. Marilyn Yalom. Philadelphia: Pennsylvania State Univ., 1985, pp. 71–88, 119–20.

Theses and Dissertations/Thèses

Baer, Elizabeth R. "The Journey Inward: The Quest Motif in Lessing, Rhys and Atwood." Diss. Indiana 1981.

Connor, Margaret Susan Carpenter. "Inside Out: Eye Imagery and Female Identity in Margaret Atwood's Poetry." M.A. Thesis North Texas State 1982.

Gronvigh, Joanne. "Thematic Development

in the Work of Margaret Atwood." M.A. Thesis Dalhousie 1977, esp. pp. 8–13, 74–86.

Interviews/Entretiens

Collective. "An *Atlantis* Interview with Margaret Atwood." *Atlantis: A Women's Studies Journal/Journal d'études sur la femme* [Acadia Univ.], 5, No. 2 (Spring/printemps 1980), 202–11.

Govier, Katherine. "Margaret Atwood: 'There's Nothing in the Book That Hasn't Already Happened.'" *Quill & Quire*, Sept. 1985, pp. 66–67.

Hammond, Karla. "An Interview with Margaret Atwood." *The American Poetry Review*, 8, No. 5 (Sept.–Oct. 1979), 27–29.

——— . "A Margaret Atwood Interview with Karla Hammond." *Concerning Poetry* [Western Washington Univ.], 12, No. 2 (Fall 1979), 73–81.

Landsberg, Michèle. "Late Motherhood." *Chatelaine*, Oct. 1977, pp. 44–46, 119–23, 125.

Matheson, Sue. "An Interview with Margaret Atwood." HERizons: *The Manitoba Women's News Magazine*, Jan.–Feb. 1986, pp. 20–22.

Miner, Valerie. "Atwood in Metamorphosis: An Authentic Canadian Fairy Tale." In *Her Own Woman: Profiles of Ten Canadian Women.* Ed. Myrna Kostash, Melanie McCracken, Valerie Miner, Erna Paris, and Heather Robertson. Toronto: Macmillan, 1975, pp. 173–94. Rpt. (abridged — "The Many Facets of Margaret Atwood") in *Chatelaine*, June 1975, pp. 32–33, 66, 68, 70.

Porter-Ladousse, Gillian. "The Unicorn and the Booby Hatch: An Interview with Margaret Atwood." *Etudes Canadiennes/Canadian Studies* [Univ. de Bordeaux III], No. 5 (déc. 1978), pp. 97–111.

Sandler, Linda. "Interview with Margaret Atwood." *The Malahat Review* [Univ. of Victoria], [Margaret Atwood: A Symposium], No. 41 (Jan. 1977), pp. 7–27.

Slinger, Helen. "Interview with Margaret Atwood." *Maclean's*, 6 Sept. 1976, pp. 4–7.

Slopen, Beverley. "Margaret Atwood." *Publisher's Weekly* [New York], 23 Aug. 1976, pp. 6–8.

Swan, Susan. "Margaret Atwood: The Woman as Poet." *Communiqué*, No. 8 (May 1975), pp. 8–11, 45–46.

Timson, Judith. "*Chatelaine's* Woman of the Year 1981: The Magnificent Margaret Atwood." *Chatelaine*, June 1981, pp. 42–43, 56, 60, 64–65, 68, 70.

van Varseveld, Gail. "Talking with Atwood." *Room of One's Own*, 1, No. 2 (Summer 1975), 66–70.

Reviews/Comptes rendus

Bell, Millicent. "The Girl on the Wedding Cake." Rev. of *The Edible Woman. New York Times Book Review*, 18 Oct. 1970, p. 51.

Blott, Anne. "Journey to Light." Rev. of *Interlunar. The Fiddlehead*, No. 146 (Winter 1985), pp. 90–95.

Cameron, Elspeth. "In Darkest Atwood." Rev. of *Murder in the Dark. Saturday Night*, March 1983, pp. 70–72.

Carpenter, Mary Wilson. Letter. Rev. of *The Handmaid's Tale. The Women's Review of Books* [Wellesley, Mass.], Sept. 1986, p. 5.

Charest, Aline. Compte rendu de *La vie avant l'homme. F.F.Q.* [La Fédération des Femmes du Québec], 2, no 1 (fév. 1982), 14.

Cole, Susan G. "Margaret Atwood: In Vertebrates Veritas." Rev. of *Life Before Man. Broadside: A Feminist Review* [Toronto], March 1980, p. 14.

Cotnoir, Louise. "Rien de confortable." Compte rendu de *La vie avant l'homme. Spirale*, no 23 (mars 1982), p. 11.

Davidson, Jane. "The Anguish of Identity." Rev. of *Surfacing. The Financial Post* [Toronto], 24 Feb. 1973, p. C5.

Delany, Paul. "Clearing a Canadian Space." Rev. of *Surfacing. New York Times Book Review*, 4 March 1973, p. 5.

du Plessix Gray, Francine. "Nature as the

Nunnery." Rev. of *Surfacing. New York Times Book Review,* 17 July 1977, pp. 3, 29.

Gousse, Diane. Compte rendu de *Lady Oracle. Des luttes et des rires de femmes,* 4, no 2 (déc.–jan. 1980–81), 52.

Greene, Gayle. "Choice of Evils." Rev. of *The Handmaid's Tale. The Women's Review of Books* [Wellesley, Mass.], July 1986, pp. 14–15.

Hofsess, John. "The Hand That Holds the Pen." Rev. of *Second Words: Selected Critical Prose,* by Margaret Atwood; and *The New Oxford Book of Canadian Verse: In English,* ed. Margaret Atwood. *Books in Canada,* Feb. 1983, pp. 12–13.

Jackson, Marni. "Critic's Choice: Margaret Atwood's *The Handmaid's Tale.*" *Chatelaine,* Oct. 1985, p. 4.

Jeannotte, M. Sharon. "An Emotional Divide." Rev. of *Lady Oracle. The Sphinx: A Magazine of Literature and Society,* [Canadian Literature Special], 2, No. 3 (Winter 1977), 81–85.

Klein, Carroll. "A Fertility Tale." Rev. of *The Handmaid's Tale. Broadside: A Feminist Review* [Toronto], Dec.–Jan. 1985–86, p. 13.

Larkin, Joan. "Soul Survivor." Rev. of *Power Politics* and *Surfacing. Ms.* [New York], May 1973, pp. 33–35.

Marshall, Joyce. Rev. of *Life Before Man. Branching Out: Canadian Feminist Quarterly,* 7, No. 1 (1980), 48–49.

Mitcham, Allison. "Woman in the North." Rev. of *Surfacing. Alive* [Guelph, Ont.], No. 39 ([Fall 1974]), p. 7. Rpt. (revised — "Margaret Atwood: Woman in the North") in *The Northern Imagination: A Study of Northern Canadian Literature.* By Allison Mitcham. Moonbeam, Ont.: Penumbra, 1983, pp. 95–99.

Morley, Patricia. Rev. of *Dancing Girls and Other Stories. World Literature Written in English* [Univ. of Texas at Arlington], [Women Writers of the Commonwealth], 17 (April 1978), 188–90.

Muzychka, Martha. Rev. of *The Handmaid's Tale. Breaking the Silence,* 4, Nos. 3–4 (Spring–Summer 1986), 27–28.

Newman, Christina. "In Search of a Native Tongue." Rev. of *Surfacing. Maclean's,* Sept. 1972, p. 88.

Ouellette-Michalska, Madeleine. Compte rendu de *La vie avant l'homme. Châtelaine,* mai 1982, p. 18.

Sandler, Linda. "Atwoodian Parody of the 1950s." Rev. of *Lady Oracle. Saturday Night,* Sept. 1976, p. 59.

Scott, Gail. "Ontario Gothic." Rev. of *Life Before Man. Spirale,* No. 10 (juin 1980), pp. 1, 4.

Sheard, Sarah. "Captives & Keepers." Rev. of *The Handmaid's Tale. Brick* [Toronto], No. 25 (Fall 1985), pp. 24–26.

Thomas, Audrey. "Topic of Cancer." Rev. of *Bodily Harm. Books in Canada,* Oct. 1981, pp. 9–12.

Thomas, Clara. "Feminist or Heroine?". Rev. of *Lady Oracle. Essays on Canadian Writing,* No. 6 (Spring 1977), pp. 28–31.

Vendler, Helen. "Do Women Have Distinctive Subjects, Roles and Styles?." Rev. of *Half Lives,* by Erica Jong; *Impossible Buildings,* by Judith Johnson Sherwin; and *Power Politics,* by Margaret Atwood. *New York Times Book Review,* 12 Aug. 1973, pp. 6–7.

Waelti-Walters, Jennifer. "Double-Read: On Margaret Atwood's *Bodily Harm.*" *Tessera,* No. 1 [*Room of One's Own,* 8, No. 4] (1983), 116–22.

Weir, Lorraine. "True Dilemmas." Rev. of *True Stories. Canadian Literature,* [Caribbean Connections], No. 95 (Winter 1982), pp. 112–13.

Miscellaneous/Matière diverse

Webb, Phyllis. "Letters to Margaret Atwood." *Open Letter,* Ser. 2, No. 5 (Summer 1973), pp. 71–73. Rpt. in *Wilson's Bowl.* By Phyllis Webb. Toronto: Coach House, 1980, pp. 36–38.

Avison, Margaret

Articles and Sections of Books/ Articles et sections de livres

Mansbridge, Francis. "Margaret Avison: An Annotated Bibliography." In *The Annotated Bibliography of Canada's Major Authors.* Ed. Robert Lecker and Jack David. Vol. VI. Toronto: ECW, 1985, 13–66.

Barfoot, Joan

Interviews/ Entretiens

Bolgan, Anne. "An Interview with Joan Barfoot." *Fireweed: A Feminist Literary & Cultural Journal*, [Women and Language], Nos. 5–6 (Winter–Spring 1979–80), pp. 159–63.

Reviews/Comptes rendus

Jackson, Marni. "Diary of Another Mad Housewife." Rev. of *Dancing in the Dark*. *Maclean's*, 18 Oct. 1982, p. 76.

McLay, Catherine. "Surviving and Surfacing." Rev. of *Abra*. *Journal of Canadian Fiction*, No. 33 (1981–82), pp. 134–37.

Mitchell, Penni. Rev. of *Duet for Three*. *HERizons: The Manitoba Women's News Magazine*, July–Aug. 1986, p. 35.

Pearce, Gail. Rev. of *Dancing in the Dark*. *Quill & Quire*, Sept. 1982, p. 58.

Beaulieu, Germaine

Reviews/Comptes rendus

Alonzo, Anne-Marie. "Ici les Amazons." Compte rendu d'*Archives distraites*. *La vie en rose*, avril 1985, pp. 55–56.

Beresford-Howe, Constance

Articles and Sections of Books/ Articles et sections de livres

Beresford-Howe, Constance. "Stages in an Education." In *A Fair Stake: Autobiographical Essays by McGill Women*. Ed. Margaret Gillett and Kay Sibbald. Montreal: Eden, 1984, pp. 30–39.

Martin, Sandra. "Eve, Well Enough Alone." *Quill & Quire*, Aug. 1974, p. 16.

Mulhallen, Karen. "A Funny Thing Happened to Constance Beresford-Howe on Her Way to Freedom." *Books in Canada*, Jan. 1978, pp. 31–32.

Robson, Barbara. "Author Corrects Critics." *Winnipeg Free Press*, 29 May 1982, p. 29.

Ryval, Michael. "Constance Beresford-Howe's Subversion & Sensibility." *Quill & Quire*, July 1981, p. 62.

Woodcock, Connie. "Constance Beresford-Howe: Practising What She Teaches." *McGill News*, 2, No. 1 (Spring 1978), 10.

Reviews/Comptes rendus

Branden, Victoria. "Glory Be to the Mother." Rev. of *The Marriage Bed*. *Books in Canada*, Nov. 1981, pp. 18–19.

French, William. Rev. of *The Marriage Bed*. *The Globe and Mail* [Toronto], 12 Sept. 1981, p. E15.

McCormick, Marion. "'Marriage' Lauds Domesticity." Rev. of *The Marriage Bed*. *The Gazette* [Montreal], 12 Sept. 1981, p. 38.

Wachtel, Eleanor. "Marriage Bed Might Put You to Sleep." Rev. of *The Marriage Bed*. *The Vancouver Sun*, 26 Feb. 1982, p. L37.

Waterston, Elizabeth. Rev. of *The Marriage Bed*. *World Literature Written in English* [Univ. of Guelph], 21 (Autumn 1982), 611–12.

Williamson, David. "Novel Reaffirms Virtues of Motherhood." Rev. of *The Marriage Bed*. *Winnipeg Free Press*, 25 Sept. 1981, p. L5.

Bersianik, Louky [Lucile Durand]

Articles and Sections of Books/
Articles et sections de livres

Ahmed, Maroussia. "'Transgresser, c'est progresser.'" *Incidences* [Univ. d'Ottawa], [Romancières québécoises], NS 4, nos 2–3 (mai–déc. 1980), 119–27.
———. See also/voir aussi Hadjukowski-Ahmed, Maroussia.
Bersianik, Louky [Lucile Durand]. "La mémoire courte." Lettre sur *L'Euguélionne*. *La vie en rose*, juil.–août 1985, p. 50.
Hadjukowski-Ahmed, Maroussia. "Louky Bersianik: Feminist Dialogisms." In *Traditionalism, Nationalism and Feminism: Women Writers of Quebec*. Ed. Paula Gilbert Lewis. Contributions in Women's Studies, No. 53. Westport, Conn.: Greenwood, 1985, pp. 205–25.
———. Voir aussi/see also Ahmed, Maroussia.
Leclerc, Lorraine. "Louky Bersianik: de la mythologie vers le 'je.'" *Femmes du Québec*, 1, no 6 (jan.–fév. 1980), 5–6.
Voldeng, Evelyne. "La parodie carnavalesque dans *L'Euguélionne*." Dans *Féminité, subversion, écriture*. Ed. Suzanne Lamy et Irène Pagès. Montréal: Remue-ménage, 1983, pp. 119–26.
Waelti-Walters, Jennifer. "The Food of Love: Plato's Banquet and Bersianik's Picnic." *Atlantis: A Women's Studies Journal/ Journal d'études sur la femme* [Acadia Univ.], 6, No. 1 (Fall/automne 1980), 96–103.
———. Introduction. In *The Euguélionne*. By Louky Bersianik. Trans. Gerry Denis, Alison Hewit, Donna Murray, and Martha O'Brien. Victoria: Porcépic, [1981], pp. [5–8].

Theses and Dissertations/Thèses

Arbour, Kathryn Mary. "French Feminist Re-Visions: Wittig, Rochefort, Bersianik and D'Eaubonne Re-Write Utopia." Diss. Michigan 1984.

Renault-Wall, Odile. "*L'Euguélionne* de Louky Bersianik: Une écriture au féminin." Thèse de maîtrise McMaster 1980.
Scott, Howard. "Louky Bersianik's *L'Euguélionne*: Problems of Translating the Critique of Language in New Quebec Feminist Writing." M.A. Thesis Concordia 1984.

Interviews/Entretiens

Bersianik, Louky [Lucile Durand]. "Lucile Durand interviewe Louky Bersianik." *Lettres québécoises: Revue de l'actualité littéraire*, no 26 (été 1982), pp. 53–55.
Smith, Donald. "Louky Bersianik et la mythologie du future: De la théorie-fiction à l'émergence de la femme positive." *Lettres québécoises: Revue de l'actualité littéraire*, [Littérature féministe, Littérature au féminin], no 27 (automne 1982), pp. 61–69.

Reviews/Comptes rendus

Alonzo, Anne-Marie. Compte rendu du *Pique-nique sur l'Acropole: Cahiers d'Ancyl*. *La Gazette des femmes*, 2, no 1 (avril 1980), 4.
Céllard, Jacques. "La Vie du langage: Parole de femmes." Compte rendu de *L'Euguélionne*. *Le Monde* [Paris], 1–2 août 1976, p. 13.
Cloutier, Cécile. "*L'Euguélionne*: texte et significations." *Revue de l'Université d'Ottawa/University of Ottawa Quarterly*, [Conférence des femmes-écrivains en Amérique], 50 (jan.–mars/Jan.–March 1980), 95–98.
Desautels, Denise. Compte rendu d'*Axes et eau*. *Arcade*, [désirs et passions], no 10 (oct. 1985), pp. 53–54.
Emond, Ariane. Compte rendu des *Agénésies du vieux monde*, par Louky Bersianik; et *Notes pour une ontologie du féminisme radical*, par Mary Daly. *La vie en rose*, mars–avril–mai 1982, p. 66.
Forsyth, Louise H. "*The Euguélionne*: Out of This World." *Broadside: A Feminist Review* [Toronto], April 1982, p. 16.

Frémont, Gabrielle. Compte rendu du *Pique-nique sur l'Acropole: Cahiers d'Ancyl. Livres et auteurs québécois 1979*. Ed. André Berthiaume. Québec: Les Presses de l'Univ. Laval, 1980, pp. 283–85.

Gariépy-Dubuc, Madeleine. Compte rendu de *L'Euguélionne. Status of Women News/Statut: Bulletin de la femme*, 5, no 1 (Sept. 1978), 25–26.

Groult, Bénoite. "Alice et Zazie au Québec." Compte rendu de *L'Euguélionne. F Magazine*, no 6 (juin 1978), pp. 64–65.

Martin, Agathe. Compte rendu de *L'Euguélionne*. Dans *Livres et auteurs québécois 1976*. Ed. Marcel Bélanger. Québec: Les Presses de l'Univ. Laval, 1977, pp. 50–53.

Merivale, Patricia. "Ideologies." Rev. of *The Euguélionne. Canadian Literature*, [B.C. Writers/Reviews Issue], No. 102 (Autumn 1984), pp. 131–32.

Messner, Céline. Compte rendu d'*Axes et eau. Canadian Women's Studies/les cahiers de la femme* [Centennial College], [Affirmative Action/Action positive], 6, no 4 (Winter/hiver 1985), 127.

Ouellette-Michalska, Madeleine. Compte rendu du *Pique-nique sur l'Acropole. Châtelaine*, mars 1980, p. 36.

Richard, Robert Gerald. Rev. of *L'Euguélionne. Atlantis: A Women's Studies Journal/Journal d'Études sur la Femme* [Acadia Univ.], 2, No. 1 (Fall/automne 1976), 127–29.

Ross, Martine. "Ainsi parlait l'Euguélionne." *Les têtes de pioche*, 1, no 3 (mai 1976), p. 7.

Royer, Jean. "La féminine intégrale." Compte rendu des *Agénésies du vieux monde." Le Devoir* [Montréal], 6 mars 1982, pp. 15, 28.

Théoret, France. "Entre l'excès du verbe et de la communication." Compte rendu du *Pique-nique sur l'Acropole: Cahiers d'Ancyl. Spirale*, no 6 (fév. 1980), p. 7.

Trépanier, Monique. "Le *Pique-nique sur l'Acropole* ou le plaisir du corps." *En-trelles: revue féministe de l'outaouais*, 2, no 3 (mai 1980), 8.

Urbas, Jeannette. Rev. of *The Euguélionne.*

Canadian Women's Studies/les cahiers de la femme [Centennial College], [Multiculture], 4, No. 2 (Winter 1982), 93–94.

Bertrand, Claudine

Reviews/Comptes rendus

Messner, Céline. Compte rendu d'*Idole errante. Canadian Women's Studies/les cahiers de la femme* [Centennial College], [post Nairobi], 7, nos 1–2 (Spring–Summer 1986), 232–33.

Binnie-Clark, Georgina

Articles and Sections of Books/ Articles et sections de livres

Jackel, Susan. Introduction. In *Wheat and Woman*. By Georgina Binnie-Clark. Social History of Canada, No. 30. Toronto: Univ. of Toronto Press, 1980, pp. v–xxxvii.

Blais, Marie-Claire

Articles and Sections of Books/ Articles et sections de livres

Atwood, Margaret. "Marie-Claire Blais Is Not for Burning." *Maclean's*, Sept. 1975, pp. 26–29.

Boivin, Aurelien, Lucie Robert et Ruth Major-Lapierre. "Bibliographie de Marie-Claire Blais." *voix & images: littérature québécoise*, 8 (hiver 1983), 249–95.

Demers, France. "Vos femmes écrivains sont plus évoluées que leurs confrères." *La Patrie* [Montréal], 8 oct. 1967, p. 55.

Forsyth, Louise H. "Some Reflections on the Novels of Marie-Claire Blais." *Resources for Feminist Research/Documentation sur la recherche féministe*, [The Lesbian Issue/Être Lesbienne], 12, No. 1 (March/mars 1983), 16–18.

Gould, Karen. "The Censored Word and the Body Politic: Reconsidering the Fiction of Marie-Claire Blais." *Journal of Popular Culture*, [Canadian Women Writers], 15, No. 3 (Winter 1981), 14–27.

Green, Mary Jean. "Redefining the Maternal: Women's Relationships in the Fiction of Marie-Claire Blais." In *Traditionalism, Nationalism and Feminism: Women Writers of Quebec*. Ed. Paula Gilbert Lewis. Contributions in Women's Studies, No. 53. Westport, Conn.: Greenwood, 1985, pp. 125–39.

Hofsess, John. "I Am, Simply, a Writer." *Books in Canada*, Feb. 1979, pp. 8–10.

Lewis, Paula Gilbert. "From Shattered Reflections to Female Bonding: Mirroring in Marie-Claire Blais's *Visions d'Anna*." *Québec Studies*, 1, No. 2 (1984), 94–104.

Major-Lapierre, Ruth. Voir/see Boivin, Aurelien, Lucie Robert et Ruth Major-Lapierre.

Paradis, Suzanne. "La jeune fille écrivain: Marie-Claire Blais." *Le Devoir* [Montréal], 22 juin 1963, p. 9.

Racicot, Ginette. "Place aux femmes." *Vie et carrières*, mai 1968, pp. 14–15.

Robert, Lucie. Voir/see Boivin, Aurelien, Lucie Robert et Ruth Major-Lapierre.

Russell, George. "Nightmare's Child." *Weekend Magazine* [*The Globe and Mail*] [Toronto], 23 Oct. 1976, pp. 10–13.

Slama, Béatrice. "*La Belle Bête* ou la double scène." *voix & image: littérature québécoise*, 8 (hiver 1983), 211–28.

Waelti-Walters, Jennifer. "Beauty and Madness in M.-C. Blais' *La Belle bête*." *Journal of Canadian Fiction*, [Les romanciers Québécois et leurs oeuvres], Nos. 25–26 (1979), pp. 186–98.

———. "Tuer des innocents: The Morality of Wanton Murder in Beauvoir's *Les Bouches inutiles* and Blais' *l'Exécution*." NEMLA, New York. April 1982.

Theses and Dissertations/Thèses

Tremblay, Victor Laurent. "La Révolte contre le patriarcat dans l'oeuvre de Marie-Claire Blais." Thèse de maîtrise British Columbia 1980.

Interviews/Entretiens

Pilotte, Hélène. "L'insoumise des lettres canadiennes: Entrevue avec la romancière à succès Marie-Claire Blais." *Châtelaine*, août 1966, pp. 21–23, 51–54.

Reviews/Comptes rendus

"Châtelaine en pantoufles." Compte rendu de *David Sterne*. *Châtelaine*, sept. 1967, p. 4.

Escomel, Gloria. Compte rendu de *Sourd dans la ville*. *La Gazette des femmes*, 2, no 2 (juin 1980), 4.

Godard, Barbara. Rev. of *Durer's Angels*. *Waves*, 6, No. 1 (Autumn 1977), 77–80.

———. Rev. of *Les nuits de l'Underground*, by Marie-Claire Blais. *Fireweed: A Feminist Literary & Cultural Journal*, [Women and Language], Nos. 5–6 (Winter–Spring 1979–80), pp. 195–96.

Gories, Doris. Rev. of *A Literary Affair* and *Nights in the Underground*. *Branching Out: Canadian Magazine for Women*, 7, No. 1 (1980), 50–51.

Gose, Elliot. "The Witch Within." Rev. of *Mad Shadows*. *Canadian Literature*, No. 7 (Winter 1961), pp. 72–74.

Gower, Doris E. Rev. of *A Literary Affair* and *Nights in the Underground*. *Branching Out: Canadian Feminist Quarterly*, 7, No. 1 (1980), 50–51.

Huot, Maurice. "De Christine de Pisan à Marie-Claire Blais." Compte rendu de *L'Insoumise*. *Le Droit* [Ottawa], 30 juil. 1966, p. 12.

Mailhot, Michèle A. "Châtelaine a lu pour vous: Images du Québec et du Canada." Compte rendu de *Tête Blanche*. *Châtelaine*, fév. 1961, p. 13.

Nabahi, Férechté. Compte rendu de *Sommeil d'hiver*. *Canadian Women's Studies/les cahiers de la femme* [Centennial College], [post Nairobi], 7, nos 1–2 (Spring–Summer 1986), 230–31.

Poulin, Gabrielle. "Saphisme, mystique et littérature." Compte rendu des *Nuits de*

*l'Underground. Lettres québécoises:
Revue de l'actualité littéraire*, [Littérature
féminine, Littérature au féminin], no 12
(nov. 1978), pp. 6–8.

Théoret, France. "Roman québécois: Mères
et filles en procès." Compte rendu de *Visions d'Auna. Spirale*, no 27 (sept. 1982),
p. 7.

Blewett, Jean

Reviews/Comptes rendus

Waterloo, Stanley. Rev. of *Heart Songs. The
Canadian Magazine of Politics, Science,
Art and Literature* [Toronto], Dec. 1897,
pp. 190–92.

Boisjoli, Charlotte

Reviews/Comptes rendus

Tremblay, Chantalle. "Sept nouvelles atta-
chantes." Compte rendu de *La chatte
blanche. Entrelles: revue féministe de
l'outaouais*, 4, no 1 (fév. 1982), 11.

Bolt, Carol

Interviews/Entretiens

Lister, Rota. "An Interview with Carol
Bolt." *World Literature Written in English* [Univ. of Texas at Arlington],
[Women Writers of the Commonwealth],
17 (April 1978), 144–53.
Wallace, Robert. See/voir Zimmerman, Cynthia, and Robert Wallace.
Zimmerman, Cynthia, and Robert Wallace.
"Carol Bolt." In their *The Work: Conversations with English-Canadian Playwrights*. Toronto: Coach House, 1982,
pp. 264–76.

Bosco, Monique

Articles and Sections of Books/
Articles et sections de livres

Escomel, Gloria. "Monique Bosco, l'icono-
claste." *voix & images: littérature québécoise*, 9, no 3 (printemps 1984), 47–54.
——— . "Monique Bosco ou la Femme en
quête de son double." *Liberté*, 20, no 2
[no 116] (mars 1978), 88–95.
——— . "Monique Bosco ou le miroir
brisé." *la nouvelle barre du jour*, no 65
(avril 1978), pp. 90–97.
Gallays, François. "Le corps scellés: Analyse
de trois romans de Monique Bosco." *voix
& images: littérature québécoise*, 9, no 3
(printemps 1984), 35–45.
Pavlovic, Myrianne. "Bibliographie de Monique Bosco." *voix & images: littérature
québécoise*, 9, no 3 (printemps 1984),
55–82.
Royer, Jean. "Monique Bosco: Le livre
comme autoportrait." *Le Devoir* [Mon-
tréal], 22 mars 1986, p. 26.
Verduyn, Christl. "Looking Back to Lot's
Wife." *Atlantis: A Women's Studies Jour-
nal/Journal d'études sur la femme* [Mt.
St. Vincent Univ.], 6, No. 2 (Spring/prin-
temps 1981), 38–46.

Interviews/Entretiens

Brochu, André. "Portrait de Minerve peint
par elle-même: entrevue avec Monique
Bosco." *voix & images: littérature québécoise*, 9, no 3 (printemps 1984), 5–12.

Reviews/Comptes rendus

Bourbonneais, Josette. "L'Année de la
Femme, un début!". Compte rendu de
New Medea. Dimanche-Matin [Mon-
tréal], 2 fév. 1975, p. C14.
Escomel, Gloria. "Portrait de Zeus."
Compte rendu de *Zeus peint par Minerve.
La vie en rose*, avril 1985, p. 54.
Hopwood, Alison. Rev. of *Lot's Wife.
Branching Out: Canadian Magazine for
Women*, 2, No. 6 (Nov.–Dec.1975), 40.

Lépin, Stéphane. "Il était une fois Sara, la fiancée juive." Compte rendu de *Sara Sage. Le Devoir* [Montréal], 22 mars 1986, p. 26.

Sandler, Linda. "Woman as Chattel: A Feminist Novel from Quebec." Rev. of *Lot's Wife. Saturday Night*, May 1975, pp. 13–14.

Saint-Onge, Paule. "Erotisme, révolution et évasion." Compte rendu de *Les infusoires. Châtelaine*, jan. 1966, p. 60.

Bouchard, Louise

Reviews/Comptes rendus

Milot, Louise. "Le refus du récit." Compte rendu de *Les images. Lettres québécoises: Revue de l'actualité littéraire*, no 42 (été 1986), pp. 18–20.

Boucher, Denise

Books/Livres

L'Autre Parole [Rimouski], [Paroles sur *Les fées ont soif*], Cahier no 1 ([1979]). [37] pp.

Articles and Sections of Books/ Articles et sections de livres

Gobin, Pierre. "Les Fées ont soif de Denise Boucher: une relecture." *Canadian Drama/L'Art dramatique canadien* [Univ. de Waterloo], 5 (Fall/automne 1979), 220–27.

Hopkins, Elaine R. "Feminism and a Female Trinity in Denise Boucher's *Les Fées ont soif.*" *The American Review of Canadian Studies,* 14, No. 1 (Spring 1984), 63–71.

Lapierre, Solange. "Cyprine ou les racines du plaisir." *Resources for Feminist Research/Documentation sur la recherche féministe*, [Women and Language/Les Femmes et le langage], 13, no 3 (Nov./nov. 1984), 43–44.

Lefebvre, Paul. "*Les Fées ont soif*: une pièce et une débat." *Canadian Drama/L'Art dramatique canadien* [Univ. de Waterloo], 5 (Fall/automne 1979), 204–11.

Interviews/Entretiens

Pascal, Gabrielle. "Entrevue avec Denise Boucher auteur de la pièce *Les fées ont soif.*" *Études Canadiennes/Canadian Studies* [Univ. de Bordeaux III], no 8 (juin 1980), pp. 107–12.

Poeteet, Susan H. "An Interview with Denise Boucher." *Fireweed: A Feminist Literary & Cultural Journal*, [Women and Language], Nos. 5–6 (Winter–Spring 1979–80), pp. 71–74.

Reviews/Comptes rendus

Barrett, Caroline, et Denis Saint-Jacques. "Heureuse censure: *Les Fées ont soif.*" *Lettres québécoises: Revue de l'actualité littéraire*, no 13 (fév. 1979), pp. 4–6.

Camerlain, Lorraine. Compte rendu de *Les Fées ont soif. Jeu: cahiers de théâtre*, [Théâtre-femmes], no 16 (1980), pp. 217–18.

Creed, Keltie. Rev. of *Les Fées ont soif. Broadside: A Feminist Review* [Toronto], July 1981, p. 14.

Ethier, Jean-Réné. "Fées ou sorcières?". Compte rendu de *Les Fées ont soif. Relations*, jan. 1979, pp. 20–27.

Gagnon, Madeleine. "Quand le pouvoir patriarcal s'en prend aux Fées . . . ." Compte rendu de *Les Fées ont soif. Le Devoir* [Montréal], 8 déc. 1978, p. 5.

Garebian, Keith. Rev. of *The Fairies Are Thirsty. Quill & Quire*, April 1983, p. 26.

Maranda, Jeanne. Compte rendu de *Cyprine. Canadian Women's Studies/les cahiers de la femme* [Centennial College], 1, no 1 (automne/Fall 1978), 113.

Saint-Jacques, Denis. Voir/see Barrett, Caroline, et Denis Saint-Jacques.

Bourget, Elisabeth

Reviews/Comptes rendus

des Rivières, Marie-José. Compte rendu de

Bernadette et Juliette ou la vie, c'est comme la vaisselle, c'est toujours à recommencer. Lettres québécoises: Revue de l'actualité littéraire, no 17 (printemps 1980), pp. 35–36.

Brennan, Pegeen

Reviews/Comptes rendus

Godard, Barbara. "Reclaiming the Cave." Rev. of *Zarkeen*. *Kinesis*, April 1984, pp. 20, 25.

Sutherland, Brigitte. "Zarkeen: Creating in Caves . . . Birthing Patriarchy." *HERizons: The Manitoba Women's News Magazine*, July 1983, p. 44.

Brewster, Elizabeth

Interviews/Entretiens

Pearce, Jon. "A Particular Image of the Self: Elizabeth Brewster." In his *Twelve Voices*. Ottawa: Borealis, 1980, pp. 7–33.

Reviews/Comptes rendus

Matyas, Cathy. "Lives of Girls and Women." Rev. of *A House Full of Women*. *Books in Canada*, Dec. 1983, pp. 23–24.

Brooke, Frances

Books/Livres

McMullen, Lorraine. *An Odd Attempt in a Woman: The Literary Life of Frances Brooke*. Vancouver: Univ. of British Columbia Press, 1984. 243 pp.

Articles and Sections of Books/
Articles et sections de livres

Blondel, Madeleine. *Images de la femme dans le roman anglais de 1740 à 1771*. 2 tomes. Lille/Paris: Univ. de Lille III/

Librairie Honoré Champion, 1976, 3, 227, 229, 315, 316, 366, 637, 701, 732, 769, 996.

Blue, Charles S. "Canada's First Novelist." *The Canadian Magazine* [Toronto], Nov. 1921, pp. 3–12.

Edwards, Mary Jane. "Frances Brooke's *The History of Emily Montague*: A Biographical Context." *English Studies in Canada*, 7 (Summer 1981), 171–82.

Fauchéry, Pierre. *La destinée féminine dans le roman européen du dix-huitième siècle: Essai de gynécomythie romanesque*. Paris: Armand Colin, 1972, pp. 74, 291, 299, 311, 421.

Marshall, Linda. Rev. of *An Odd Attempt in a Woman: The Literary Life of Frances Brooke*, by Lorraine McMullen. *Resources for Feminist Research/Documentation sur la recherche féministe*, [Review Issue/Comptes rendus], 14, No. 2 (July/juil. 1985), 24–25.

M[cMullen]., L[orraine]. "Frances Brooke." *A Dictionary of British and American Women Writers 1660–1800* (1985).

McMullen, Lorraine. "All's Right at Last: An Eighteenth Century Canadian Novel." *Journal of Canadian Fiction*, No. 21 (1977–78), pp. 95–104.

——— . "Double Image: Frances Brooke's Women Characters." *World Literature Written in English* [Univ. of Guelph], 21 (Summer 1982), 356–63.

——— . "Frances Brooke (1724–1789)." In *Canadian Writers and Their Works*. Ed. Robert Lecker, Jack David, and Ellen Quigley. Fiction Series. Vol. I. Downsview, Ont.: ECW, 1983, 25–60.

——— . "Frances Brooke's Early Fiction." *Canadian Literature*, [The Structure of Fiction], No. 86 (Autumn 1980), pp. 31–40.

New, William H. "Frances Brooke's Chequered Gardens." *Canadian Literature*, [National Origins], No. 52 (Spring 1972), pp. 24–38.

——— . "*The Old Maid*: Frances Brooke's Apprentice Feminism." *Journal of Canadian Fiction*, 2, No. 3 (Summer 1973), 9–12.

Rogers, Katharine M. "Sensibility and Feminism: The Novels of Frances Brooke." *Genre: A Quarterly Devoted to Generic Criticism* [Univ. of Oklahoma], 11 (Summer 1978), 159–71.

Séjourné, Phillipe. *Aspects Généraux du roman féminin en Angleterre de 1740 à 1800*. Publications des annales de la faculté des lettres, Nouvelle série, no 52. Aix-en-Provence: Ophrys, 1966, pp. 43, 60, 63, 94, 99, 105, 153–54, 187, 203, 214, 221, 222, 236, 246–47, 250, 251–52, 257–58, 260, 269, 270, 272, 303, 304, 308, 313, 315–16, 318, 323, 324, 325, 326, 327, 331, 338, 347, 349, 350, 351, 367, 368, 369, 371, 403, 416–18, 430, 437, 438, 440, 441, 446, 464–65, 468, 479, 484, 496, 500, 501, 504, 508, 540–41, 542.

Brossard, Nicole

Articles and Sections of Books/ Articles et sections de livres

Abel, Marie-Christine. "La Passion insolite de . . . Nicole Brossard: le désert mauve." *Le Devoir* [Montréal], 25 jan. 1986, p. 34.

Bayard, Caroline. "Nicole Brossard et l'utopie du langage." *Revue de l'Université d'Ottawa/University of Ottawa Quarterly*, [Conférence des femmes-écrivains en Amérique], 50 (jan.–mars/Jan.–March 1980), 82–88.

———. "Nicole Brossard: La théorie et la pratique." *Lettres québécoises: Revue de l'actualité littéraire*, no 13 (fév. 1979), pp. 19–22.

———. "Subversion Is the Order of the Day." *Essays on Canadian Writing*, Nos. 7–8 (Fall 1977), pp. 17–25.

———. "Vingt ans pour la trajectoire d'une subversion de Paul Marie Lapointe à Nicole Brossard." *Études Canadiennes/Canadian Studies* [Univ. de Bordeaux III], no 12 (juin 1982), pp. 135–43.

Beausoleil, Claude. "La parole des amantes." *Les deux rives* [Paris], no 1 (printemps–été 1984), pp. 13–14.

———. "Pourquoi une colloque?". *Les deux rives* [Paris], no 1 (printemps–été 1984), pp. 15–16.

Bersianik, Louky [Lucile Durand]. "Fieffée désirante." *la nouvelle barre du jour*, nos 118–119 (nov. 1982), pp. 99–112.

Bonenfant, Joseph. "Nicole Brossard, hauteur d'un text." *Voix et images du pays, 9* (1975), 223–35.

Causse, Michèle. "Le monde comme volonté et comme représentation." *Vlasta* [Paris], no 1 (printemps 1983), pp. 10–25; surtout pp. 18–25.

Cotnoir, Louise. "Lecture tangentielle." *la nouvelle barre du jour*, nos 118–119 (nov. 1982), pp. 121–27.

Dufresne, Francine. "Pense-bête pour les écrivaines féministes." *Le Devoir* [Montréal], 10 juin 1978, p. 25.

Dupré, Louise. "Les utopies du réel." *la nouvelle barre du jour*, nos 118–119 (nov. 1982), pp. 83–89.

Duranleau, Irène. "Le texte moderne et Nicole Brossard." *études littéraires* [Univ. Laval], 14 (avril 1981), 105–21.

Fisette, Jean. "L'Ecrevisse et l'Impossible: glosses autour de deux textes de Nicole Brossard." *voix & images: littérature québécoise, 11*, no 1 (automne 1985), 63–75.

Forsyth, Louise. "Beyond the Myths and Fictions of Traditionalism and Nationalism: The Political in the Work of Nicole Brossard." In *Traditionalism, Nationalism and Feminism: Women Writers of Quebec*. Ed. Paula Gilbert Lewis. Contributions in Women's Studies, No. 53. Westport, Conn.: Greenwood, 1985, pp. 157–72.

———. "Fernand Ouellette et Nicole Brossard — La poésie à caractère spéculaire: deux moments, deux écritures." Colloque sur la Poésie de l'Hexagone, Toronto. Nov. 1979.

———. "The Fusion of Reflexive Writing and Theoretical Reflection: Nicole Brossard and Feminist Criticism in Quebec." MLA Conference, New York. 29 Dec. 1981.

———. "Nicole Brossard and the Emergence of Feminist Criticism in Quebec since 1970." Dialogue, York Univ., Downsview, Ont. 17 Oct./oct. 1981. Printed ("Nicole Brossard and the Emergence of Feminist Literary Theory in Quebec since 1970") in *Gynocritics/Gynocritiques: Feminist Approaches to Canadian and Quebec Women's Writing/ Démarches féministes à l'écriture des Canadiennes et Québécoises.* Ed. Barbara Godard. Toronto: ECW, 1987, pp. 211–20.

——— . "The Novels of Nicole Brossard: An Active Voice." *Room of One's Own,* 4, No. 1 (1978), 30–38.

——— . "Regards, reflets, reflux, reflexions — exploration de l'oeuvre de Nicole Brossard." *la nouvelle barre du jour,* nos 118–119 (nov. 1982), 11–25.

Godard, Barbara. "*L'Amèr* or the Exploding Chapter: Nicole Brossard at the Site of Feminist Deconstruction." *Atlantis: A Women's Studies Journal/Journal d'études sur le femme* [Mt. St. Vincent Univ.], 9, No. 2 (Spring/printemps 1984), 23–34.

——— . "'Je est un autre': Nicole Brossard au Canada anglais." *la nouvelle barre du jour,* nos 118–119 (nov. 1982), 150–55.

——— . "Nicole Brossard: Amantes and L'Amèr." *Broadside: A Feminist Review* [Toronto], April 1981, pp. 14–15.

——— . "Women Loving Women Writing: Nicole Brossard." *Resources for Feminist Research/Documentation sur la recherche féministe,* [The Lesbian Issue/ Être Lesbienne], 12, No. 1 (March/mars 1983), 20–22.

Kravetz, Marc. "Nicole Brossard: une revue, des livres, un journal." *Magazine littéraire,* mars 1978, pp. 98–99.

Lamy, Suzanne. "Glossaire pour Nicole." *la nouvelle barre du jour,* nos 118–119 (nov. 1982), 63–70.

Lequin, Lucie. "Femmage: Nicole Brossard: Les Mots-étreints." *Canadian Women's Studies/les cahiers de la femme* [Centennial College], 1, no 3 (Spring/printemps 1979), 56–59.

Moisan, Lise. See/voir Feminist Literary Theory/Théorie littéraire féministe: Articles and Sections of Books/Articles et

sections de livres.

Poulin, Gabrielle. "La Femme et l'écriture." Compte rendu de *Liberté,* [Actes de la Rencontre Québécoise internationale des écrivains], 18, nos 4–5 [nos 106–107] (juil.–oct. 1976). *Le Droit* [Ottawa], 4 déc. 1976, p. 18.

Royer, Jean. "Nicole Brossard: la traversée des inédits." *Le Devoir* [Montréal], 16 déc. 1978, pp. 25–26.

——— . "La tentation du roman." *Les deux rives* [Paris], no 1 (printemps–été 1984), pp. 11–12.

Saucier, Michèle. "Lecture intimes *L'AMÈR — LE SENS APPARENT — AMANTES.*" *la nouvelle barre du jour,* nos 118–119 (nov. 1982), pp. 27–43.

Strachan, Fiona. "Bibliographie." *la nouvelle barre du jour,* [Traces, écriture de Nicole Brossard], nos 118–119 (nov. 1982), pp. 203–17.

Vasseur, François. "J'écris." *la nouvelle barre du jour,* no 99 (fév. 1981), pp. 65–71.

Villemaire, Yolande. "Le french kiss de la Vénus rouge." *Cul-Q,* nos 8–9 (1976), pp. 63–85.

——— . "Vénus est une jeune femme rouge toujours plus belle." *la nouvelle barre du jour,* nos 118–119 (nov. 1982), pp. 45–61.

Wilson, Jean. "Nicole Brossard: Fantasies and Realities." *Broadside: A Feminist Review* [Toronto], June 1981, pp. 11, 18. Rpt. in *Broadside: A Sampler* [Toronto], May 1982, pp. 20–23.

Theses and Dissertations/Thèses

Delepoulle, Anne-Marie. "La rage d'écrire ou le défi féminin dans l'oeuvre de Nicole Brossard." Thèse du troisième cycle Paris XII [Val de Marne] 1983.

Saucier, Michèle. "L'oeil love volubilis: Lectures de/avec Nicole Brossard." Thèse de maîtrise Sherbrooke 1981.

Interviews/Entretiens

Bayard, Caroline, et Jack David. "Nicole Brossard: Entrevue." *Les lettres québécoises: Revue de l'actualité littéraire,* no 4 (nov. 1976), pp. 34–37. Rpt. in *Avant-postes/Out-posts*. Par Caroline Bayard et Jack David. Three Solitudes: Contemporary Literary Criticism in Canada/Série sur les littératures de la séparation, no 4. Erin, Ont.: Porcépic, 1978, pp. 59–74.

David, Jack. Voir/see Bayard, Caroline, et Jack David.

Delepoulle, Anne-Marie. "Entretien avec Nicole Brossard." *Etudes Canadiennes/Canadian Studies* [Univ. de Bordeaux III], no 16 (juin 1984), pp. 67–71.

"Entretien avec Nicole Brossard sur *Picture theory*." *la nouvelle barre du jour*, nos 118–119 (nov. 1982), pp. 177–201.

Fisette, Jean. Voir/see Van Schendel, Michel, et Jean Fisette.

Roy, André. "La Fiction vive: entretien avec Nicole Brossard sur sa prose." *Journal of Canadian Fiction*, [Les romanciers Québécois et leurs oeuvres], nos 25–26 (1979), pp. 31–40.

Royer, Jean. "Nicole Brossard: la tentation du roman." *Le Devoir* [Montréal], 30 oct. 1982, pp. 17–18. Repris dans *Ecrivains contemporains: Entretiens 3: 1980–1983*. Par Jean Royer. Montréal: L'Hexagone, 1985, pp. 163–69.

Van Schendel, Michel, et Jean Fisette. "Un livre à venir — Rencontre avec Nicole Brossard." *voix et images: études québécoises,* 3 (sept. 1977), 3–18.

Reviews/Comptes rendus

Alonzo, Anne-Marie. Compte rendu du *Sens apparent*. *La Gazette des femmes*, 2, no 5 (oct. 1980), 4.

——— . "Une plaque tournante." Compte rendu de *La lettre aérienne*. *La vie en rose*, déc.–jan. 1985–86, p. 52.

Bayard, Caroline. "*Domaine d'écriture*: ou jouer serré." *Lettres québécoises,* 41 (printemps 1986), 42–43.

Beausoleil, Claude. "Nicole Brossard: la parole des amantes." Compte rendu d'*Amantes*. *Le Devoir* [Montréal], 25 oct. 1980, p. 26.

——— . "La Spirale ardente." Compte rendu du *Sens apparent*. *Le Devoir* [Montréal], 10 mai 1980, p. 24.

Gaudet, Gerald. "Nicole Brossard: une pensée qui se lit comme de la fiction." Compte rendu de *La lettre aérienne*. *Le Devoir* [Montréal], 21 déc. 1985, p. 24.

Haeck, Philippe. "Nicole Brossard: Ecrire, lire, aimer." Compte rendu du *Sens apparent* et *Amantes*. *Estuaire*, no 19 (printemps 1981), pp. 105–07.

LaRue, Monique. "La forme ardente de la fiction." Compte rendu du *Sens apparent*. *Spirale*, no 10 (juin 1980), pp. 1, 6.

Royer, Jean. "*French Kiss*: toucher au délire." *Le Soleil* [Québec], 28 sept. 1974, p. D10.

Saint-Martin, Lori. "Une histoire d'amour." Compte rendu de *La lettre aérienne*. *Spirale*, no 58 (fév. 1986), p. 7.

Smart, Patricia. "Tout dépend de l'angle de vision: Nicole Brossard. *La lettre aérienne*." *voix & images: littérature québécoise*, no 32 (hiver 1986), pp. 330–33.

Théoret, France. "Le style et le désir." Compte rendu du *Centre blanc*. *Spirale*, no 1 (sept. 1979), p. 7.

——— . "Un roman sans ombres." Compte rendu de *Picture Theory*. *Spirale*, no 31 (fév. 1983), p. 3.

Théry, Chantal. "*La lettre aérienne* de Nicole Brossard: Minuit moins une ou l'imagynaire à la rescousse de la planète." *Lettres québécoises*, 41 (printemps 1986), 74–76.

Voldeng, Evelyn. "The Elusive Source Text." Rev. of *These Our Mothers or: The Disintegrating Chapter*, trans. Barbara Godard. *Canadian Literature*, [Poets & Politics], No. 105 (Summer 1985), pp. 138–39.

Weinstein, Norm. "Forging New Feminist Texts." Rev. of *Turn of a Pang*, trans. Patricia Claxton; *A Book*, trans. Larry Shouldice; *Daydream Mechanics*, trans. Larry Shouldice; and *These Our Mothers or: The Disintegrating Chapter*, trans. Barbara Godard. *Brick* [Toronto], No. 25 (Fall 1985), pp. 41–42.

Brouillet, Christine

Reviews/Comptes rendus

Ouellette-Michalska, Madeleine. Compte rendu de *Ma chère voisine*. *Châtelaine*, juil. 1982, p. 17.

Cameron, Anne (pseud. Cam Hubert)

Articles and Sections of Books/ Articles et sections de livres

Messenger, Ann. "B. A. Cameron/Cam Hubert: Poet of the Afflicted." *Canadian Drama/L'Art dramatique canadien* [Univ. of Waterloo], 5 (Fall/automne 1979), 94–103.

Interviews/Entretiens

Wachtel, Eleanor. "Politically Incorrect: An Interview with Anne Cameron." *Room of One's Own*, 6, No. 4 (1981), 35–44.

Wilson, Jean. "Now We Get Some Truths: An Interview with Anne Cameron." *Broadside: A Feminist Review* [Toronto], June 1982, p. 12.

Reviews/Comptes rendus

De Wiel, Alexa. "Sacred Stories Shared." Rev. of *Daughters of Copper Woman*. *Broadside: A Feminist Review* [Toronto], April 1982, p. 16.

Herringer, Barbara. "Weaving the Old Magic." Rev. of *Daughters of Copper Woman*. *The Radical Reviewer: A Feminist Journal of Critical & Creative Work*, Nos. 7–8 (1982), p. 2.

Kane, K. O. "Anne Cameron: And This Is Fiction Also." *The Radical Reviewer*, No. 6 (Spring 1982), pp. 5–7.

Lyons, Moe. Rev. of *Daughters of Copper Woman*. *Hysteria* [Kitchener, Ont.], 2, No. 2 (Spring 1983), 19–21.

Sand, Cy-Thea. "Anne Cameron: Sharing the Cowgirl Fantasy." Rev. of *The Jour-*

ney. *Kinesis*, Dec.–Jan. [1982–83], p. 19.

Twigg, Alan. "Nanaimo's Favourite Daughter: Eloquent and Immovable." *Quill & Quire*, June 1982, p. 38.

Virgo, Sean. "To Keep Our Spirits Up." Rev. of *Dreamspeaker*. *Books in Canada*, March 1979, p. 14.

Whitt, Laurie Anne. "Old Woman/White Man." Rev. of *Daughters of Copper Woman*. *Brick* [Ilderton, Ont.], No. 19 (Fall 1983), pp. 17–22.

Campbell, Maria

Articles and Sections of Books/ Articles et sections de livres

Bataille, Gretchen M., and Kathleen Mullen Sands. "The Long Road Back: Maria Campbell." In their *American Indian Women: Telling Their Lives*. Lincoln: Univ. of Nebraska Press, 1984, pp. 113–26.

Sands, Kathleen Mullen. See/voir Bataille, Gretchen M., and Kathleen Mullen Sands.

Casgrain, Thérèse

Reviews/Comptes rendus

Brown, Elizabeth. Rev. of *A Woman in a Man's World*. *Status of Women News/ Statut de la femme*, [Violence against Women — Rape], 4, No. 2 (Nov. 1977), 19.

Chamberland, Aline

Reviews/Comptes rendus

Saint-Martin, Lori. "Une histoire d'horreur." Compte rendu de *La Fissure*. *Spirale*, no 58 (fév. 1986), p. 13.

Chiasson, Herménegilde

Interviews/Entretiens

Robichaud, Anne-Marie. "Entretien avec Herménegilde Chiasson." *Si Que: études françaises* [Univ. de Moncton], no 4 (automne 1979), pp. 65–68.

Choquette, Adrienne

Books/Livres

Paradis, Suzanne. *Adrienne Choquette lue par Suzanne Paradis: une analyze de l'oeuvre littéraire d'Adrienne Choquette.* Notre-Dames-des-Laurentides: Les Presses Laurentiennes, 1978. 220 pp.

Clarke, Margaret

Reviews/Comptes rendus

Carlsen, Jorn. "Signposts." Rev. of *The Cutting Season. Canadian Literature*, [The Times Between], No. 107 (Winter 1985), pp. 165–67.

Coleman, Helena

Articles and Sections of Books/ Articles et sections de livres

Allison, W. T. "A New Canadian Poet." *The Canadian Magazine of Politics, Science, Art and Literature* [Toronto], Feb. 1907, pp. 404–08.

Collectif

Interviews/Entretiens

Beauchamp, Hélène, et Judith Renaud. "justement! oui, encore! entretien cuisines." *Jeu: cahiers de théâtre*, [Théâtre-femmes], no 16 (1980), pp. 97–115.

Renaud, Judith. Voir/see Beauchamp, Hélène, et Judith Renaud.

Reviews/Comptes rendus

Bélanger, Claire. Compte rendue de *Si Cendrillon pouvait mourir!. Des luttes et des rires de femmes*, 3, no 5 (juin–juil.–août 1980), 61.

Camerlain, Lorraine. Compte rendu de *La nef des sorcières. Jeu: cahiers de théâtre*, [Théâtre-femmes], no 16 (1980), pp. 216–17.

des Rivières, Marie-José. Compte rendu de *A ma mère, à ma mère, à ma mère, à ma voisine*, [par Dominique Gagnon, Louise Laprade, Nicole Lecavalier, et Pol Pelletier]. *Resources for Feminist Research/ Documentation sur la recherche féministe*, [Reviews Issue/Comptes rendus], 10, no 3 (Nov./nov. 1981), 16.

——— . Compte rendu de *Si Cendrillon pouvait mourir!* le show des femmes de Thetford Mines." *Resources for Feminist Research/Documentation sur la recherche féministe*, [Reviews Issue/ Comptes rendus], 10, no 3 (Nov./nov. 1981), 16–17.

Laplante-L'Hérault, Juliette. Compte rendu de *Si Cendrillon pouvait mourir!. Canadian Women's Studies/les cahiers de la femme* [Centennial College], 3, no 2 (1981), 117–18.

Lequin, Lucie. Compte rendu de *La Vrai Vie des masquées. Canadian Women's Studies/les cahiers de la femme* [Centennial College], 2, no 2 (1980), 99.

Conan, Laure (Voir/see Anger, Felicité)

Cotnoir, Louise

Interviews/Entretiens

Casanova, Sylvie, Marie-Christine Lombardo, et Jean-Yves Reuzeau. "Ecriture québécoises d'aujourd'hui: Entretien avec Louise Cotnoir." *Les deux rives* [Paris], no 1 (printemps–été 1984), p. 48.

Lombardo, Marie-Christine. Voir/see Casanova, Sylvie, Marie-Christine Lombardo, et Jean-Yves Reuzeau.

Reuzeau, Jean-Yves. Voir/see Casanova, Sylvie, Marie-Christine Lombardo, et Jean-Yves Reuzeau.

Reviews/Comptes rendus

Alonzo, Anne-Marie. "Cotnoir scribe et témoin." Compte rendu de *Plusieures* et *Le rendez-vous par correspondance/les prénoms*. *La vie en rose*, avril 1985, pp. 53–54.

Crawford, Isabella Valancy

Articles and Sections of Books/ Articles et sections de livres

Cogswell, Fred. "Feminism in Isabella Valancy Crawford's 'Said the Canoe.'" The Crawford Symposium, Univ. of Ottawa, Ottawa. 8 May 1977. Printed in *The Crawford Symposium*. Ed. Frank Tierney. Reappraisals: Canadian Writers, No. [4]. Ottawa: Univ. of Ottawa Press, 1979, pp. 79–85.

Dunn, Margo. "Crawford's Early Works." The Crawford Symposium, Univ. of Ottawa, Ottawa. 7 May 1977. Printed in *The Crawford Symposium*. Ed. Frank Tierney. Reappraisals: Canadian Writers, No. [4]. Ottawa: Univ. of Ottawa Press, 1979, pp. 19–32.

———. "Valancy Crawford: The Lifestyle of a Canadian Poet." *Room of One's Own*, 2, No. 1 (1976), 11–19.

Thomas, Clara. "Crawford's Achievement." The Crawford Symposium, Univ. of Ottawa, Ottawa. 7 May 1977. Printed in *The Crawford Symposium*. Ed. Frank Tierney. Reappraisals: Canadian Writers, No. [4]. Ottawa: Univ. of Ottawa Press, 1979, pp. 131–36.

Reviews/Comptes rendus

Marshall, Linda. Rev. of *Selected Stories of Isabella Valancy Crawford*, ed. Penny Petrone. *World Literature Written in English* [Univ. of Texas at Arlington], [Women Writers of the Commonwealth], 17 (April 1978), 197–98.

Culleton, Beatrice

Reviews/Comptes rendus

Cameron, Anne. "Metis Heart." Rev. of *April Raintree* and *Spirit of the White Bison*. *Canadian Literature*, [Popular Culture], No. 108 (Spring 1986), pp. 164–66.

Curzon, Sarah Anne

Articles and Sections of Books/ Articles et sections de livres

Edgar, Lady. "Transaction No. 2: Sketch of Mrs. Curzon's Life and Work." Deeds Speak. 1899. Printed in *Transactions: 1896–1916*. Ed. Women's Canadian Historical Society. Toronto: Woman's Canadian Historical Society of Toronto, 1916, pp. 3–4.

de la Roche, Mazo

Articles and Sections of Books/ Articles et sections de livres

Greene, Margaret Laurence. "Sophisticated Ladies: Mazo de la Roche." In her *The School of Femininity*. N.p.: Frederick A. Stokes, 1936, pp. 293–96. Rpt. Toronto: Musson, 1972, pp. 293–96.

Livesay, Dorothy. "Mazo de la Roche, 1879–1961." In *The Clear Spirit: Twenty Canadian Women and Their Times*. Ed. Mary Quayle Innis. Toronto: Canadian Federation of University Women/Univ. of

Toronto Press, 1966, pp. 242–59.

de l'Incarnation, Mère Marie (Voir/see Marie Guyart de l'Incarnation)

Delisle, Jeanne-Mance

Articles and Sections of Books/ Articles et sections de livres

Trépanier, Monique. "Du théâtre: un réel ben beau ben triste, Jeanne-Mance Delisle." *Entrelles: revue féministe de l'outaouais*, 3, no 1 (fév. 1981), 13.

Déry, Francine

Reviews/Comptes rendus

Cotnoir, Louise. Compte rendu du *Noyau*. *Arcade*, [désirs et passions], no 10 (oct. 1985), pp. 56–57.

Di Michele, Mary

Reviews/Comptes rendus

Smith, Paul. Rev. of *Mimosa and Other Poems*. *Dalhousie Review*, 61 (Winter 1981–82), 760.

Dougall, Lily

Articles and Sections of Books/ Articles et sections de livres

Macpherson, Katharine L. "Lily Dougall and Her Work." *The Canadian Magazine of Politics, Science, Art and Literature* [Toronto], Sept. 1906, pp. 478–80.

Duley, Margaret

Articles and Sections of Books/ Articles et sections de livres

Feder, Alison. "Margaret Duley: Still

Unknown Novelist?". *Room of One's Own*, 5, No. 3 (1980), 60–69.

Duncan, Sara Jeannette

Books/Livres

Fowler, Marian. *Redney: A Life of Sara Jeannette Duncan*. Toronto: House of Anansi, 1983. 333 pp.

Tausky, Thomas E. *Sara Jeannette Duncan: Novelist of Empire*. Port Credit, Ont.: P. D. Meany, 1980. 300 pp.

Articles and Sections of Books/ Articles et sections de livres

Brydon, Diana. "The Colonial Heroine: The Novels of Sara Jeannette Duncan and Mrs. Campbell Praed." ACUTE Annual Meeting, Univ. of Western Ontario, London, Ont. May 1978. Printed in *Canadian Literature*, [The Structure of Fiction], No. 86 (Autumn 1980), pp. 41–48.

Fraser, Wayne. "A New Deal for Women Is a New Deal for Canada: Sara Jeannette Duncan as Nationalist, Feminist, and Novelist." Conference of Interamerican Writers, Mexico. 3 June 1981.

McMullen, Lorraine. Rev. of *Sara Jeannette Duncan: Novelist of Empire*, by Thomas E. Tausky. *Atlantis: A Women's Studies Journal/Journal d'études sur la femme* [Mt. St. Vincent Univ.], 7, No. 1 (Fall/ automne 1981), 38–41.

Vauthier, Simone. "Sara Jeannette Duncan's 'A Mother in India.'" *Canadian Women's Studies/les cahiers de la femme* [Centennial College], 6, No. 1 (Fall 1984), 101–02.

Theses and Disserations/Thèses

McKenna, Isobel Kerwin. "Sara Jeannette Duncan: The New Woman. A Critical Biography." Diss. Queen's 1981.

Reviews/Comptes rendus

Gerson, Carole. "Empire & Bumble-

Puppy." Rev. of *The Pool in the Desert*. *Canadian Literature*, [Italian-Canadian Connections], No. 106 (Fall 1985), pp. 104–05.

Martens, Debra. "The Elusive Ideal." Rev. of *The Pool in the Desert*. *Brick* [Ilderton, Ont.], No. 24 (Spring 1985), pp. 24–26.

Ryan, K. Rev. of *The Pool in the Desert*. *Kinesis*, June 1985, p. 24.

Dunham, Mabel

Articles and Sections of Books/
Articles et sections de livres

Evans, J. A. S. "The World of Mabel Dunham." *Room of One's Own*, 5, No. 4 (1980), 41–47.

Dupré, Louise

Reviews/Comptes rendus

Pagès, Irène. Compte rendu de *La peau familière*. *Canadian Women's Studies/les cahiers de la femme* [Centennial College], [Aging/Le 3ᵉᵐᵉ âge], 5, no 3 (Spring/printemps 1984), 91–92.

Durand, Lucile (Voir/see Bersianik, Louky)

Endres, Robin

Articles and Sections of Books/
Articles et sections de livres

Endres, Robin Belitsky. "Notes Towards an Androgynous Theatre: Self Profile." *Fireweed: A Feminist Quarterly*, [Women and Performance], No. 7 (Summer 1980), pp. 8–13.

Engel, Marian

Articles and Sections of Books/
Articles et sections de livres

Cameron, Elspeth. "Midsummer Madness: Marian Engel's *Bear*." *Journal of Canadian Fiction*, No. 21 (1977–78), pp. 83–94.

French, William. "Can Lit's Female Flag-bearers Win Salutes from Australia." *The Globe and Mail* [Toronto], 8 April 1980, Sec. Entertainment, p. 19.

Hofsess, John. "Escape from the Fifties." *The Canadian* [*The Toronto Star*], 30 Oct. 1976, pp. 22–23.

Hutchinson, Ann. "Marian Engel, Equilibriste." *Book Forum* [New York], 4 (1978), 46–55.

Lee, Betty. "Marian Engel: Writer at Work." *Chatelaine*, April 1981, pp. 55, 168, 172, 174.

Monk, Patricia. "Engel's *Bear*: A Furry Tale." *Atlantis: A Women's Studies Journal/Journal d'études sur la femme* [Acadia Univ.], 5, No. 1 (Fall/automne 1979), 29–39.

Munro, Alice. "An Appreciation." *Room of One's Own*, [Special Issue on Marian Engel], 9, No. 2 (June 1984), 32–33.

Osachoff, Margaret Gail. "The Bearness of *Bear*." *The University of Windsor Review*, 15, Nos. 1–2 (1979–80), 13–21.

Palting, Diana. See/voir van Herk, Aritha, and Diana Palting.

Ryval, Michael. "A Satiric Engel on Toronto Society: Profile of Marian Engel." *Quill & Quire*, March 1981, p. 60.

Thomas, Clara. "The Girl Who Wouldn't Grow Up: Marian Engel's *The Glassy Sea*." In *Present Tense: A Critical Anthology*. Vol. IV of *The Canadian Novel*. Ed. John Moss. Toronto: NC, 1985, pp. 157–67.

van Herk, Aritha, and Diana Palting. "Marian Engel: Beyond Kitchen Sink Realism." *Branching Out: Canadian Magazine for Women*, [Special Issue on Women and Art], 5, No. 2 (1978), 12–13, 40.

Wengel, Annette. "Marian Engel: A Select

Bibliography." *Room of One's Own*, [Special Issue on Marian Engel], 9, No. 2 (June 1984), 92–99.

Wiseman, Adele. "Marian Engel: 1933–1985." *Canadian Literature*, [Popular Culture], No. 108 (Spring 1986), pp. 198–200.

Theses and Dissertations/Thèses

Gagnon, Suzanne Marie E. "The Problem of Self-Realization and the Journey Motif in the Novels of Marian Engel." M.A. Thesis McGill 1978.

Interviews/Entretiens

Gibson, Graeme. "Marian Engel." In his *Eleven Canadian Novelists*. Toronto: House of Anansi, 1973, pp. 85–114.

Klein, Carroll. "A Conversation with Marian Engel." *Room of One's Own*, [Special Issue on Marian Engel], 9, No. 2 (June 1984), 9–30.

Reviews/Comptes rendus

Cheda, Sherrill. Rev. of *The Glassy Sea*. *Canadian Women's Studies/les cahiers de la femme* [Centennial College], 1, No. 3 (Spring/printemps 1979), 106.

Gordon, Alison. "Through Endless Agony with an Engel Heroine." Rev. of *The Glassy Sea*. *Saturday Night*, Nov. 1978, pp. 61–63.

Irvine, Lorna. Rev. of *Lunatic Villas*. *World Literature Written in English* [Univ. of Guelph], 21 (Autumn 1982), 613–16.

Kirkwood, Hilda. Rev. of *Lunatic Villas*. *The Canadian Forum*, Feb. 1982, pp. 43–44.

Kostash, Myrna. "That Nice Woman Next Door." Rev. of *Joanne: Last Days of a Modern Marriage*. *Books in Canada*, May 1975, pp. 6–8.

Lamy, Suzanne. "En bref." Compte rendu de *L'Ours*. *Spirale*, no 47 (nov. 1984), p. 2.

Mellanby, Layne. "Lives Not Lifestyles in Lunatic Villas." *Broadside: A Feminist Review* [Toronto], Aug.–Sept. 1981, p. 11.

Pratt, Annis. "How to Weather Gynophobia." Rev. of *The Glassy Sea*. *The Feminist Connection* [Madison, Wisc.], 1, No. 3 (Nov. 1980), 13, 20.

Ross, Catherine. "Mary and Martha." Rev. of *The Glassy Sea*. *Journal of Canadian Fiction*, No. 33 (1981–82), pp. 138–41.

van Daele, Christa. "The Princess of Serendip: Marian Engel in Review." Rev. of *Bear* and *Inside the Easter Egg. Branching Out: Canadian Magazine for Women,* 3, No. 2 (April–June 1976), 41–42.

Vance, Sylvia. "A Novel Worth the Wait." Rev. of *The Glassy Sea*. *Branching Out: Canadian Magazine for Women*, [Fifth Anniversary Issue], 6, No. 1 (1979), 52.

Waterston, Elizabeth. Rev. of *Room of One's Own*, [Special Issue on Marian Engel], 9, No. 2 (June 1984). *Resources for Feminist Research/Documentation sur la recherche féministe*, [Review Issue/Comptes rendus], 14, No. 2 (July/juil. 1985), 17–18.

Wiseman, Adele. "Pooh at Puberty." Rev. of *Bear*. *Books in Canada*, April 1976, pp. 6–8.

Fadette, Henriette (née Dessaules)

Articles and Sections of Books/ Articles et sections de livres

Verduyn, Christl. "La Religion dans le Journal d'Henriette Fadette (1874–1880)." *Atlantis: A Women's Studies Journal/ Journal d'études sur la femme* [Mt. St. Vincent Univ.], 8, no 2 (Spring/printemps 1983), 45–50.

Ferron, Madeleine

Articles and Sections of Books/ Articles et sections de livres

Legaré, Céline. "Madeleine Ferron doit interrompre un roman pour faire la campagne électorale de son mari Robert Cliché." *La Patrie* [Montréal], 26 mai 1968,

p. 21.

"Madeleine Ferron, une femme gaie qui sait concilier divers métiers." *Le Soleil* [Québec], 11 oct. 1966, p. 31.

Reviews/Comptes rendus

Roy, Monique. Compte rendu du *Chemin des Dames*. *Status of Women News/Statut de la femme*, 5, no 2 (Dec. 1978), 30.

Fidelis (See/voir Machar, Agnes Maule)

Fleming, Agnes May

Articles and Sections of Books/
Articles et sections de livres

Nowlan, Michael O. "For Export: Words/ Les exportateurs: des mots." *Le Nouveau/New Brunswick* [Fredericton N.B. Information Services], 8, nos 1–2 (Spring–Summer/printemps–été 1983), 27–31.

Fraser, Sylvia

Articles and Sections of Books/
Articles et sections de livres

Gane, M.D. "In the Palace of the Snow Queen." *Weekend Magazine* [*The Globe and Mail*] [Toronto], 7 Feb. 1976, pp. 8–11.
Irvine, Lorna. "Assembly Line Stories: Pastiche in Sylvia Fraser's *The Candy Factory*." *Canadian Literature*, [Faces of Realism/Facing Realities], No. 89 (Summer 1981), pp. 45–55.
——— . "Politicizing the Private: Sylvia Fraser's *Pandora*." *MOSAIC: A Journal for the Interdisciplinary Study of Literature* [Univ. of Manitoba], 17, No. 2 (Spring 1984), 223–33.

Interviews/Entretiens

Twigg, Alan. "Sylvia Fraser: Female." In his *For Openers: Conversations with 24 Canadian Writers*. Madeira Park, B.C.: Harbour, 1981, pp. 117–25.

Reviews/Comptes rendus

Cowan, Doris. "Someday Her Prince Will Come." Rev. of *A Casual Affair. Books in Canada*, April 1978, pp. 14–15.
Hedenstrom, Joanne. Rev. of *The Emperor's Virgin. Branching Out: Canadian Feminist Quarterly*, 7, No. 2 (1980), 55.
Smith, Rebecca. "Some Thoughtful Tales." Rev. of *A Casual Affair. Branching Out: Canadian Magazine for Women*, 5, No. 3 (1978), 38–39.

Gagnon, Madeleine

Articles and Sections of Books/
Articles et sections de livres

"Bibliographie de Madeleine Gagnon." *voix & images: littérature québécoise*, 7 (automne 1981), 53–58.
Boulanger, Madeleine. "Madeleine Gagnon: Les constantes d'une écriture . . . ." *voix & images: littérature québécoise*, 8 (automne 1982), 45–51.
——— . "Madeleine Gagnon: Words of Women, Words of Life." *ellipse*, Nos. 33–34 (1985), pp. 32–37.
Desjardins, Louise. "La lettre de l'amour et la crise du coeur." *voix & images: littérature québécoise*, 8 (automne 1982), 35–43.
Frémont, Gabrielle. "Madeleine Gagnon: Du politique à l'intime." *voix & images: littérature québécoise*, 8 (automne 1982), 23–34.
Gagnon, Madeleine. "dire ces femmes d'où je viens." *Magazine Littéraire*, no 134 (mars 1978), pp. 11, 94–96.
Gould, Karen. "Madeleine Gagnon's Po(e)litical Vision: Portrait of an Author and an Era." In *Traditionalism, Nationalism and Feminism: Women Writers of Quebec*. Ed. Paula Gilbert Lewis. Contributions in Women's Studies, No. 53. Westport, Conn.: Greenwood, 1985,

pp. 185–204.

———. "Unearthing the Female Text: Madeleine Gagnon's *Lueur*." *L'Esprit créateur*, 23, No. 3 (Fall 1983), 86–94.

Roy, Monique. "Femmage: Madeleine Gagnon." *Canadian Women's Studies/les cahiers de la femme* [Centennial College], 1, no 1 (automne/Fall 1978), 48–51.

———. "Madeleine Gagnon: La Solitude peuplée d'écriture." *La vie en rose*, mai 1986, pp. 46–47.

Interviews/Entretiens

Major, Ruth. Voir/see Robert, Lucie, et Ruth Major.

Pontbriand, Michèle. "Entrevue de Madeleine Gagnon." *MOEBIUS*, no 26 (automne 1985), pp. 1–16.

Robert, Lucie, et Ruth Major. "Percer le mur du son du sens, une entrevue avec Madeleine Gagnon." *voix & images: littérature québécoise*, 8 (automne 1982), 5–21.

Roy, Monique. "Madeleine Gagnon, écrivain: 'Je ne suis pas un oracle.'" *La Gazette des femmes*, 1, no 3 (jan. 1980), 17–18.

Reviews/Comptes rendus

Bayard, Caroline. "La lettre et l'Ò, vertige et utopie." Compte rendu de *Au coeur de la lettre. Lettres québécoises: Revue de l'actualité littéraire*, no 26 (été 1982), pp. 37–40.

Bédard, Nicole. Compte rendu de *L'Antre. Livres et auteurs québécois 1978*. Ed. André Berthiaume. Québec: Les Presses de l'Univ. Laval, 1979, pp. 118–20.

Cotnoir, Louise. "Une écriture traversière." Compte rendu de *Au coeur de la lettre. Spirale*, no 23 (mars 1982), p. 5.

Fournier, Danielle. Compte rendu de *La Lettre infinie. Arcade*, [désirs et passions], no 10 (oct. 1985), pp. 57–58.

Lareau, Danielle. Compte rendu de *Lueur. La Gazette des femmes*, 1, no 1 (1979), 5.

Mailhot, Michèle. Compte rendu de *L'Antre. Canadian Women's Studies/les cahiers de la femme* [Centennial College], 1, no 2

(Winter/hiver 1978–79), 104.

Nepveu, Pierre. "La jeune poésie: L'Antre et la sorcière: Madeleine Gagnon et Francine Déry." *Lettres québécoises: Revue de l'actualité littéraire*, no 12 (nov. 1978), pp. 15–16.

Royer, Jean. "Madeleine Gagnon: Explorer les premières traces du langage." Compte rendu de *Lueur. Le Devoir* [Montréal], 26 mai 1979, pp. 17–18.

Gallant, Mavis

Articles and Sections of Books/ Articles et sections de livres

Knelman, Martin. "The Article Mavis Gallant Didn't Want Written: In Pursuit of Our Elegant, Expatriate Storyteller." *Saturday Night*, Nov. 1978, pp. 25–31.

Interviews/Entretiens

Lawrence, Karen. "From the Other Paris: Interview with Mavis Gallant." *Branching Out: Canadian Magazine for Women*, 3, No. 1 (Feb.–March 1976), 18–19.

Royer, Jean. "Mavis Gallant: 'La vie n'est pas un roman.'" *Le Devoir* [Montréal], 21 mai 1983, pp. 19, 36. Repris ("Mavis Gallant: 'La vie est une suite de nouvelles'") dans *Ecrivains contemporains: Entretiens 3: 1980–1983*. Par Jean Royer. Montréal: L'Hexagone, 1985, pp. 54–60.

Reviews/Comptes rendus

Leslie, Geneviève. Rev. of *From the Fifteenth District: A Novella and Eight Short Stories. Status of Women News/Statut de la femme*, 6, No. 2 (Spring 1980), 30–31.

Giguère, Diane

Articles and Sections of Books/ Articles et sections de livres

Beauregard, Hermine. "De Maria Chapdelaine à Elaine Bédard." *Liberté*, 7, no 4 [no 40] (juil. 1965), 353–61.

——— . "Faute d'avoir des enfants, j'écris des livres: Diane Giguère." *Le Petit journal* [Montréal], 11 avril 1965, pp. 57, 59.

Reviews/Comptes rendus

Mailhot, Michèle A. "Châtelaine a lu pour vous: deux romans couleurs du temps." Compte rendu de *Le temps des jeux*, par Diane Giguère; et *Délivrez-nous du mal*, par Claude Jasmin. *Châtelaine*, fév. 1962, p. 18.

Gilboord, Margaret Gibson

Reviews/Comptes rendus

Swartz, Shirley. "Who Was Then the Crazy One? Gilboord's *The Butterfly Ward*." *Branching Out: Canadian Magazine for Women*, 3, No. 4 (Sept.–Oct. 1976), 44.

Glass, Joanna

Articles and Sections of Books/ Articles et sections de livres

Somerville, Jane. "Reflections of Joanna Glass." *The Globe and Mail* [Toronto], 16 Oct. 1982, p. E3.

Gotlieb, Phyllis

Articles and Sections of Books/ Articles et sections de livres

Miller, Judith. "Strangely Familiar: The Science Fiction Novels of Phyllis Gotlieb." *Hysteria* [Kitchener, Ont.], 2, No. 1 (Winter 1982–83), 5–8.

Gotlieb, Sondra

Articles and Sections of Books/ Articles et sections de livres

French, William. "Innocent in Washington."

The Globe and Mail [Toronto], 29 Jan. 1983, p. 10.

Govier, Katherine

Reviews/Comptes rendus

Smith, Rebecca. "More Than a Geneology." Rev. of *Random Descent. Branching Out: Canadian Magazine for Women*, 6, No. 4 (1979), 43.

Greffard, Madeleine

Reviews/Comptes rendus

Bourassa, André G. "Le lourd passif des hommes: *Passé dû* de Madeleine Greffard." *Lettres québécoises: Revue de l'actualité littéraire*, no 19 (automne 1980), pp. 36–39.

Guèvremont, Germaine

Articles and Sections of Books/ Articles et sections de livres

Herlan, James J. "*Le Survenant* as Ideological Messenger: A Study of Germaine Guèvremont's Radio Serial." In *Traditionalism, Nationalism and Feminism: Women Writers of Quebec*. Ed. Paula Gilbert Lewis. Contributions in Women's Studies, No. 53. Westport, Conn.: Greenwood, 1985, pp. 37–51.

Pelletier-Dlamini, Louis. "Germaine Guèvremont: Rencontre avec l'auteur du *Survenant*." *Châtelaine*, avril 1967, pp. 32–33, 84, 86, 88.

Rubinger, Catherine. "Germaine Guèvremont et l'univers féminin." *Le Devoir* [Montréal], 31 oct. 1967, Supp. littéraire, p. 22.

Williamson, Richard C. "The Stranger Within: Sexual Politics in the Novels of Germaine Guèvremont." *Québec Studies*, 1, No. 1 (Spring 1983), 246–56.

Theses and Dissertations/Thèses

Rubinger, Catherine. "Germaine Guèvre-mont: portrait de la femme dans le roman canadien-français." Thèse de matrîse McGill 1967.

Gunnars, Kristjana

Interviews/Entretiens

Casey, Jane. "An Interview with Kristjana Gunnars." *CV/II*, [Manitoba Poetry Issue], 8, No. 3 (Sept. 1984), 36–39.

Guyart de l'Incarnation, Marie

Articles and Sections of Books/ Articles et sections de livres

Chabot, Marie-Emmanuel. "Marie Guyart de l'Incarnation." Dans *The Clear Spirit: Twenty Canadian Women and Their Times*. Ed. Mary Quayle Innis. Toronto: Canadian Federation of University Women/Univ. of Toronto Press, 1966, pp. 25–41.

Couillard, Marie. "Le discours mystique de Marie de l'Incarnation: Paroles de femme et/ou érotomanie?". Dans *La femme, son corps et la religion: approches pluridisciplinaires*. Ed. Elisabeth J. Lacelle. Montréal: Bellarmin, 1983, pp. 163–73.

Ha-Milton, Reina

Reviews/Comptes rendus

Gousse, Diane. Compte rendu de *Lettre d'amour de Femmes. Des luttes et des rires des femmes*, 4, no 3 (fév.–mars 1981), 52–53.

Trépanier, Monique. "Reina Ha-Milton: une révolte très grande." Compte rendu de *Lettre d'amour de Femmes. Entrelles: Revue féministe de l'outaouais*, 3, no 2 (mai 1981), 12.

Harris, Claire

Reviews/Comptes rendus

Brand, Dionne. Rev. of *Translation into Fiction* and *Fables from the Women's Quarters. Canadian Women's Studies/les cahiers de la femme* [Centennial College], [post Nairobi], 7, Nos. 1–2 (Spring–Summer 1986), 222–24.

Thomas, Deb. "Small Press Poetry Review." Rev. of *Fable from the Women's Quarters. Kinesis*, Oct. 1985, p. 29.

Harrison, Susan Frances (pseud. Seranus)

Articles and Sections of Books/ Articles et sections de livres

Wetherald, A. Ethelwyn. "Some Canadian Literary Women — I: Seranus." *The Week: A Canadian Journal of Politics, Society and Literature* [Toronto], 22 March, 1888, pp. 267–68.

Hart, Julia Catherine (Beckwith)

Articles and Sections of Books/ Articles et sections de livres

Bennett, C. L. "An Unpublished Manuscript of the First Canadian Novelist." *The Dalhousie Review*, 43 (Autumn 1963), 317–32.

Harvey, Pauline

Interviews/Entretiens

Bertrand, Claudine, et Josée Bonneville. "Entrevue: Pauline Harvey ou la passion de l'écriture." *Arcade*, [désirs et passions], no 10 (oct. 1985), pp. 47–50.

Bonneville, Josée. Voir/see Bertrand, Claudine, et Josée Bonneville.

Milot, Louise. "Pauline Harvey: Interview." *Lettres québécoises: Revue de l'actualité littéraire*, no 40 (hiver 1985–86), pp. 47–49.

Reviews/Comptes rendus

Bonneville, Josée. Compte rendu d'*Encore une partie pour Berri. Arcade*, [désirs et passions], no 10 (oct. 1985), pp. 58–59.

Roy, Michèle. "Des jeux graves et fous." Compte rendu d'*Encore une partie pour Berri. La vie en rose*, déc.–jan. 1985–86, pp. 52–53.

Harvor, Beth

Articles and Sections of Books/
Articles et sections de livres

Harvor, Beth. "'My Craft and Sullen Art': The Writers Speak. Beth Harvor." *Atlantis: A Women's Studies Journal/ Journal d'études sur la femme* [Acadia Univ.], 4, No. 1 (Fall/automne 1978), 147–50.

Hébert, Anne

Books/Livres

Major, Jean-Louis. *Anne Hébert et le miracle de la parole.* Collection "Lignes québécoises." Montréal: Les Presses de l'Univ. de Montréal, 1976. 114 pp.

Articles and Sections of Books/
Articles et sections de livres

Bishop, Neil B. "Distance, point de vue, voix et idéologie dans *Les fous de Bassan*, d'Anne Hébert." *voix & images: littérature québécoise*, 9, no 2 (hiver 1984), 113–29.

———. "Les Enfants du sabbat et la problématique de la libération chez Anne Hébert." *Etudes Canadiennes/Canadian Studies* [Univ. de Bordeaux III], no 8 (juin 1980), pp. 33–46.

Bourbonnais, Nicole. "La femme métony-mique chez Anne Hébert et Renée Vivien." NEMLA Conference, New York. April 1982.

Cohen, Matt. "Queen in Exile." *Books in Canada*, Aug.–Sept. 1983, pp. 9–12.

Couillard, Marie. "*Les Enfants du sabbat* d'Anne Hébert: un récit de subversion fantastique." *Incidences* [Univ. d'Ottawa], [Romancières québécoises], NS 4, nos 2–3 (mai–déc. 1980), 77–83.

English, Judith, et Jacqueline Viswanathan. "Deux Dames du Précieux-Sang: à propos des *Enfants du Sabbat* d'Anne Hébert." *Présence francophone: Revue littéraire*, no 22 (printemps 1981), pp. 111–19.

Féral, Josette. "Clôture du moi, clôture du texte dans l'oeuvre d'Anne Hébert." *voix & images: études québécoises*, 1 (déc. 1975), 265–83. Repris dans *Littérature*, no 20 (déc. 1975), pp. 102–17.

Green, Mary Jean. "The Witch and the Princess: The Feminine Fantastic in the Fiction of Anne Hébert." *The American Review of Canadian Studies*, 15, No. 2 (Summer 1985), 137–46.

Iqbal, Françoise Maccabée. "*Kamouraska*, 'la fausse représentation démasquée.'" *voix et images: études québécoises*, 4 (avril 1979), 460–78.

Major, Ruth. "*Kamouraska* et *Les Enfants du sabbat*: faire jouer la transparence." *voix & images: littérature québécoise*, 7 (printemps 1982), 459–70.

McDonald, Marci. "Anne Hébert: Charting the Rage Within." *City Woman*, Spring 1981, pp. 55–61, 74.

Morissette, Brigitte. "Prix Femina '82: Lointaine et proche. Anne Hébert." *Châtelaine*, fév. 1983, pp. 47, 48, 50, 52, 54.

Pascal, Gabrielle. "Soumission et révolte dans les romans d'Anne Hébert." *Incidences* [Univ. d'Ottawa], [Romancières québécoises], NS 4, nos 2–3 (mai–déc. 1980), 59–75.

Pascal-Smith, Gabrielle. "La condition féminine dans *Kamouraska* d'Anne Hébert." *The French Review*, 54 (oct. 1980), 85–92.

Paterson, Janet M. "Bibliographie critique des études consacrées aux romans d'Anne Hébert." *voix & images: études québé-*

coises, 5 (automne 1979), 187–92.

———. "Bibliographie d'Anne Hébert." *voix & images: littérature québécoise*, 7 (printemps 1982), 505–10.

———. "L'écriture de la jouissance dans l'oeuvre romanesque d'Anne Hébert." *Revue de l'Université d'Ottawa/University of Ottawa Quarterly*, [Conférence des femmes-écrivains en Amérique], 50 (jan.–mars/Jan.–March 1980), 69–73.

Pépin, Fernande. "La Femme dans l'espace imaginaire de la dramatique d'Anne Hébert: *Le Temps sauvage*." *Canadian Drama/L'Art dramatique canadien* [Univ. de Waterloo], 5 (Fall/automne 1979), 164–78.

Rosenstreich, Susan L. "The Poet in Pieces: Anne Hébert's Marginal Poetics." NEMLA Conference, New York. April 1982. Printed ("Counter-Tradition: The Marginal Poetics of Anne Hébert") in *Traditionalism, Nationalism and Feminism: Women Writers of Quebec*. Ed. Paula Gilbert Lewis. Contributions in Women's Studies, No. 53. Westport, Conn.: Greenwood, 1985, pp. 63–70.

Sacks, Murray. "Love on the Rocks: Anne Hébert's *Kamouraska*." In *Traditionalism, Nationalism and Feminism: Women Writers of Quebec*. Ed. Paula Gilbert Lewis. Contributions in Women's Studies, No. 53. Westport, Conn.: Greenwood, 1985, pp. 109–23.

Smart, Patricia. "La Poésie d'Anne Hébert: une perspective féminine." *Revue de l'Université d'Ottawa/University of Ottawa Quarterly*, [Conférence des femmes-écrivains en Amérique], 50 (jan.–mars/Jan.–March 1980), 62–68.

Viswanathan, Jacqueline. Voir/see English, Judith, et Jacqueline Viswanathen.

Theses and Dissertations/Thèses

Amar, Wendy. "L'amour dans l'oeuvre d'Anne Hébert." M.A. Thesis McGill 1975.

Aonzo, Jeannine. "La Femme dans les romans d'Anne Hébert." Thèse de maîtrise McGill 1981.

Davis, Pauline Marie. "L'Affrontement des sexes dans les romans d'Anne Hébert." M.A. Thesis Calgary 1983.

Lefebvre, Louisette B. "Le Thème de la femme dans l'oeuvre romanesque d'Anne Hébert." Thèse de maîtrise Québéc à Trois-Rivières 1976.

Interviews/Entretiens

Royer, Jean. "Anne Hébert: la passion est un risque, mais c'est un risque indispensable." *Le Devoir* [Montréal], 11 déc. 1982, pp. 21, 40. Repris ("La passion d'écrire") dans *Ecrivains contemporains: Entretiens 3: 1980–1983*. Par Jean Royer. Montréal: L'Hexagone, 1985, pp. 18–22.

Vanasse, André. "L'écriture et l'ambivalence, entrevue avec Anne Hébert." *voix & images: littérature québécoise*, 7 (printemps 1982), 441–48.

Reviews/Comptes rendus

Lamy, Suzanne. "Le pouvoir des noms propres." Compte rendu de *Héloïse*. *Spirale*, no 10 (juin 1980), pp. 1, 4.

Micros, Marianne. "Rape and Ritual." Rev. of *Children of the Black Sabbath* and *Poems* by Anne Hébert. *Essays on Canadian Writing*, Nos. 7–8 (Fall 1977), pp. 31–35.

Poulin, Gabrielle. "D'Elisabeth à soeur Julie: *Les Enfants du sabbat* d'Anne Hébert." *Le Droit* [Ottawa], 17 avril 1976, p. 20.

———. "La 'Nouvelle Héloïse' québécoise: Une lecture des *Enfants du sabbat*." *Relations*, mars 1976, pp. 92–94. Repris dans *Roman du Pays 1968–1979*. Par Gabrielle Poulin. Montréal: Bellarmin, 1980, pp. 299–306.

Henley, Gail

Reviews/Comptes rendus

Pringle, Heather. "God's Pawn Goes Home." Rev. *Where the Cherries End Up*. *Branching Out: Canadian Magazine for Women*, 6, No. 1 (1979), 53.

Henry, Ann

Articles and Sections of Books/
Articles et sections de livres

Mann, Maureen. "Ann Henry: A Canadian Paycock." *Canadian Drama/L'Art dramatique canadien* [Univ. of Waterloo], 5 (Fall/automne 1979), 129–38.

Henshaw, Julia W.

Articles and Sections of Books/
Articles et sections de livres

M., B. "Canadian Celebrities: Julia W. Henshaw." *The Canadian Magazine of Politics, Science, Art and Literature* [Toronto], Jan. 1902, pp. 220–21.

L'Heureux, Christine

Articles and Sections of Books/
Articles et sections de livres

Leclerc, José. "La très belle utopie de Christine L'Heureux, écrivaine québécoise." *Canadian Women's Studies/les cahiers de la femme* [Centennial College], [The Future/le futur], 6, no 2 (Spring 1985), 24–26.

Hollingsworth, Margaret

Interviews/Entretiens

Zimmerman, Cynthia, and Robert Wallace. "Margaret Hollingsworth." In their *The Work: Conversations with English-Canadian Playwrights*. Toronto: Coach House, 1982, pp. 90–101.
Wallace, Robert. See/voir Zimmerman, Cynthia, and Robert Wallace.

Reviews/Comptes rendus

Kaplan, Jon. "Double Dose of Hollings-

worth." Rev. of *Alli Alli Oh* and *Islands. Now* [Toronto], 9–15 Jan. 1986, p. 9.

Hospital, Janette Turner

Interviews/Entretiens

"Cashing In: An Interview with Janette Turner Hospital." *The Lunatic Gazette* [Erin, Ont.], Ser. 2, 1, No. 2 (Nov.–Dec. 1982), 5.

Reviews/Comptes rendus

Jackson, Marni. "Exiles in an Exotic Dream." Rev. of *The Ivory Swing. Maclean's,* 4 Oct. 1982, p. 72.
Klein, Carroll. See/voir Feminist Literary Theory/Théorie littéraire féministe: Reviews/Comptes rendus.
Timson, Judith. Rev. of *The Ivory Swing. Chatelaine*, Oct. 1982, p. 4.

Howes, Mary

Reviews/Comptes rendus

Kroetsch, Robert. "From Magpies to Booby Coots." Rev. of *Lying in Bed*, by Mary Howes; EXTREME POSITIONS, by bp Nichol; *A Grand Memory for Forgetting*, by Stephen Scobie; and *Gaullimaufry*, by Jon Whyte. *Books in Canada*, Jan. 1982, p. 9.

Hubert, Cam (See/voir Cameron, Anne)

Ireland, Anne

Reviews/Comptes rendus

Muench, Heidi. Rev. of *A Certain Mr. Takahashi*. HERizons: *The Manitoba Women's News Magazine*, Jan.–Feb. 1986, p. 45.

Itter, Carole

Reviews/Comptes rendus

Haggerty, Joan. Rev. of *Whistle Daughter Whistle*. *Room of One's Own*, 9, No. 1 (Feb. 1984), 73–76.

Jacob, Suzanne

Articles and Sections of Books/ Articles et sections de livres

Ouellette-Michalska, Madeleine. "Mais qui donc est Laura Laur?". *Les deux rives* [Paris], no 1 (printemps–été 1984), pp. 26–27.
Pedneault, Hélène. "Inhabituelle: Suzanne Jacob." *La vie en rose*, mai 1986, pp. 41–42.
Royer, Jean. "Le corps traversé des mots." *Les deux rives* [Paris], no 1 (printemps–été 1984), p. 25.

Reviews/Comptes rendus

Hogue, Jacqueline. Compte rendu de *Laura Laur*. *Canadian Women's Studies/les cahiers de la femme* [Centennial College], [Belles lettres], 5, no 1 (Fall/automne 1983), 77–78.

Jameson, Anna

Books/Livres

Thomas, Clara. *Love and Work Enough: The Life of Anna Jameson*. Preface Clara Thomas. Studies and Texts, No. 14. Toronto: Univ. of Toronto Press, 1967. vii–x, 252 pp. Rpt. Prefaces Clara Thomas. Toronto: Univ. of Toronto Press, 1978. vii–viii, ix–xii, 252 pp.

Articles and Sections of Books/ Articles et sections de livres

Thomas, Clara. "Anna Jameson: Art Histor-ian and Critic." *Woman's Art Journal*, 1, No. 1 (Spring–Summer 1980), 20–22.

Jiles, Paulette

Articles and Sections of Books/ Articles et sections de livres

Armstrong, Luanne. "Learning to Navigate: The Work of Paulette Jiles." *HERizons: The Manitoba Women's News Magazine*, July–Aug. 1986, p. 27.

Johnson, Pauline

Books/Livres

Keller, Betty. *Pauline, a Biography of Pauline Johnson*. Vancouver: Douglas & McIntyre, 1981. 317 pp.
Van Steen Marcus. *Pauline Johnson, Her Life and Work*. 1965; rpt. Toronto: Hodder and Stoughton, 1973. 279 pp.

Articles and Sections of Books/ Articles et sections de livres

Loosley, Elizabeth. "Pauline Johnson 1861–1913." In *The Clear Spirit: Twenty Canadian Women and Their Times*. Ed. Mary Quayle Innis. Toronto: Canadian Federation of University Women/Univ. of Toronto Press, 1966, pp. 74–90.
Ruoff, A. LaVonne Brown. "The Mocassin Makers: Pauline Johnson's Portrayal of Women." MLA Conference, New York. Dec. 1983.

Theses and Dissertations/Thèses

Baker, Marilyn. "Pauline Johnson: A Biographical, Thematic, and Stylistic Study." M.A. Thesis Sir George Williams 1974.

Joudry, Patricia

Articles and Sections of Books/ Articles et sections de livres

Wagner, Anton. "Patricia Joudry: Biographical Checklist." *Canadian Theatre Review* [York Univ.], No. 23 (Summer 1979), pp. 45–58.

Zinman, Rosalind. "Images of Women: A Study in Sound and Symbol: CBC Radio Production 'Mother Is Watching.'" Canadian Research Institute for the Advancement of Women/Institut canadien de recherche pour l'avancement des femmes, Montréal. Nov. 1984. Printed in *Femmes: images, modèles/Women: images, role-models. Actes du Colloque 1984/Proceedings of the 1984 Conference.* Ed. Evelyne Tardy. Ottawa: CRIAW/ICRAF, 1985, pp. 105–14.

Jutras, Jeanne d'Arc

Reviews/Comptes rendus

Saint-Denis, Janou. Compte rendu du *Georgie. Canadian Women's Studies/les cahiers de la femme* [Centennial College], 1, no 1 (automne/Fall 1978), 112–13.

Kamboureli, Smaro

Reviews/Comptes rendus

Hryniuk, Angela. "Second Skin." Rev. of *In the Second Person. Brick* [Toronto], No. 27 (Spring 1986), pp. 43–44.

Kane, K. O.

Interviews/Entretiens

Herringer, Barbara. "A Poet's Vision: Interview with K. O. Kane." *The Radical Reviewer*, No. 4 (Fall 1981), pp. 1, 4–5.

Kemp, Penny

Reviews/Comptes rendus

Meigs, Mary. Rev. of *Binding Twine. Room*

of One's Own, 10, No. 2 (Dec. 1985), 88–90.

Kerslake, Susan

Reviews/Comptes rendus

Sand, Cy-Thea. Rev. of *The Book of Fears. Kinesis*, May 1985, p. 30.

Kogawa, Joy

Reviews/Comptes rendus

Corbeil, Carole. "Kogawa: A Tale of Two Worlds." Rev. of *Obasan. The Globe and Mail* [Toronto], 14 May 1983, p. E1.

Kostash, Myrna

Interviews/Entretiens

Smyth, Donna E. "Interview with Myrna Kostash — 'A Western, Ukrainian, Regionalist, Feminist, Socialist Writer.'" *Atlantis: A Women's Studies Journal/ Journal d'études sur la femme* [Acadia Univ.], 6, No. 2 (Spring/printemps 1981), 178–85.

Warland, Betsy. "A Ukrainian Feminist Makes Cultural Connections: An Interview with Myrna Kostash." *HERizons: The Manitoba Women's News Magazine*, July–Aug. 1986, pp. 21–22, 26.

Laberge, Marie

Interviews/Entretiens

Dionne, André. "Marie Laberge, dramaturge: Entrevue." *Lettres québécoises: Revue de l'actualité littéraire*, no 25 (printemps 1982), pp. 62–66.

Laforest, Marie-Thérèse (Voir/see Sainte-Marie-Eleuthère, Soeur)

Lahofer, Althea

**Articles and Sections of Books/
Articles et sections de livres**

Toews, Charlyn. "Althea Lahofer: A Thoroughly Modern Poet." HERIZONS: The Manitoba Women's News Magazine, July–Aug. 1986, pp. 20, 23.

Lalonde, Michèle

Interviews/Entretiens

Mezei, Kathy. "Interview with Michèle Lalonde." Room of One's Own, [Québécoises], 4, Nos. 1–2 (1978), 19–29.

Lambert, Betty

**Articles and Sections of Books/
Articles et sections de livres**

"Betty Lambert 1933–1983." Canadian Theatre Review, No. 39 (Spring 1984), pp. 6–7.

Interviews/Entretiens

Svendson [sic], Jennifer. "Betty Lambert 1933–1983." Kinesis, Dec.–Jan. [1983–84], p. 26.
Worthington Bonnie. "Battling Aristotle: A Conversation." Room of One's Own, 8, No. 2 (1983), 54–66.

Reviews/Comptes rendus

Beer, Frances. Rev. of Crossings. Canadian Women's Studies/les cahiers de la femme [Centennial College], [Law and Politics/La loi et la politique], 2, No. 4 (1980), 108.
Svendsen [sic], Jenifer [sic]. "Tragedy: Woman's Rage Turned Inward." Rev. of Jenny's Story. The Radical Reviewer, No. 6 (Spring 1982), p. 18.

Lamy, Suzanne

Reviews/Comptes rendus

Simon, Sherry. Compte rendu de Quand je lis, je m'invente. Canadian Women's Studies/les cahiers de la femme [Centennial College], [The Future/le futur], 6, no 2 (Spring 1985), 108.

La Rue, Monique

Interviews/Entretiens

Royer, Jean. "Monique La Rue: Le corps des mots." Le Devoir [Montréal], 26 juin 1982, pp. 13, 24. Repris dans Ecrivains contemporains: Entretiens 3: 1980–1983. Par Jean Royer. Montréal: L'Hexagone, 1985, pp. 314–20.

Reviews/Comptes rendus

Ouellette-Michalska, Madeleine. Compte rendu de La Cohorte fictive. Livres et auteurs québécois 1979. Ed. André Berthiaume. Québec: Les Presses de l'Univ. Laval, 1980, pp. 56–58.

Lasnier, Rina

**Articles and Sections of Books/
Articles et sections de livres**

Gilroy, James P. "The Pursuit of the Real in Rina Lasnier's Presence de l'absence." In Traditionalism, Nationalism and Feminism: Women Writers of Quebec. Ed. Paula Gilbert Lewis. Contributions in Women's Studies, No. 53. Westport, Conn.: Greenwood, 1985, pp. 53–62.
Paradis, Suzanne. "Eloge de Rachel." Liberté, 18, no 6 [no 108] (nov.–déc. 1976), 12–20.

Interviews/Entretiens

Bonenfant, Joseph, et Richard Giguère.

"Est-il chose plus belle qu'une orange? Rencontre avec Rina Lasnier." *voix et images: études québécoises,* 4 (sept. 1978), 3–32. Rpt. trans. M. L. Taylor ("Conversation with Rina Lasnier") in *ellipse,* No. 22 (1978), pp. 32–61.

Giguère, Richard. Voir/see Bonenfant, Joseph, et Richard Giguère.

Laurence, Margaret

Books/Livres

Buss, Helen M. *Mother and Daughter Relationships in the Manawaka World of Margaret Laurence.* ELS Monograph Series, No. 34. Victoria: Univ. of Victoria, 1986. 88 pp.

Morley, Patricia. *Margaret Laurence.* Twayne's World Authors Series, No. 591. Boston: G. K. Hall, 1981. 171 pp.; esp. pp. 130–33.

Thomas, Clara. *The Manawaka World of Margaret Laurence.* Toronto: McClelland and Stewart, 1975. 212 pp.

Articles and Sections of Books/
Articles et sections de livres

Ayre, John. "Bell, Book and Scandal." *Weekend Magazine* [*The Globe and Mail*] [Toronto], 28 Aug. 1976, pp. 8–12.

Bailey, Nancy. "Fiction and the New Androgyne: Problems and Possibilities in *The Diviners.*" *Atlantis: A Women's Studies Journal/Journal d'études sur la femme* [Acadia Univ.], 4, No. 1 (Fall/automne 1978), 10–17.

——— . "Margaret Laurence, Carl Jung and the Manawaka Women." *Studies in Canadian Literature,* 2 (Summer 1977), 306–21.

Bennett, Donna A. "The Failures of Sisterhood in Margaret Laurence's Manawaka Novels." *Atlantis: A Women's Studies Journal/Journal d'études sur la femme* [Acadia Univ.], 4, No. 1 (Fall/automne 1978), 103–09.

Blodgett, Harriet. "The Real Lives of Mar-

garet Laurence's Women." *Critique* [Atlanta, Ga.], 23, No. 1 (Fall 1981), 5–17.

Cameron, Donald. "The Many Lives of Margaret Laurence." *Weekend Magazine* [*The Globe and Mail*] [Toronto], 20 July 1974, pp. 3–5.

Coldwell, Joan. "The Beauty of the Medusa: Twentieth Century." *English Studies in Canada,* 11 (Dec. 1985), 422–37.

Czarnecki, Mark. "Margaret Laurence and the Book Banners." *Chatelaine,* Oct. 1985, pp. 55, 186–91.

Demetrakopoulos, Stephanie. "Accepting Femininity: Margaret Laurence's *The Stone Angel.*" In her *Listening to Our Bodies: The Rebirth of Feminine Wisdom.* Boston: Beacon, 1983, pp. 79–87.

Demetrakopoulos, Stephanie A. "Laurence's Fiction: A Revisioning of Feminine Archetypes." *Canadian Literature,* No. 93 (Summer 1982), pp. 42–57.

Engel, Marian. "It's the Grit: Laurence Is Unforgettable Because She Is Us." *The Globe and Mail* [Toronto], 19 April 1975, p. 37. Rpt. (abridged) in *Margaret Laurence: The Writer and Her Critics.* Ed. William New. Critical Views on Canadian Writers, No. 10. Toronto: McGraw-Hill Ryerson, 1977, pp. 219–21.

——— . "Steps to the Mythic: *The Diviners* and *A Bird in the House.*" *Journal of Canadian Studies/Revue d'études canadiennes,* [Margaret Laurence], 13, No. 3 (automne/Fall 1978), 72–74.

Frye, Joanne S. "Beyond Telelogy: *Violet Clay* and *The Stone Angel.*" In her *Living Stories, Telling Lies: Women and the Novel in Contemporary Experience.* Ann Arbor: Univ. of Michigan Press, 1986, pp. 109–42; esp. pp. 130–42.

Greene, Gayle. "The Contemporary Woman Writer as Prospero: Margaret Laurence's *The Diviners.*" MLA Conference, New York. Dec. 1983.

Hughes, Kenneth James. "Politics and *A Jest of God.*" *Journal of Canadian Studies/ Revue d'études canadiennes,* [Margaret Laurence], 13, No. 3 (automne/Fall 1978), 40–54.

Kearns, Judy. "Rachel and Social Determination: A Feminist Reading of *A Jest of God.*" *Journal of Canadian Fiction*, [The Work of Margaret Laurence], No. 27 (1980), pp. 101–23.

Maeser, Angelika. "Finding the Mother: The Individuation of Laurence's Heroines." *Journal of Canadian Fiction*, [The Work of Margaret Laurence], No. 27 (1980), pp. 151–66.

Miner, Valerie. "The Matriarch of Manawaka." *Saturday Night*, May 1974, pp. 17–20.

Morley, Patricia. "Margaret Laurence: Feminist, Nationalist and Matriarch of Canadian Letters." *Laurentian University Review/Revue de l'Université Laurentienne*, [Women: Images and Insights], 14, No. 2 (Feb./fév. 1982), 24–33.

——. "No Mean Feat." *Canadian Newsletter of Research on Women/Recherches sur la Femme — Bulletin d'Information Canadien*, 7, No. 2 (July 1978), 25.

Perrotin, Françoise. "Quelques personnages masculins chez Margaret Laurence." *Annales du CRAA* [Univ. de Bordeaux III], NS no 7, 1982, pp. 81–89.

Rocard, Marcienne. "Women and Woman in *The Stone Angel.*" *Etudes Canadiennes/Canadian Studies* [Univ. de Bordeaux III], No. 11 (déc. 1981), pp. 77–78.

Rooke, Constance. "A Feminist Reading of *The Stone Angel.*" *Canadian Literature*, [Wilson, Laurence, Gallant, Glassco], No. 93 (Summer 1982), pp. 26–41.

Stevenson, Warren. "The Myth of Demeter and Persephone in *A Jest of God.*" *Studies in Canadian Literature*, 1 (Winter 1976), 120–23.

Thomas, Clara. "Beyond Feminism: Margaret Laurence's Heroines." *Existere* [Vanier College, York Univ.], April 1979, pp. 16–18.

——. "Proud Lineage: Willa Cather and Margaret Laurence." *The Canadian Review of American Studies*, 2, No. 1 (Spring 1971), 3–12.

Vauthier, Simone. "Names and Naming in *The Stone Angel.*" *Recherches Anglaises et Américaines*, 14 (1981), 237–54.

Warwick, Susan J. "Margaret Laurence: An Annotated Bibliography." In *The Annotated Bibliography of Canada's Major Authors.* Ed. Robert Lecker and Jack David. Vol. 1. Downsview, Ont.: ECW, 1979, 47–101.

Wigmore, Donnalu. "Margaret Laurence: The Woman Behind the Writing." *Chatelaine*, Feb. 1981, pp. 28–29, 52, 54.

Theses and Dissertations/Thèses

Birch, Frances Ann. "Principal Female Protagonists in the Novels of Brian Moore and Margaret Laurence." M.A. Thesis Toronto 1974.

Curry, Gwen Cranfill. "Journeys towards Freedom: A Study of Margaret Laurence's Fictional Women." Diss. Indiana 1980.

Janes, Kathryn. "Margaret Laurence: A Bibliography." M.A. Thesis San José State 1975.

Long, Tanya. "The Heroine in the Novels of Margaret Laurence." M.Phil. Thesis Toronto 1973.

Pell, Barbara Helen. "Margaret Laurence's Treatment of the Heroine." M.A. Thesis Waterloo 1972.

Tremblay, Anne. "Feminine Self-Consciousness in the Works of Margaret Laurence." M.A. Thesis McGill 1976.

Interviews/Entretiens

Atwood, Margaret. "Face to Face: An Interview with Margaret Laurence." *Maclean's*, May 1974, pp. 38–39, 43–46.

Gibson, Graeme. "Margaret Laurence." In his *Eleven Canadian Novelists.* Toronto: House of Anansi, 1973, pp. 181–208; esp. pp. 199–200.

Law, Harriet. "Our Myths: Our Selves." *Indirections*, 2, No. 2 (Winter 1977), 33–42.

Lever, Bernice. "Margaret Laurence." *Waves*, 3, No. 2 (Winter 1975), 4–12.

Sheppard, June. "June Sheppard Talks with Margaret Laurence." *Branching Out: Canadian Magazine for Women*, 1, No. 1 (Dec. 1973), 20–21.

Bagley, Laurie. "Morag Gunn: A Canadian Venus at Last?". Rev. of *The Diviners*. *Branching Out: Canadian Magazine for Women*, 3, No. 1 (Feb.–March 1976), 39–40.

Engel, Marian. "The Girl Who Escaped from Manawaka Is at the Core of Margaret Laurence's New Novel." Rev. of *The Fire-Dwellers*. *Saturday Night*, May 1969, pp. 38–39.

———. "Margaret Laurence: Her New Book Divines Women's Truths." Rev. of *The Diviners*. *Chatelaine*, May 1974, p. 25.

Grosskurth, Phyllis. "A Looser, More Complex, More Sexually Uninhibited Laurence: And Never an Atwood Victim." Rev. of *The Diviners*. *The Globe and Mail* [Toronto], 4 May 1974, p. 35.

Piercy, Marge. "Gritty Places and Strong Women." Rev. of *The Diviners*. *The New York Times Book Review*, 23 June 1974, p. 6. Rpt. in *Margaret Laurence: The Writer and Her Critics*. Ed. William New. Critical Views on Canadian Writers, No. 10. Toronto: McGraw-Hill Ryerson, 1977, p. 224.

Le Blanc, Emilie C. (Voyez/see Marichette)

LeBlanc, Louise

Reviews/Comptes rendus

Lafortune-Martel, Agathe. Compte rendu de *37½ AA*. *Canadian Women's Studies/les cahiers de la femme* [Centennial College], [Belles lettres], 5, no 1 (Fall/automne 1983), 77.

Langevin, Lysanne. "Le rire à l'eau de rose." Compte rendu de *37½ AA*. *Spirale*, no 37 (oct. 1983), p. 4.

Le Franc, Marie

Books/Livres

Collet, Paulette. *Marie Le Franc: Deux patries, deux exils*. Sherbrooke: Cosmos, 1977. 198 pp.

Articles and Sections of Books/ Articles et sections de livres

Salonne, Marie-Paule. "Chez Marie Le Franc, Bretagne et Canada." *La revue populaire*, juin 1930, pp. 7–9, 82.

Le Normand, Michelle

Articles and Sections of Books/ Articles et sections de livres

"A propos de femmes de lettres." *Le Devoir* [Montréal], 3 jan. 1931, p. 1.

Fadette, [Henriette]. "Plumes féminines: Michelle Le Normand." *Le Devoir* [Montréal], 10 jan. 1920, p. 5.

Letarte, Geneviève

Reviews/Comptes rendus

La Grenade, Carole. Compte rendu du *Station Transit*. *Canadian Women's Studies/ les cahiers de la femme* [Centennial College], [Aging/Le 3ème âge], 5, no 3 (Spring/printemps 1984), 89.

Livesay, Dorothy

Books/Livres

Livesay, Dorothy. *Right Hand Left Hand*. Erin, Ont.: Porcépic, 1977. 280 pp.

Articles and Sections of Books/ Articles et sections de livres

Banting, Pamela. "Dorothy Livesay's

Notations of Love and the Stance Dance of the Female Poet in Relation to Language." *CV/II*, [Manitoba Poetry Issue], 8, No. 3 (Sept. 1984), 14–18.

Dykk, Lloyd. "A Gallant Poet Speaks Her Mind." *The Vancouver Sun*, 11 Sept. 1981, pp. L40–L41.

Foulks, Debbie. "Livesay's Two Seasons of Love." *Canadian Literature*, [Women and Literature], No. 74 (Autumn 1977), pp. 63–73.

Hawkes, Cheryl. "Poet's Progress." *Starweek Magazine* [*The Toronto Star*], 13–20 March 1982, p. 9.

Kisuk, Alex. "Some Theoretical Considerations on Reading Dorothy Livesay's Poetry: 'green blades scissoring / the sun.'" *Journal of Literary Theory* [Royal Military College of Canada], 4 (1983), 47–61.

Marshall, Joyce. "Dorothy Livesay: A Bluestocking Remembers." *Branching Out: Canadian Feminist Quarterly*, 7, No. 1 (1980), 18–21.

Mitchell, Beverley. "'How Silence Sings' in the Poetry of Dorothy Livesay 1926–1973." *The Dalhousie Review*, 54 (Autumn 1974), 510–28.

Ricketts, Alan. "Dorothy Livesay: An Annotated Bibliography." In *The Annotated Bibliography of Canada's Major Authors*. Ed. Robert Lecker and Jack David. Vol. IV. Downsview, Ont.: ECW, 1983, 129–203.

Robertson, Heather. "Dorothy Livesay: 'My Aim Was to Merge the Political and the Lyrical. I'm an Unabashed Romantic.'" *Quill & Quire*, March 1983, pp. 4, 6.

Thomas, Audrey. "Open Letter to Dorothy Livesay." *Room of One's Own*, 5, No. 3 (1980), 70–73.

Thompson, Lee Briscoe. "A Coat of Many Cultures: The Poetry of Dorothy Livesay." *Journal of Popular Culture*, 15, No. 3 (Winter 1981), 53–61.

Whiteman, Bruce. "The Tradition: The Beginnings of Modernism (2) Dorothy Livesay." *Poetry Canada Review*, 7, No. 2 (Winter 1985–86), 23.

Whitney, Joyce. "Death and Transfiguration: The Mature Love Poems of Dorothy Livesay." *Room of One's Own*, [The Dorothy Livesay Issue], 5, Nos. 1–2 (1979), 100–12.

Wilson, Jean. "Introduction: Travelling Lives." *Room of One's Own*, [The Dorothy Livesay Issue], 5, Nos. 1–2 (1979), 5–12.

Zimmerman, C. D., and S. C. Zimmerman. "Remember Dorothy?". *The Canadian Forum*, Sept. 1980, pp. 33–34.

Zimmerman, Susan. "Livesay's Houses." *Canadian Literature*, [Fifteenth Anniversary Issue], No. 61 (Summer 1974), pp. 32–45.

——— . See also/voir aussi Zimmerman, C. D., and S. C. Zimmerman.

Interviews/Entretiens

Barber, Marsha. "An Interview with Dorothy Livesay." *Room of One's Own*, [The Dorothy Livesay Issue], 5, Nos. 1–2 (1979), 13–34.

Lever, Bernice. "An Interview with Dorothy Livesay." *The Canadian Forum*, [Women's Issue], Sept. 1975, pp. 45–52.

Marshall, Joyce. "Dorothy Livesay: A Bluestocking Remembers." *Branching Out: Canadian Feminist Quarterly*, 7, No. 1 (1980), 18–21.

Twigg, Alan. "Dorothy Livesay: Matrona." In his *For Openers: Conversations with 24 Canadian Writers*. Madiera Park, B.C.: Harbour, 1981, pp. 127–37.

Reviews/Comptes rendus

Aubert, Rosemary. Rev. of *The Woman I Am. Quill & Quire*, Dec. 1977, p. 34.

Keitner, Wendy. Rev. of *The Phases of Love. CV/II*, 8, No. 1 (May 1984), 50–51.

Laing, Karen. Rev. of *Feeling the World/ New Poems*. HERizons: *The Manitoba Women's News Magazine*, April–May 1986, p. 44.

Loeffler, Sheryl. Rev. of *The Phases of Love. Quill & Quire*, June 1983, p. 34.

Marshall, Joyce. "Remembering Ancestors." Rev. of *Right Hand Left Hand. Branching*

Out: Canadian Magazine for Women, [Special Issue on Women and Art], 5, No. 2 (1978), 41.

Morley, Patricia. "Learning and Loving During the Lost Years." Rev. of *Right Hand Left Hand. Atlantis: A Women's Studies Journal/Journal d'études sur la femme* [Acadia Univ.], 3, No. 2, Pt. 1 (Spring/printemps 1978), 145–50.

Morton, Mary Lee. "Livesay Distorted." Rev. of *The Woman I Am. Branching Out: Canadian Magazine for Women*, 5, No. 3 (1978), 41.

Murray, Heather. Rev. of *Feeling the World/New Poems. Canadian Women's Studies/les cahiers de la femme* [Centennial College], [Women's Studies/Conference: Les Études de la femme/Colloque], 6, No. 3 (Summer–Fall 1985), 112–13.

Read, Daphne. Rev. of *Ice Age. World Literature Written in English* [Univ. of Texas at Arlington], [Women Writers of the Commonwealth], 17 (April 1978), 191–96.

Loranger, Françoise

Articles and Sections of Books/Articles et sections de livres

Coates, Carrol F. "From Feminism to Nationalism: The Theatre of Françoise Loranger. 1965–1970." In *Traditionalism, Nationalism and Feminism: Women Writers of Quebec.* Ed. Paula Gilbert Lewis. Contributions in Women's Studies, No. 53. Westport, Conn.: Greenwood, 1985, pp. 83–94.

Lowther, Patricia

Articles and Sections of Books/Articles et sections de livres

Grescoe, Paul. "Eulogy for a Poet." *The Canadian* [*The Toronto Star*], 5 June 1976, pp. 13, 16–19.

Reviews/Comptes rendus

Jones, Elizabeth. Rev. of *A Stone Diary. Atlantis: A Women's Studies Journal/Journal d'études sur la femme* [Acadia Univ.], 3, No. 1 (Fall/automne 1977), 232–36.

MacEwen, Gwendolyn

Interviews/Entretiens

Keeney Smith, Patricia. "An Interview with Gwendolyn MacEwen." *Cross-Canada Writers' Quarterly*, 5, No. 1 (1983), 14–17.

Reviews/Comptes rendus

Ravel, Aviva. "From Playwrights." Rev. of *Trojan Women. Canadian Literature*, [Faces of Realism/Facing Realities], No. 89 (Summer 1981), pp. 158–59.

Machar, Agnes Maule (pseud. Fidelis)

Articles and Sections of Books/Articles et sections de livres

Guild, Leman A. "Canadian Celebrities: Agnes Maule Machar (Fidelis)." *The Canadian Magazine of Politics, Science, Art and Literature* [Toronto], Oct. 1906, pp. 499–501.

MacCallum, F. L. "Agnes Maule Machar." *The Canadian Magazine of Politics, Science, Art and Literature* [Toronto], March 1924, pp. 354–56.

Wetherald, A. Ethelwyn. "Some Canadian Literary Women — II. Fidelis." *The Week: A Canadian Journal of Politics, Society and Literature* [Toronto], 5 April 1888, pp. 300–01.

MacPhail, Agnes

Reviews/Comptes rendus

Kaplan, Jon. "Witty, Wise Agnes Mac-

Phail." Rev. of *Agnes MacPhail*, by Theresa Sears and Don Switzer. *Now* [Toronto], 3–9 April 1986, p. 23.

Macpherson, Jay

Reviews/Comptes rendus

Atwood, Margaret. "In the Fields of Light." Rev. of *Poems Twice Told:* The Boatman *&* Welcoming Disaster. *Books in Canada*, April 1982, pp. 14–15.

Maheux-Forcier, Louise

**Articles and Sections of Books/
Articles et sections de livres**

Bosco, Monique. "Depuis peu le roman connaît la sexualité." Compte rendu d'*Inutile et adorable*, par Robert Fournier; et *Amadou*, par Louise Maheux-Forcier. *Le Magazine Maclean*, fév. 1964, p. 46.

Bourbonnais, Nicole. "Ophélie . . . ressuscitée." Dans *La femme, son corps et la religion: approches pluridisciplinaires.* Ed. Elisabeth J. Lacelle. Montréal: Bellarmin, 1983, pp. 174–83.

Cagnon, Maurice. "Louise Maheux-Forcier and the Poetics of Sensuality." *Québec Studies*, 1, No. 1 (Spring 1983), 286–97. Rpt. in *Traditionalism, Nationalism and Feminism: Women Writers of Quebec.* Ed. Paula Gilbert Lewis. Contributions in Women's Studies, No. 53. Westport, Conn.: Greenwood, 1985, pp. 95–107.

Interviews/Entretiens

Royer, Jean. "Louise Maheux-Forcier: Seul l'amour n'est pas absurde." *Le Devoir* [Montréal], 30 jan. 1982, pp. 15, 28. Repris dans *Ecrivains contemporains: Entretiens 3: 1980–1983.* Par Jean Royer. Montréal: L'Hexagone, 1985, pp. 48–53.

Reviews/Comptes rendus

Sirois, Denise. Compte rendu de *En Toutes lettres* et *Appasionata. Des luttes et des rires de femmes*, 4, no 3 (fév.–mars 1981), 51.

Templeton, Wayne. "Figures That Crumble." Rev. of *Letter by Letter. The Vancouver Sun*, 31 Dec. 1982, p. L28.

Mailhot, Michèle

**Articles and Sections of Books/
Articles et sections de livres**

Verthuy, Maïr. "Michèle Mailhot ou comment passer inaperçue." Dialogue, York Univ., Downsview, Ont. 16 Oct./oct. 1981. Printed ("Michèle Mailhot: A Cautionary Tale") in *Gynocritics/Gynocritiques: Feminist Approaches to Canadian and Quebec Women's Writing/Démarches féministes à l'écriture des Canadiennes et Québécoises.* Ed. Barbara Godard. Toronto: ECW, 1987, pp. 131–41.

Maillet, Andrée

**Articles and Sections of Books/
Articles et sections de livres**

Francion, Lise Morin. "Le mâle orgueil d'être femme: les *Remparts de Québec.*" *Le Progrès du golfe* [Rimouski], 26 mars 1965, p. 5.

Interviews/Entretiens

Pilotte, Hélène. "Andrée Maillet — une romancière québécoise fait le portrait amer de notre bourgeoisie (entrevue)." *Châtelaine*, oct. 1972, pp. 34–35, 66–67, 80–81.

Reviews/Comptes rendus

Saint-Onge, Paule. "Châtelaine a lu pour vous: Andrée Maillet." Compte rendu de *Nouvelles montréalaises. Châtelaine*, avril 1966, p. 98.

Maillet, Antonine

Articles and Sections of Books/ Articles et sections de livres

Crecelius, Kathryn. "L'histoire et son double dans *Pelagie-la-charette*." *Studies in Canadian Literature*, 6, no 2 ([Fall] 1981), 211–20. Présenté NEMLA Conference, New York. April 1982.

Fitzpatrick, Marjorie A. "Antonine Maillet and the Epic Heroine." In *Traditionalism, Nationalism and Feminism: Women Writers of Quebec*. Ed. Paula Gilbert Lewis. Contributions in Women's Studies, No. 53. Westport, Conn.: Greenwood, 1985, pp. 141–55.

——— . "Antonine Maillet: The Search for a Narrative Voice." *Journal of Popular Culture*, 15, No. 3 (Winter 1981), 4–13.

Godard, Barbara Thompson. "The Tale of a Narrative: Antonine Maillet's *Don l'Orignal*." *Atlantis: A Women's Studies Journal/Journal d'études sur la femme* [Acadia Univ.], 5, No. 1 (Fall/automne 1979), 51–69.

Lanken, Dane. "L'Acadienne." *Quest: Canada's Urban Magazine*, Dec. 1982, pp. 34–42.

Webster, Jackie. "Antonine Maillet: First Lady of Acadian Literature." *Le Nouveau/New Brunswick*, 5, No. 2 (Summer 1980), 1–5.

Interviews/ Entretiens

Cowan, Doris. "Interview with Antonine Maillet." *Books in Canada*, May 1982, pp. 24–26.

Collin, Françoise. "Antonine Maillet: Interview." *Les Cahiers du GRIF* [Brussels], no 12 (juin 1976), pp. 44–48. Continué dans no 13.

——— . "Antonine Maillet: Interview." *Les Cahiers du GRIF* [Brussels], no 13 (oct. 1976), pp. 41–43. Continuation de no 12.

Jacquot, Martine. "Last Story-Teller: An Interview with Antonine Maillet." *Waves*, 14, No. 4 (Spring 1986), 92–95.

Leblanc-Rainville, Simone. "Entretien avec Antonine Maillet." *La Revue de l'Université de Moncton*, 7, no 2 (mai 1974), 13–24.

Reviews/Comptes rendus

Cellard, Jacques. "Vierges folles et femmes fortes." Compte rendu de *Corde-de-Bois*. *Le Monde des livres*, 16 sept. 1977, p. 15.

Ouellette-Michalska, Madeleine. "Antonine Maillet: Un roman parfait cent ans trop tard . . . ." Compte rendu de *Cent ans dans les bois*. *Le Devoir* [Montréal], 21 nov. 1981, p. 23.

Mallet, Marilu

Interviews/ Entretiens

Royer, Jean. "Marilu Mallet: Ouvrir une tradition de la différence." *Le Devoir* [Montréal], 12 fév. 1983, pp. 16, 32. Repris dans *Ecrivains contemporains: Entretiens 3: 1980–1983*. Par Jean Royer. Montréal: L'Hexagone, 1985, pp. 89–94.

Mandel, Miriam

Reviews/Comptes rendus

Tostevin, Lola Lemire. Rev. of *The Collected Poems of Miriam Mandel*. *Contemporary Verse 2*, 9, No. 2 (Fall 1985), 51–53.

Marchessault, Jovette

Articles and Sections of Books/ Articles et sections de livres

Gaboriau, Linda. "Jovette Marchessault: A Luminous Wake in Space." *Canadian Theatre Review*, [Feminism: Canadian Theatre], No. 43 (Summer 1985), pp. 91–99.

Godard, Barbara. Bibliography. In *Lesbian Triptych*. By Jovette Marchessault. Trans.

Yvonne Klein. Toronto: Women's, 1985, pp. 97–100.

———. "Flying Away with Language." In *Lesbian Triptych*. By Jovette Marchessault. Trans. Yvonne Klein. Toronto: Women's, 1985, pp. 9–28.

Le Clézio, Marie. "Poétique et/ou politique: Le théâtre de Jovette Marchessault." *NDQ: North Dakota Quarterly* [Univ. of North Dakota], 52, no 3 (Summer 1984), 100–06.

Marchessault, Jovette. "Il m'est encore impossible de chanter, mais j'écris." *Jeu: cahiers de théâtre*, [Théâtre-femmes], no 16 (1980), pp. 207–10.

Orenstein, Gloria. "Jovette Marchessault ou La quête ecstatique de la nouvelle chamane féministe." *Bulletin de la société des professeurs français en Amérique*, 1 (Fall 1979), 37–57. Rpt. trans. ("Jovette Marchessault: The Ecstatic Vision-Quest of the New Feminist Shaman") in *Gynocritics/Gynocritiques: Feminist Approaches to Canadian and Quebec Women's Writing/Démarches féministes à l'écriture des Canadiennes et Québécoises*. Ed. Barbara Godard. Toronto: ECW, 1987, pp. 179–97.

Interviews/Entretiens

Bell, Gay. "Power, Magic and Visibility: From Biting Satirical Diatribes to Warm Evocations of the Natural Earth, Québécoise Playwright Jovette Marchessault Captures the Strength of Lesbian Energy. An Interview." *The Body Politic* [Toronto], Jan. 1986, pp. 35, 37.

———. "Where Nest the Wet Hens." Interview with Michelle Rossignol and Jovette Marchessault. *Broadside: A Feminist Review* [Toronto], Feb. 1982, pp. 12–13.

Royer, Jean. "Jovette Marchessault: Le chaos brulant de la mémoire." *Le Devoir* [Montréal], 31 oct. 1981, pp. 21, 40. Repris dans *Ecrivains contemporains: Entretiens 3: 1980–1983*. Par Jean Royer. Montréal: L'Hexagone, 1985, pp. 204–10.

Smith, Donald. "Jovette Marchessault: de la femme tellurique à la démythification sociale." *Lettres québécoises: Revue de l'actualité littéraire*, [Littérature féministe, Littérature au féminin], no 27 (automne 1982), pp. 52–58.

Théoret, France. "Répercuter les premiers mots: Interview avec Jovette Marchessault." *Spirale*, no 20 (juin 1981), p. 18.

Reviews/Comptes rendus

Alonzo, Anne-Marie. "Oeuvre de chair." Compte rendu d'*Anaïs, dans la queue de la comète*. *La vie en rose*, fév. 1986, p. 52.

Constantin, Louise. Compte rendu de *Tryptique lesbien*. *Des luttes et des rires de femmes*, 4, no 5 (juin–juil.–août 1981), 43–44.

Dumont, Monique. "Une filiation d'écritures." Compte rendu de *La Saga des poules mouillées*. *Spirale*, no 20 (juin 1981), p. 19.

Forsyth, Louise H. "Women Reclaim Their Culture in Quebec: A Saga of Night Cows and Wet Hens." *Spirale: A Women's Art and Culture Quarterly*, NS 1, No. 2 (Autumn 1981), 12–13 (English; 13, 15 (français).

H[ale]., A[manda]. "Daydreams and Night Cows." Rev. of *Lesbian Triptych*. *Broadside: A Feminist Review* [Toronto], May 1985, p. 13.

Hale, Amanda. "Voices, Vices and Voyeurs." Rev. of *The Edge of the Earth Is Too Near, Violette Leduc*, prod. Nightwood Theatre, dir. Cynthia Grant, Theatre Centre, Toronto, 14 May–1 June 1986. *Broadside: A Feminist Review* [Toronto], June 1986, p. 11.

Orenstein, Gloria. "Plant Mother: Mythic Vision." Rev. of *La mère des herbes*. *New Women's Times Feminist Review*, Sept.–Oct. 1980, pp. 8–9.

———. "The Telluric Women of Jovette Marchessault." Rev. of the Telluric sculptures. *Fireweed: A Feminist Literary & Cultural Journal*, [Women and Language], Nos. 5–6 (Winter–Spring 1979–80), pp. 164–67.

R[ioux]., E[liette]. Compte rendu de *Comme une enfant de la terre*. *Les Têtes de pi-*

oche: *Journal des femmes*, no 5 (sept. 1976), p. 8.

Théoret, France. "Un livre impatient." Compte rendu de *La mère des herbes*. *Spirale*, no 10 (juin 1980), pp. 1, 6.

Marichette [Emilie C. Le Blanc]

Articles and Sections of Books/ Articles et sections de livres

Gérin, Pierre. "Une écrivaine acadienne à la fin du dix-neuvième siècle: Marichette." *Atlantis: A Women's Studies Journal/ Journal d'études sur la femme* [Mt. St. Vincent Univ.], 10, no 1 (Fall 1984), 38.

Marlatt, Daphne

Articles and Sections of Books/ Articles et sections de livres

Cole, Christina. "Daphne Marlatt as Penelope, Weaver of Words." *Open Letter*, Ser. 6, No. 1 (Spring 1985), pp. 5–19.

Godard, Barbara. "'Body I': Daphne Marlatt's Feminist Poetics." *The American Review of Canadian Studies*, 15, No. 4 (Winter 1985), 481–96. Repris (abrégé — "'Mon Corps est mots': la poétique féminine de Daphne Marlatt") dans *ellipse*, nos 33–34 (1985), pp. 88–100.

Interviews/Entretiens

Arnason, David, Denis Cooley, and Robert Enright. "There's this and this connexion: an interview with Daphne Marlatt." *CV/II*, 3, No. 1 (Spring 1977), 28–33.

Bowering, George. "Given This Body: An Interview with Daphne Marlatt." *Open Letter*, [Three Vancouver Writers], Ser. 4, No. 3 (Spring 1979), pp. 32–88.

Reviews/Comptes rendus

Duncan, Frances. Rev. of *Steveston*. *Brick* [Toronto], No. 26 (Winter 1986), pp. 56–57.

Hall, Chris. "Three from the West Coast." Rev. of *What Matters: Writing 1968–70*, by Daphne Marlatt; *House of Water*, by Robert Tyhurst; and *A Poor Photographer*, by John Barton. *The University of Windsor Review*, 16, No. 2 (Spring 1982), 119–22.

Hatch, Ronald. "Poet's Pilgrimage to a Mythical Past." Rev. of *How Hug a Stone*. *The Vancouver Sun*, 13 Aug. 1983, p. H12.

Potter, Robin. "Retrieving Wholeness." Rev. of *How Hug a Stone*. *Brick* [Ilderton, Ont.], No. 22 (Fall 1984), pp. 27–29.

Marshall, Joyce

Reviews/Comptes rendus

Hopwood, Alison L. Rev. of *A Private Place*. *Branching Out: Canadian Magazine for Women*, 3, No. 4 (Sept.–Oct. 1976), 43–44.

Martin, Claire

Articles and Sections of Books/ Articles et sections de livres

"Châtelaine en pantoufles: Claire Martin." *Châtelaine*, juin 1965, p. 3.

Gagnon, Lysiane. "La romancière Claire Martin fait le point." *Le Magazine de la Presse* [*La Presse*] [Montréal], 30 déc. 1967, pp. 3–5.

Koski, Jaija. "*Avec ou sans amour* de Claire Martin: cohérence de recueil." ACQL/ALCQ, Univ. de Guelph, Guelph, Ont. 5 juin 1984.

"L'homme est absent de la littérature canadienne-française." *Le Devoir* [Montréal], 20 avril 1965, p. 7.

Pilotte, Hélène. "La romancière Claire Martin analyste de l'amour et de la femme." *Châtelaine*, juin 1965, pp. 29, 46–49.

Urbas, Jeannette. "Le Jeu et la guerre dans l'oeuvre de Claire Martin." *Voix et images du pays*, 8 (1974), 133–47.

Theses and Dissertations/Thèses

Thibaudeau, Huguette. "Les femmes dans l'oeuvre de Claire Martin." M.A. Thesis British Columbia 1975.

Interviews/Entretiens

Dorion, Gilles. Voir/see Iqbal, Françoise, et Gilles Dorion.
Iqbal, Françoise, et Gilles Dorion. "Claire Martin: Une Interview." *Canadian Literature*, [Journals: Self and Society], No. 82 (Autumn 1979), pp. 59–77.

Reviews/Comptes rendus

Homel, David. "Silhouettes on the Shade." Rev. of *Best Man*. *Books in Canada*, Aug.–Sept. 1983, p. 29.
Légaré, Céline. "Claire Martin ou le procès de l'éducation féminine." Compte rendu de *La Joue droite*. *La Patrie* [Montréal], 18 sept. 1966, p. 20.
Saint-Onge, Paule. "Châtelaine a lu pour vous." Compte rendu de *La Joue de droite*. *Châtelaine*, nov. 1966, p. 17.
Sénécal, Louise-Marie. "Claire Martin ou le refus du rôle traditionnel de mère." Compte rendu de *Dans un gant de fer*. *Le Devoir* [Montréal], 19 déc. 1964, pp. 13, 14.

Masel, Dona Paul

Reviews/Comptes rendus

Miller, Judith. Rev. of *Yes: A Play in Search of Mary*. *Hysteria* [Kitchener, Ont.], 2, No. 4 (1983–84), 26.

Massé, Carole

Articles and Sections of Books/ Articles et sections de livres

Fournier, Danielle. "Carole Massé: le texte

de la langue maternelle." *Dalhousie French Studies*, [Numéro spécial: La poésie québécoise depuis 1975], 1985, pp. 167–72.
Royer, Jean. "Carole Massé: Accéder à sa propre voix." *Le Devoir* [Montréal], 5 avril 1986, pp. 21, 27.

Reviews/Comptes rendus

David, Carole. "La mise en scène d'une histoire désirante." Compte rendu de *Dieu*. *Spirale*, no 4 (déc. 1979), p. 7.
Martin, Agathe. "Femmes figurantes à délire *Dieu*." *Canadian Women's Studies/les cahiers de la femme* [Centennial College], [Femme et Santé/Women and Health], 1, No. 4 (Summer/été 1979), 92–93.

McClung, Nellie

Articles and Sections of Books/ Articles et sections de livres

Matheson, Gwen, and V. E. Lang. "Nellie McClung: 'Not a Nice Woman.'" In *Women in the Canadian Mosaic*. Ed. Gwen Matheson. Toronto: Peter Martin, 1976, pp. 1–20.

Theses and Dissertations/Thèses

Verkvuysse, Patricia Louise. "Small Legacy of Truth: The Novels of Nellie McClung." M.A. Thesis New Brunswick 1975.

Reviews/Comptes rendus

Matheson, Gwen. "Nellie McClung." Rev. of *In Times Like These*. *Canadian Dimension*, [Women: A Special Issue], 10, No. 8 (June 1975), 42–48.

McFee, Oonah

Articles and Sections of Books/ Articles et sections de livres

Ruston, Ruth Ellen. "Not Your Average

Tortured Writer." *The Canadian* [*The Toronto Star*], 2 July 1977, pp. 12–13.

Reviews/Comptes rendus

McMullen, Lorraine. "This Long-Ago Rainbow World: Oonah McFee's *Sandbars*." *World Literature Written in English* [Univ. of Texas at Arlington], [Women Writers of the Commonwealth], 17 (April 1978), 199–202.

Smyth, Donna E. "Speak, Memory." Rev. of *Sandbars*. *Journal of Canadian Fiction*, No. 20 (1977), pp. 159–60.

McIlwraith, Jean

Articles and Sections of Books/ Articles et sections de livres

MacMurchy, Marjory. "Canadian Celebrities. xxiv: Miss Jean N. McIlwraith." *The Canadian Magazine of Politics, Science, Art and Literature* [Toronto], June 1901, pp. 131–34.

McLean, Anne

Interviews/Entretiens

Schrier, Louise. "An Interview with Anne McLean." *Hejira* [McGill Faculty of Nursing], 3, No. 1 (Winter 1985–86), 22–29.

Reviews/Comptes rendus

Ruvinsky, Joan. "Divine Depravity." Rev. of *A Nun's Diary. Brick* [Toronto], No. 25 (Fall 1985), pp. 38–39.

Meigs, Mary

Interviews/Entretiens

Herringer, Barbara. "I Have Opened My Soul to Interpretation . . . ." *The Radical Reviewer*, No. 5 (Winter 1981–82),

pp. 8–9, 12–13.

Reviews/Comptes rendus

Alonzo, Anne-Marie. "Portrait Sexagénaire." Compte rendu de *Lily Briscoe: un autoportrait. La vie en rose*, mars 1985, p. 60.

Béland, Claude. Compte rendu de *Lily Briscoe: un autoportrait*. MOEBIUS, no 26 (automne 1985), pp. 125–26.

Cliche, Elène. "Une célibataire souveraine." Compte rendu de *Lily Briscoe: un autoportrait. Spirale*, no 51 (avril 1985), p. 5.

Donald, C. M. Rev. of *The Medusa Head. Canadian Women's Studies/les cahiers de la femme* [Centennial College], [The Future/le futur], 6, No. 2 (Spring 1985), 105–06.

Pope, Dan. "Loving the Wrong Person." Rev. of *The Medusa Head. Matrix*, No. 21 (Fall 1985), pp. 71–72.

Sand, Cy-Thea. "Artist and Lesbian: A Coming Out." Rev. of *Lily Briscoe: A Self Portrait. The Radical Reviewer*, No. 5 (Winter 1981–82), pp. 1, 5.

Merrill, Helen

Articles and Sections of Books/ Articles et sections de livres

Garvin, John. "Canadian Poets: xix. Helen M. Merrill." *Public Health Journal*, Oct. 1915, pp. 519–23.

Metalious, Grace

Articles and Sections of Books/ Articles et sections de livres

Toth, Emily. "Fatherless and Dispossessed: Grace Metalious as a French-Canadian Writer." *Journal of Popular Culture*, 15, No. 3 (Winter 1981), 28–38.

Michel, Pauline

Reviews/Comptes rendus

Maranda, Jeanne. Compte rendu du *Mirage*. *Canadian Women's Studies/les cahiers de la femme* [Centennial College], [Women and Work/La Femme et le travail], 1, no 2 (Winter/hiver 1978–79), 106.

Monette, Madeleine

Reviews/Comptes rendus

Kurtzman, Lyne. Compte rendu du *Double suspect. Des luttes et des rires de femmes*, 4, no 1 (oct.–nov. 1980), 52–53.
Ouellette-Michalska, Madeleine. Compte rendu de *Petites violences*. *Châtelaine*, mars 1983, p. 16.

Montgomery, L. M.

Articles and Sections of Books/ Articles et sections de livres

Burns, Jane. "Anne and Emily: L. M. Montgomery's Children." *Room of One's Own*, 3, No. 3 (1977), 37–38, 43–48.
MacLulich, T. D. "L. M. Montgomery's Portraits of the Artist: Realism, Idealism and the Domestic Imagination." *English Studies in Canada*, 11 (Dec. 1985), 459–73.
Miller, Judith. "Montgomery's Emily: Voices and Silences." *Studies in Canadian Literature*, 9, No. 2 (1984), 158–68.
Rubio, Mary Henley. "L. M. Montgomery: Where Does the Voice Come From?". Nordic Association for Canadian Studies/Association Nordic d'études canadiennes, Univ. of Aarhus, Denmark. 1984. Printed in *Canadiana: Studies in Canadian Literature/Etudes de la Littérature Canadienne*. Ed. Jørn Carlsen and Knud Larsen. Aarhus, Den.: Dept. of English, Univ. of Aarhus, 1985, pp. 109–19.
———— . See also/voir aussi Rubio, Mary,

and Elizabeth Waterson.
Rubio, Mary, and Elizabeth Waterston. Introduction. In *The Selected Journals of L. M. Montgomery: Vol. I, 1889–1910*. Ed. Mary Rubio and Elizabeth Waterston. Toronto: Oxford Univ. Press, 1985, pp. xiii–xxiv.
Waterston, Elizabeth. "Lucy Maud Montgomery, 1874–1942." In *The Clear Spirit: Twenty Canadian Women and Their Times*. Ed. Mary Quayle Innis. Toronto: Canadian Federation of University Women/Univ. of Toronto Press, 1966, pp. 198–220.
———— . See also/voir aussi Rubio, Mary, and Elizabeth Waterston.
Weber, E. "L. M. Montgomery as Letter-Writer." *The Dalhousie Review*, 22 (1942), 300–10.
Whitaker, Muriel A. "Queer Children." *Canadian Children's Literature*, 1, No. 3 (Autumn 1975), 50–59.

Theses and Dissertations/Thèses

Goddard-Scanlon, Leslie S. "Alternatives: The Search for a Heroine in the Novels of Lucy Maude Montgomery." M.A. Thesis Carleton 1978.

Reviews/Comptes rendus

Cameron, Elspeth. Rev. of *The Selected Journals of L. M. Montgomery*, ed. Mary Rubio and Elizabeth Waterston. *Saturday Night*, Nov. 1985, pp. 73–75.
Cowan, Anne. Rev. of *The Selected Journals of L. M. Montgomery*, ed. Mary Rubio and Elizabeth Waterston. *The Reader* [Vancouver], 5, No. 2 (June 1986), 15–16.

Moodie, Susanna (See also/voir aussi Stricklands)

Books/Livres

Hopkins, Beth, and Anne Joyce. *Daughter by Adoption: A Play Based on the Writings of Susanna Moodie (1803–1885)*

pièce basée sur les écrits de Susanna Moodie (1803–1885). ACQL/ALCQ, Univ. of Guelph, Guelph, Ont. 6 June 1984. Printed. Toronto: Playwrights Canada, 1981. 25 pp.

Shields, Carol. *Susanna Moodie: Voice and Vision*. Ottawa: Borealis, 1977. 81 pp.

Articles and Sections of Books/ Articles et sections du livres

Ballstadt, Carl, Elizabeth Hopkins, and Michael Peterman. "Afterword: 1884–1885." In *Susanna Moodie: Letters of a Lifetime*. Ed. Carl Ballstadt, Elizabeth Hopkins, and Michael Peterman. Toronto: Univ. of Toronto Press, 1985, pp. 353–57.

––––– . "The Frowns of an Untoward Fortune: 1863–1869." In *Susanna Moodie: Letters of a Lifetime*. Ed. Carl Ballstadt, Elizabeth Hopkins, and Michael Peterman. Toronto: Univ. of Toronto Press, 1985, pp. 195–205.

––––– . "Muse on Canadian Shores: 1833–1851." In *Susanna Moodie: Letters of a Lifetime*. Ed. Carl Ballstadt, Elizabeth Hopkins, and Michael Peterman. Toronto: Univ. of Toronto Press, 1985, pp. 69–90.

––––– . "My pen as a resource: 1852–1862." In *Susanna Moodie: Letters of a Lifetime*. Ed. Carl Ballstadt, Elizabeth Hopkins, and Michael Peterman. Toronto: Univ. of Toronto Press, 1985, pp. 103–23.

––––– . "The soul is always young: 1869–1882." In *Susanna Moodie: Letters of a Lifetime*. Ed. Carl Ballstadt, Elizabeth Hopkins, and Michael Peterman. Toronto: Univ. of Toronto Press, 1985, pp. 255–65.

––––– . "The Wild Suffolk Girl: 1826–1832." In *Susanna Moodie: Letters of a Lifetime*. Ed. Carl Ballstadt, Elizabeth Hopkins, and Michael Peterman. Toronto: Univ. of Toronto Press, 1985, pp. 1–17.

Hopkins, Elizabeth. See/voir Ballstadt, Carl, Elizabeth Hopkins, and Michael Peterman.

Peterman, Michael A. "Susanna Moodie (1803–1885)." In *Canadian Writers and Their Works*. Ed. Robert Lecker, Jack David, and Ellen Quigley. Introd. George Woodcock. Fiction Series. Vol. I. Downsview, Ont.: ECW, 1983, 63–104.

––––– . See/voir Ballstadt, Carl, Elizabeth Hopkins, and Michael Peterman.

Mouré, Erin

Interviews/Entretiens

Billings, Robert. "Changes the Surface: A Conversation with Erin Mouré." *Waves*, 14, No. 4 (Spring 1986), 36–44.

Regan, Stephen. "Poet Erin Mouré Tracks Her Progress from Brown Paper Bags to the Wide Open Prairie." *Books in Canada*, April 1981, pp. 30–31.

Reviews/Comptes rendus

Tregebov, Rhea. Rev. of *Wanted Alive*. *Fireweed: A Feminist Quarterly*, [Writing], No. 17 (Summer–Fall 1983), pp. 109–13.

Munro, Alice

Articles and Sections of Books/ Articles et sections de livres

Allentuck, Marcia. "Resolution and Independence in the Work of Alice Munro." *World Literature Written in English* [Univ. of Texas at Arlington], 16 (Nov. 1977), 340–43.

Birbalsingh, Frank. "Women in Alice Munro's Lives of Girls and Women." Nordic Association for Canadian Studies/ Association Nordic d'études canadiennes, Univ. of Aarhus, Denmark. 1984. Printed in *Canadiana: Studies in Canadian Literature/Etudes de la Littérature Canadienne*. Ed. Jørn Carlsen and Knud Larsen. Aarhus, Den.: Dept. of English, Univ. of Aarhus, 1985, pp. 131–38.

Cook, D.E. "Alice Munro: A Checklist (to

December 31 1974)." *Journal of Canadian Fiction*, No. 16 (1976), pp. 131–36.

Daziron, Héliane. "Alice Munro's 'The Flats Road.'" *Canadian Women's Studies/les cahiers de la femme* [Centennial College], [International], 6, No. 1 (Fall 1984), 103–04.

DeSalvo, Louise. "Literature and Sexuality: Teaching the Truth about the Body." *Media & Methods*, Sept. 1979, pp. 32–33, 64–67.

Fleenor, Julianne E. "Rape Fantasies as Initiation Rite: Female Imagination in *Lives of Girls and Women*." *Room of One's Own*, 4, No. 4 (1979), 35–49.

Frye, Joanne S. "Growing Up Female: *Lives of Girls and Women* and *The Bluest Eyes*." In her *Living Stories, Telling Lies: Women and the Novel in Contemporary Experience*. Ann Arbor: Univ. of Michigan Press, 1986, pp. 77–108; esp. pp. 83–97.

Godard, Barbara. "'Heirs of the Living Body': Alice Munro and the Question of a Female Aesthetic." Alice Munro Conference, Univ. of Waterloo, Waterloo, Ont. 20 March 1982. Printed in *The Art of Alice Munro: Saying the Unsayable*. Ed. Judith Miller. Waterloo: Univ. of Waterloo Press, 1984, pp. 43–71.

Gold, Joseph. "Our Feeling Exactly: The Writing of Alice Munro." Alice Munro Conference, Univ. of Waterloo, Waterloo, Ont. 20 March 1982. Printed in *The Art of Alice Munro: Saying the Unsayable*. Ed. Judith Miller. Waterloo: Univ. of Waterloo Press, 1984, pp. 1–13.

Perrakis, Phyllis Sternberg. "Portrait of The Artist as a Young Girl: Alice Munro's *Lives of Girls and Women*." *Atlantis: A Women's Studies Journal/Journal d'études sur la femme* [Mt. St. Vincent Univ.], 7, No. 2 (Spring/printemps 1982), 61–67.

Rasporich, Beverly J. "Child-Women and Primitives in the Fiction of Alice Munro." *Atlantis: A Women's Studies Journal/Revue des Études sur la Femme* [Acadia Univ.], 1, No. 2 (Spring/printemps 1976), 4–14.

Wallace, Bronwen. "Women's Lives: Alice Munro." In *The Human Elements: Critical Essays*. 1st ser. Ed. David Helwig. Ottawa: Oberon, 1978, pp. 52–67. Rpt. (excerpt — "Men, Women, and Body English in Alice Munro") in *Books in Canada*, Aug.–Sept. 1978, p. 13.

Wayne, Joyce. "Huron County Blues." *Books in Canada*, Oct. 1982, pp. 9–12.

"'Writing's something I did, like the ironing.'" *The Globe and Mail* [Toronto], 11 Dec. 1982, p. E1.

Theses and Dissertations/Thèses

Rankin, Linda Marie. "Sexual Roles in the Fiction of Alice Munro." M.A. Thesis New Brunswick 1978.

Tanaszi, Margaret Jane. "Emancipation of Consciousness in Alice Munro's *Lives of Girls and Women*." M.A. Thesis Queen's 1972.

Wilson, Patricia A. "Women of Jubilee: A Commentary on Female Roles in the Work of Alice Munro." M.A. Thesis Guelph 1975.

Interviews/Entretiens

Gerson, Carole. "Who Do You Think You Are?: Review/Interview with Alice Munro." *Room of One's Own*, 4, No. 4 (1979), 2–7.

Gibson, Graeme. "Alice Munro." In his *Eleven Canadian Novelists*. Toronto: House of Anansi, 1973, pp. 237–64. Rpt. (excerpts — "The Authors on Their Writing") in *Personal Fictions: Stories by Munro, Wiebe, Thomas & Blaise*. Ed. Michael Ondaatje. Toronto: Oxford Univ. Press, 1977, p. 224.

Metcalf, John. "A Conversation with Alice Munro." *Journal of Canadian Fiction*, 1, No. 4 (Fall 1972), 54–62.

Murch, Kem. "Taped Interview with Alice Munro." *The London Ontario Women's Centre Review*, Feb. 1975, pp. [8–19]. Rpt. (revised — "Name: Alice Munro; Occupation: Writer") in *Chatelaine*, Aug. 1975, pp. 42–43, 69–72.

Sand, Cy-Thea. "Alice Munro Talks about Her Work, Her Life." *Kinesis*, Dec.–Jan. [1982–83], pp. 20–21.

Twigg, Alan. "Alice Munro: What Is." In his *For Openers: Conversations with 24 Canadian Writers*. Madeira Park, B.C.: Harbour, 1981, pp. 13–20.

Reviews/Comptes rendus

Collins, Anne. "The Fantasy of Perfect Mastery." Rev. of *The Moons of Jupiter*. *Maclean's*, 18 Oct. 1982, pp. 74–75.

Edwards, Caterina. "Language and Self." Rev. of *Who Do You Think You Are?*. *Branching Out: Canadian Magazine for Women*, [Special Fiction Issue], 6, No. 3 (1979), 43.

Gerson, Carole. "Who Do You Think You Are?: Review/Interview with Alice Munro." Rev. of *Who Do You Think You Are?*. *Room of One's Own*, 4, No. 4 (1979), 2–7.

Grady, Wayne. "A House of Her Own." Rev. of *The Moons of Jupiter*. *Books in Canada*, Oct. 1982, pp. 12, 14.

Sand, Cy-Thea. "Munro's Latest Preoccupied with Romantic Love." Rev. of *The Moons of Jupiter*. *Kinesis*, Nov. 1982, pp. 21, 29.

Solecki, Sam. "Lives of Girls and Women." Rev. of *The Moons of Jupiter*. *The Canadian Forum*, Oct. 1982, pp. 24–25.

Thomas, Clara. "Woman Invincible." Rev. of *Lives of Girls and Women*. *Journal of Canadian Fiction*, 1, No. 4 (Fall 1972), 95–96.

Timson, Judith. Rev. of *The Moons of Jupiter*. *Chatelaine*, Nov. 1982, p. 10.

Tudor, Kathleen. Rev. of *Something I've Been Meaning to Tell You*. *Atlantis: A Women's Studies Journal/Journal d'études sur la femme* [Acadia Univ.], 1, No. 1 (Fall/automne 1975), 129–30.

Murphy, Emily

Books/Livres

Mander, Christine. *Emily Murphy: Rebel.* Toronto: Simon & Pierre, 1985. 150 pp.

Murray, Louisa

Articles and Sections of Books/ Articles et sections de livres

Wetherald, A. Ethelwyn. "Some Canadian Literary Women — III. Louisa Murray." *The Week: A Canadian Journal of Politics, Society and Literature* [Toronto], 19 April 1888, pp. 335–36.

Murray, Suzie

Reviews/Comptes rendus

Labartino, Nancy. "Dramatisation au féminin: réécrire le monde avec son ventre." Compte rendu de *La mère morte*. *Spirale*, no 24 (avril 1982), p. 8.

Musgrave, Susan

Articles and Sections of Books/ Articles et sections de livres

Moers, Vernon. "Susan Musgrave: Poet behind the Prodigy." *Cross-Canada Writers' Quarterly*, 8, No. 2 (1986), 6–7.

Musgrave, Susan. "Beginnings: We Slept in the Same Bed, but I Guess I Was Saving Myself for the Right Man." *Today Magazine* [*The Toronto Star*], 13 March 1982, pp. 7–9.

Interviews/Entretiens

Jewinski, Ed. "An Interview with Susan Musgrave." *The New Quarterly*, 5, No. 2 (Summer 1985), 9–23.

———. "WQ Interview with Susan Musgrave." *Cross-Canada Writers' Quarterly*, 8, No. 2 (1986), 3–5.

Stott, Dorothy. "An Interview with Susan Musgrave." *Canadian Fiction Magazine*, Nos. 30–31 (1979), pp. 33–39.

Reviews/Comptes rendus

MacMillan, Carrie. Rev. of *Becky Swan's Book* and *Selected Strawberries and Other Poems*. *The Fiddlehead*, No. 119 (Fall 1978), pp. 131–34.

Stainsbury, Mary E. "Epochal Conflicts." Rev. of *A Man to Marry, A Man to Bury*. *Branching Out: Canadian Magazine for Women*, [Special Fiction Issue], 6, No. 3 (1979), 45–46.

Namjoshi, Suniti

Reviews/Comptes rendus

Goldsmith, Penny. "Uprooting Childhood's Legends." Rev. of *From the Bedside Book of Nightmares*. *Kinesis*, Oct. 1984, p. 24.

Lane, M. Travis. "'I and My Creature': Three Versions of the Human." Rev. of *The Animals Within*, by David Day; *Piling Blood*, by Al Purdy; and *From the Bedside Book of Nightmares*, by Suniti Namjoshi. *The Fiddlehead*, No. 146 (Winter 1985), pp. 106–13.

Meigs, Mary. Rev. of *Feminist Fables*, *The Authentic Lie*, and *The Jackass and the Lady*. *Room of One's Own*, 9, No. 1 (Feb. 1984), 65–68.

Nelson, Sharon H.

Reviews/Comptes rendus

Kenyon, Linda. Rev. of *Mad Women & Crazy Ladies*. *Hysteria* [Kitchener, Ont.], 2, No. 4 (Winter 1983–84), 26–27.

Nightwood Theatre

Articles and Sections of Books/ Articles et sections de livres

Mingail, Lillian. "Women's Theatre Shines." *The Toronto Journal*, 3, No. 2 (April 1986), 8.

Noël, Francine

Interviews/Entretiens

de Gramont, Monique. "Francine Noël: *Maryse*, *Sarah*, et les autres." *Châtelaine*, déc. 1985, pp. 28–31.

Trépanier, Marie-Claude. "Francine Noël: une vieille passion." *La vie en rose*, déc.–jan. 1985–86, pp. 48–49.

Reviews/Comptes rendus

Saint-Martin, Lori. Compte rendu de *Maryse*. *Resources for Feminist Research/Documentation sur la recherche féministe*, [Women and Language/Les Femmes et le langage], 13, no 3 (Nov./nov. 1984), 57–58.

Olier, Moïsette

Books/Livres

Lafrenière Suzanne. *Moïsette Olier: femme de lettres de la Mauricie*. Hull: Asticou, 1980. 224 pp.

Ostenso, Martha

Articles and Sections of Books/ Articles et sections de livres

Hesse, M.G. "The Endless Quest: Dreams and Aspirations in Martha Ostenso's *Wild Geese*." *Journal of Popular Culture*, 15, No. 3 (Winter 1981), 47–52.

Thomas, Clara. "Martha Ostenso's Trial of Strength." In *Writers of the Prairies*. Ed. Donald G. Stephens. Vancouver: Univ. of British Columbia Press, 1973, pp. 39–50.

Ouellette-Michalska, Madeleine

Articles and Sections of Books/ Articles et sections de livres

Blanchard, Louise. "Il n'y a pas d'écriture

féministe: Madeleine Ouellette-Michalska." *Le journal de Montréal,* 8 août 1981, p. 39.

Homel, David. "Quebec G. G. Winner: Utopian Feminist among the Phallocrats." *Quill & Quire,* Aug. 1982, p. 29.

Interviews/Entretiens

Haeck, Philippe. "Autour de l'origine: Entrevue avec Madeleine Ouellette-Michalska sur *L'Echappée des discours de l'oeil.*" *Lettres québécoises: Revue de l'actualité littéraire,* no 23 (automne 1981), pp. 73–76.

Royer, Jean. "Madeleine Ouellette-Michalska: Faire circuler le féminin." *Le Devoir* [Montréal], 27 juin 1981, pp. 17–18. Repris dans *Ecrivains contemporains: Entretiens 3: 1980–1983.* Par Jean Royer. Montréal: L'Hexagone, 1985, pp. 211–22.

Reviews/Comptes rendus

Alonzo, Anne-Marie. Compte rendu de *La Femme de sable* et *Le Plat de lentilles. La Gazette des femmes,* 2, no 5 (oct. 1980), 4.

Andersen, Margret. Compte rendu de *L'Echappée des discours de l'oeil. Resources for Feminist Research/Documentation sur la recherche féministe,* [Reviews Issue/Comptes rendus], 10, no 3 (Nov./nov. 1981), 27–28.

Ferretti, Andrée. Compte rendu de *L'Echappée des discours de l'oeil. Le Devoir* [Montréal], 27 juin 1981, p. 18.

Haineault, Doris-Louise. Compte rendu de *L'Echappée des discours de l'oeil. Canadian Women's Studies/les cahiers de la femme* [Centennial College], 4, no 1 (Fall 1982), 89.

Roy, Monique. "Madeleine Ouellette-Michalska: Retourner aux sources pour mieux comprendre la condition féminine." Compte rendu de *L'Échappée des discours de l'oeil. Le Livre d'ici* [Montréal], 19 août 1981, p. 2.

Ouvrard, Hélène

Reviews/Comptes rendus

Cloutier, Cécile. Compte rendu du *Coeur sauvage. Livres et auteurs canadiens 1967.* Ed. Adrien Thério. Montréal: Jumonville, 1968, pp. 60–61.

Saint-Onge, Paule. "Châtelaine a lu pour vous." Compte rendu du *Coeur sauvage. Châtelaine,* juil. 1967, p. 13.

———. "Châtelaine a lu pour vous." Compte rendu de *La fleur de peau. Châtelaine,* août 1965, p. 46.

Page, P. K.

Articles and Sections of Books/ Articles et sections de livres

Orange, John. "P. K. Page: An Annotated Bibliography." In *The Annotated Bibliography of Canada's Major Authors.* Ed. Robert Lecker and Jack David. Vol. VI. Toronto: ECW, 1985, 207–85.

Interviews/Entretiens

Keeler, Judy. "An Interview with P. K. Page." *The Canadian Forum,* Sept. 1975, pp. 33–35.

Reviews/Comptes rendus

Lawrence, Karen. Rev. of *The Sun and the Moon and Other Fictions* and *P. K. Page: Poems Selected and New. Branching Out: Canadian Magazine for Women,* 2, No. 6 (Nov.–Dec. 1975), 41.

Valiquette, Michèle. "Celebration of Imagination." Rev. of *Evening Dance of the Grey Flies. The Radical Reviewer,* No. 6 (Spring 1982), pp. 16–17.

Paquin, Alice

Interviews/Entretiens

Smith, Donald. "Alice Paquin: L'Histoire

servie par une écriture palpitante."
Lettres québécoises, 41 (printemps 1986),
44–48.

Paradis, Suzanne

Articles and Sections of Books/
Articles et sections de livres

T[heberge]., J[ean].-Y[ves]. "La femme dans
le roman." *Le Canada français* [St. Jean,
P.Q.], 8 déc. 1966, p. 34.
Verduyn, Christl. "*Miss Charlie* by Suzanne
Paradis: Subversion in Women's Writing."
Tessera, No. 1 [*Room of One's Own*, 8,
No. 4] (1983), 109–15.

Parizeau, Alice

Interviews/Entretiens

Smith, Donald. "Alice Parizeau: L'Histoire
servie par une écriture palpitante."
*Lettres québécoises: Revue de l'actualité
littéraire*, no 41 (printemps 1986), pp.
44–48.

Pelletier, Pol

Articles and Sections of Books/
Articles et sections de livres

Pelletier, Pol. "Histoire d'une féministe."
Trac Femmes, déc. 1978, pp. 92–113.

Interviews/Entretiens

Gormley, Joanne. "Talking to Pol Pelletier."
Fireweed: A Feminist Quarterly, [Women
and Performance], No. 7 (Summer 1980),
pp. 88–96.
Rubess, Banuta. "Interview with Pol
Pelletier, March 1985." *Canadian Theatre
Review*, [Feminism: Canadian Theatre],
No. 43 (Summer 1985), pp. 179–84.

Pickthall, Marjorie

Books/Livres

Pierce, Lorne. *Marjorie Pickthall: A Book of
Remembrance*. Toronto: Ryerson, 1925.
217 pp.; esp. pp. 201–17 (bibliography).

Articles and Sections of Books/
Articles et sections de livres

Lugrin, N. de Bertrand. "Marjorie Pickthall
as a Companion." *The Canadian Magazine* [Toronto], April 1925, pp. 72–73.

Pollock, Sharon

Interviews/Entretiens

Zimmerman, Cynthia, and Robert Wallace.
"Sharon Pollock." In their *The Work:
Conversations with English-Canadian
Playwrights*. Toronto: Coach House,
1982, pp. 114–26.

Reviews/Comptes rendus

Hale, Amanda. "Family Document." Rev. of
Doc. Broadside: A Feminist Review [Tor-
onto], Nov. 1984, p. 11.
Neil, Boyd. "Canadian Plays Lacking Ideas
and Critics." Rev. of *Blood Relations*.
Quill & Quire, April 1982, p. 29.

Primeau, Marguerite

Reviews/Comptes rendus

Mailhot, Michèle A. "Châtelaine a lu pour
vous: Trois femmes évoquent un destin."
Compte rendu de *Dans le muskeg*, par
Marguerite Primeau; *With: la force de
l'âge*, par S. de Beauvoir; et *Dix heures et
demi du soir en été*, par M. Duras. *Châtelaine*, juin 1961, p. 25.

Proulx, Monique

Reviews/Comptes rendus

Gultman, Naomi. Rev. of *Sans coeur et sans reproche*. *Resources for Feminist Research/Documentation sur la recherche féministe*, [Review Issue/Comptes rendus], 14, No. 2 (July/juil. 1985), 25.

Riis, Sharon

Articles and Sections of Books/ Articles et sections de livres

Berger, Sara. "Experiencing Friendships & Loyalties." *HERizons: The Manitoba Women's News Magazine*, Jan.–Feb. 1986, pp. 32–35; esp. pp. 32–33.
"Nightwood Theatre Tells the True Story of *The True Story of Ida Johnson*." *Fireweed: A Feminist Quarterly*, [Women and Performance], No. 7 (Summer 1980), pp. 30–37.

Reviews/Comptes rendus

Lawrence, Karen. "A Day in the Life of a Real Person." Rev. of *The True Story of Ida Johnson*. *Branching Out: Canadian Magazine for Women*, 4, No. 2 (May–June 1977), 40–41.
Smyth, Donna E. Rev. of *The True Story of Ida Johnson*. *World Literature Written in English* [Univ. of Texas at Arlington], [Women Writers of the Commonwealth], 17 (April 1978), 203–04.

Ringwood, Gwen Pharis

Articles and Sections of Books/ Articles et sections de livres

Anthony, Geraldine. "The Ringwood Plays of Social Protest." *Canadian Drama/ L'Art dramatique canadien* [Univ. of Waterloo], 5 (Fall/automne 1979), 112–28.

Interviews/Entretiens

Anthony, Geraldine. *Stage Voices: Twelve Canadian Playwrights Talk about Their Lives and Work*. Toronto: Doubleday, 1978, pp. 85–110.

Ritter, Erika

Articles and Sections of Books/ Articles et sections de livres

Lister, Rota Herzberg. "Erika Ritter and the Comedy of Self-Actualization." Dialogue, York Univ., Downsview, Ont. 17 OCT./ OCT. 1981. Printed in *Gynocritics/Gynocritiques: Feminist Approaches to Canadian and Quebec Women's Writing/ Démarches féministes à l'écriture des Canadiennes et Québécoises*. Ed. Barbara Godard. Toronto: ECW, 1987, pp. 143–55.

Interviews/Entretiens

Brissenden, Constance. "Erika Ritter: 'The very fact that I survive is encouraging.'" *Fireweed: A Feminist Quarterly*, [Women and Performance], No. 7 (Summer 1980), pp. 68–70.
Brown, Barry. Interview with Erika Ritter. *Books in Canada*, April 1982, pp. 26–28.
Wallace, Robert. See/voir Zimmerman, Cynthia, and Robert Wallace.
Zimmerman, Cynthia, and Robert Wallace. "Erika Ritter." In their *The Work: Conversations with English-Canadian Playwrights*. Toronto: Coach House, 1982, pp. 277–91.

Robertson, Heather

Reviews/Comptes rendus

Emberley, Heather. "Willie/Lily." Rev. of *Willie*. *HERizons: The Manitoba Women's News Magazine*, Feb. 1984, p. 40.

Rochon, Esther

Interviews/Entretiens

Lord, Michel. "Esther Rochon: Interview." *Lettres québécoises*, no 40 (hiver 1985–86), pp. 36–39.

Rosenthal, Helene

Articles and Sections of Books/ Articles et sections de livres

Rosenthal, Helene. "Being a Woman and a Poet in Canada." CRIAW Conference, Halifax, N.S. Nov. 1981.

Rostein, Nancy Gay

Reviews/Comptes rendus

Reid, Verna. "Poetic Travelogue." Rev. of *Taking Off. Branching Out: Canadian Magazine for Women*, 6, No. 4 (1979), 36–37.

Rothwell, Annie

Articles and Sections of Books/ Articles et sections de livres

Wetherald, A. Ethelwyn. "Some Canadian Literary Women — IV. Annie Rothwell." *The Week: A Canadian Journal of Politics, Society and Literature* [Toronto], 28 June 1888, pp. 494–95.

Routier, Simone

Articles and Sections of Books/ Articles et sections de livres

Diesendorf, Margaret. "Terre de Quebec, Mère Courage." *Poetry Australia* [Sydney], 3 [No. 16] (June 1967), 56–59.

Roy, Gabrielle

Books/Livres

Hesse, M. G. *Gabrielle Roy.* Twayne's Canadian Authors Series. Boston: Twayne, 1984. 113 pp. Repris trad. Michelle Tisseyre. *Gabrielle Roy par elle-même.* Préface Alain Stanké. Montréal: Stanké, 1985. 179 pp.

Lewis, Paula Gilbert. *The Literary Vision of Gabrielle Roy: An Analysis of Her Works.* Birmingham, Alabama: Summa, 1984. 319 pp.

Articles and Sections of Books/ Articles et sections de livres

Cobb, David. "'I Have, I think, a grateful heart.'" *The Canadian* [*The Toronto Star*], 1 May 1976, pp. 10–14.

Grosskurth, Phyllis. "Gabrielle Roy and the Silken Noose." *Canadian Literature*, [The Living Mosaic], No. 42 (Autumn 1969), pp. 6–13.

Hesse, M. G. "Mothers and Daughters in Gabrielle Roy's *The Tin Flute, Street of Riches*, and *The Road Past Altamont*." Twentieth Century Women Writers' Conference, Hofstra Univ., Hempstead, N.Y. Nov. 1982.

Lewis, Paula Gilbert. "Female Spirals and Male Cages: The Urban Sphere in the Novels of Gabrielle Roy." In *Traditionalism, Nationalism and Feminism: Women Writers of Quebec.* Ed. Paula Gilbert Lewis. Contributions in Women's Studies, No. 53. Westport, Conn.: Greenwood, 1985, pp. 71–81.

——— . "Feminism and Traditionalism in the Early Short Stories of Gabrielle Roy." In *Traditionalism, Nationalism and Feminism: Women Writers of Quebec.* Ed. Paula Gilbert Lewis. Contributions in Women's Studies, No. 53. Westport, Conn.: Greenwood, 1985, pp. 27–35.

——— . "*Street of Riches* and *The Road Past Altamont*: The Feminine World of Gabrielle Roy." *Journal of Women's Studies in Literature*, 1 (Spring 1979), 133–41.

───── . "Trois générations des femmes: le reflet mère-fille dans quelques nouvelles de Gabrielle Roy." *voix et images: littérature québécois*, 10, no 3 (printemps 1985), 165–76.

Pascal, Gabrielle. "La condition féminine dans l'oeuvre de Gabrielle Roy." *voix & images: littérature québécoise*, 5 (automne 1979), 143–63.

───── . "La femme dans l'oeuvre de Gabrielle Roy." *Revue de l'Université d'Ottawa/University of Ottawa Quarterly*, [Conférence des femmes-écrivains en Amérique], 50 (jan.–mars/Jan.–March 1980), 55–61.

Piccione, Marie Lyne. "La femme canadienne-française chez Gabrielle Roy et Michel Tremblay ou la remis en question des valeurs traditionelles familiales." *Études Canadiennes/Canadian Studies* [Univ. de Bordeaux III], no 2 (juin 1976), pp. 39–56.

Socken, Paul. "Gabrielle Roy: An Annotated Bibliography." In *The Annotated Bibliography of Canada's Major Authors*. Ed. Robert Lecker and Jack David. Vol. I. Downsview, Ont.: ECW, 1979, 213–63.

Ste-Marie, Paule. "De dire Gérard Bessette: les personnages de Gabrielle Roy présents à leurs corps et au monde." *Le Droit* [Ottawa], 2 mars 1966, p. 4.

Theses and Dissertations/Thèses

Bosco, Monique. "*Bonheur d'occasion* ou les échecs de la femme." Thèse de doctorat Montréal 1953.

Bride, J. Harvey. "Bio-bibliographie de Gabrielle Roy." M. Phil. Thesis Toronto 1970.

Bureau, J. J. "Le complexe de la maternité chez Luzina dans *La Petite Poule d'eau* de Gabrielle Roy." Thèse de maîtrise Montréal 1962.

Maillet, Antonine. "La femme et l'enfant dans l'oeuvre de Gabrielle Roy." Thèse de maîtrise Saint-Joseph 1959.

Interviews/Entretiens

Parizeau, Alice. "Gabrielle Roy, la grande romancière canadienne." *Châtelaine*, avril 1966, pp. 44, 118, 120–23, 137, 140.

Reviews/Comptes rendus

Grosskurth, Phyllis. "Maternity's Fond but Tedious Tune." Rev. of *Windflower*. *The Globe Magazine* [*The Globe and Mail*] [Toronto], 19 Sept. 1970, p. 20.

Neuman, Shirley. "Tender Vignettes." Rev. of *Children of My Heart*. *Branching Out: Canadian Magazine for Women*, 6, No. 4 (1979), 37–38.

Saint-Martin, Lori. "Donner naissance à sa mère." Compte rendu de De quoi t'ennuies-tu *suivi de* Ely! Ely! Ely!. *Spirale*, no 45 (sept. 1984), p. 6.

Swartz, Shirley. "The Writer as Psalmist." Rev. of *Enchanted Summer* and *Garden in the Wind*. *Branching Out: Canadian Magazine for Women*, 4, No. 4 (Sept.–Oct. 1977), 42–43.

Rule, Jane

Articles and Sections of Books/ Articles et sections de livres

Applin, Alexis, and Marlyn MacDonald. "Profile: Jane Rule on Writing." *HERizons: The Manitoba Women's News Magazine*, Oct. 1984, pp. 27–30.

Bradbury, Patricia. "Jane Rule: Passages Ruled by the Heart." *Quill & Quire*, Nov. 1985, p. 25.

Brady, Elizabeth. "'A Vision of Central Value': The Novels of Jane Rule." *Resources for Feminist Research/Documentation sur la recherche féministe*, [The Lesbian Issue/Être Lesbienne], 12, No. 1 (March/mars 1983), 13–16.

Grescoe, Paul. "One Kind of Loving." *The Canadian* [Toronto], 4 Dec. 1976, pp. 18–21.

Hofsess, John. "Calamity Jane." *Books in Canada*, Oct. 1976, pp. 3–6.

———. "Who Is Jane Rule? And How Much Does Her Sexuality Have to Do with It?". *Content*, Jan. 1977, pp. 6–8.

MacDonald, Marlyn. See/voir Applin, Alexis, and Marlyn MacDonald.

Massiah, Elizabeth. "Jane Rule: Building Community." *The Newsmagazine for Alberta Women*, May–June 1986, pp. 45–46.

Rule, Jane. "Making the Real Visible: Lesbian and Writer." *Fireweed: A Feminist Quarterly*, [Lesbian Issue], No. 13 (July 1982), pp. 101–04. Rpt. in *New Lesbian Writing*. Ed. Margaret L. Cruikshank. San Francisco: Grey Fox, 1984, pp. 96–99.

Schuster, Marilyn R. "Strategies for Survival: The Subtle Subversion of Jane Rule." *Feminist Studies*, 7 (Fall 1981), 431–50.

Sonthoff, Helen. "Celebration: Jane Rule's Fiction." *Canadian Fiction Magazine*, No. 23 (Autumn 1976), pp. 121–32.

———. "Jane Rule: A Bibliography." *Canadian Fiction Magazine*, No. 23 (Autumn 1976), pp. 133–38.

Interviews/Entretiens

Hancock, Geoff. "An Interview with Jane Rule." *Canadian Fiction Magazine*, No. 23 (Autumn 1976), pp. 57–112.

Kennedy, Sarah. "A Time of Harvest: Interview with Jane Rule." *Branching Out: Canadian Feminist Quarterly*, 7, No. 2 (1980), 25–28.

Klein, Yvonne. "An Interview with Lesbian Novelist Jane Rule." *Gay News* [Philadelphia, Pa.], 17–25 Dec. 1982, pp. 14–15, 19. Rpt. in *The Front Page* [Raleigh, N.C.], 21 Feb.–12 March 1984, pp. 1, 7.

Powell, Marilyn. "Interview: Jane Rule." *Books in Canada*, Nov. 1985, pp. 38–41.

Twigg, Alan. "Jane Rule: What Can Be." In his *For Openers: Conversations with 24 Canadian Writers*. Madeira Park, B.C.: Harbour, 1981, pp. 21–29.

Reviews/Comptes rendus

Barclay, Pat. "The Lesbian Viewpoint." Rev. of *Lesbian Images* and *Theme for Diverse Instruments*. *Victoria Times*, 8 Nov. 1975, p. 23.

Bell, Ilene. Rev. of *The Young in One Another's Arms* and *Desert of the Heart*. *Room of One's Own*, 4, No. 3 (1979), 72–74.

Biggs, Mary. "Career without Compromise." Rev. of *Inland Passage* and *A Hot-Eyed Moderate*. *The Women's Review of Books* [Wellesley, Mass.], May 1986, pp. 13–15.

Dansereau, Estelle. Rev. of *Young in One Another's Arms*. *Canadian Fiction Magazine*, No. 27 (1977), pp. 139–40.

Giacomelli, Eloah F. "Housetraps." Rev. of *Theme for Diverse Instruments*. *Branching Out: Canadian Magazine for Women*, 2, No. 5 (Sept.–Oct. 1975), 38–40.

Gollan, Donna. "Lesbian Love Stories." Rev. of *Desert Hearts* [film adaptation of *Desert of the Heart*]. *Broadside: A Feminist Review* [Toronto], April 1986, p. 10.

Harvor, Beth. "Not All Talking Heads Deserve Equal Time." Rev. of *Contract with the World*. *Books in Canada*, Nov. 1980, pp. 10–11.

Josephs, Shirley. Rev. of *The Young in One Another's Arms*. *Emergency Librarian*, 4, No. 5 (May–June 1977), 16.

Lebowitz, Andrea. "Some Recent Feminist Criticism." Rev. of *Lesbian Images*. *West Coast Review* [Simon Fraser Univ.], 10, No. 3 (Feb. 1976), 61–63.

Martin, Sandra. "The Age-Old Dilemma." Rev. of *Theme for Diverse Instruments*. *Canadian Literature*, [The Psychology of Literature], No. 72 (Spring 1977), pp. 87–89.

Morgan, Robin. Rev. of *Outlander*. *Ms.* [New York], July 1981, p. 89.

Muzychka, Martha. Rev. of *Inland Passage*. *Breaking the Silence*, 4, Nos. 3–4 (Spring–Summer 1986), 25.

Nelson, Martha. Rev. of *This Is Not for You*. *Ms.* [New York], June 1982, p. 18.

Rapoport, Janis. "Unity Through Diversity." Rev. of *Theme for Diverse Instruments*. *The Tamarack Review*, No. 68 (Spring 1976), pp. 92–95.

Ross, Catherine. "Angry Mourner." Rev. of *Contract with the World*. *Canadian Literature*, [Faces of Realism/Facing Realities], No. 89 (Summer 1981), pp. 121–23.

Scott, Jay. "Shaver Carries *Desert Hearts*." Rev. of *Desert Hearts* [film adaptation of *Desert of the Heart*]. *The Globe and Mail* [Toronto], 11 April 1986, p. D1.

Smith, Rebecca L. Rev. of *Lesbian Images* and *Theme for Diverse Instruments*. *World Literature Written in English* [Univ. of Texas at Arlington], [Women Writers of the Commonwealth], 17 (April 1978), 205–07.

Spires, Randi. "Toronto's Festival of Festivals." Rev. of *Desert Hearts* [film adaptation of *Desert of the Heart*] and *Desert of the Heart*. *Hysteria* [Kitchener, Ont.], 4, No. 2 (Autumn 1985), 14–17; esp. pp. 14–15.

"Tortured Lesbians." Rev. of *This Is Not for You*. *Chatelaine*, Nov. 1970, p. 10.

Valverde, Mariana. "Opinion, Not Dogma." Rev. of *Outlander*. *Broadside: A Feminist Review* [Toronto], July 1981, p. 16.

Wiseman, Adele. "Sisters Under the Skin." Rev. of *Lesbian Images* and *Theme for Diverse Instruments*. *Books in Canada*, Sept. 1975, pp. 3–6.

Saillant, Francine

Reviews/Comptes rendus

Dupré, Louise. "Un texte nomade." Compte rendu de *Ruptures*. *Spirale*, no 24 (avril 1982), p. 9.

Saint-Onge, Paule

Reviews/Comptes rendus

Mailhot, Michèle. "Châtelaine a lu pour vous: du rose masculin au noir féminin." Compte rendu de *La Maîtresse*. *Châtelaine*, mars 1964, p. 72.

Sainte-Marie-Eleuthère, Soeur [Marie-Thérèse Laforest]

Reviews/Comptes rendus

Falardeau, Jean-Charles. Compte rendu de *La Mère dans le roman canadien-français*. *Recherches sociographiques* [Univ. Laval], 5 (sept.–déc. 1964), 385–88.

Salverson, Laura Goodman

Reviews/Comptes rendus

Dahlie, Hallvard. Rev. of *Confessions of an Immigrant Daughter*. By Laura Goodman Salverson. Ed. K. P. Stich. *Canadian Ethnic Studies/études ethnique au Canada*, 15, No. 1 (1983), 134–36.

Saunders, Margaret Marshall

Theses and Dissertations/Thèses

Sanders, Karen E. "Margaret Marshall Sanders: Children's Literature as an Expression of Early Twentieth Century Social Reform." M.A. Thesis Dalhousie 1978.

Savard, Marie

Reviews/Comptes rendus

Alonzo, Anne-Marie. Compte rendu du *Bien à moi*. *La Gazette des femmes*, 2, no 1 (avril 1980), 4.

Dumouchel, Thérèse. Compte rendu de *Bien à moi*. *Canadian Women's Studies/les cahiers de la femme* [Centennial College], 2, no 2 (1980), 99.

Frémont, Gabrielle. Compte rendu de *Bien à moi*. *Livres et auteurs québécois 1979*. Ed. André Berthiaume. [Québec]: Les Presses de l'Univ. Laval, 1980, pp. 201–02.

Villemaire, Yolande. "Etre une heroine." Compte rendu de *Bien à moi*. *Spirale*, no 5

(Jan. 1980), p. 10.

Schrader, Helen

Articles and Sections of Books/
Articles et sections de livres

Silversides, Brock V. "Helen Schrader — Saskatoon Poet & Photographer." *Canadian Women's Studies/les cahiers de la femme* [Centennial College], [Belles lettres], 5, No. 1 (Fall/automne 1983), 23–26.

Scott, Gail

Reviews/Comptes rendus

Cody, Susan. Rev. of *Spare Parts. Quill & Quire*, Sept. 1982, p. 59.
Rule, Jane. Rev. of *Spare Parts. The Globe and Mail* [Toronto], 15 May 1982, p. 15.
St. Peter, Christine. Rev. of *Spare Parts. Canadian Women's Studies/les cahiers de la femme* [Centennial College], [Belles lettres], 5, No. 1 (Fall/automne 1983), 38–39.

Seranus (See/voir Susan Frances Harrison)

Shields, Carol

Articles and Sections of Books/
Articles et sections de livres

French, William. "Housewife, Mother of Five Confounds Theory on Writers." *The Globe and Mail* [Toronto], 21 June 1977, p. 17.
Shields, Carol. "'My Craft and Sullen Art': The Writers Speak. Carol Shields." *Atlantis: A Women's Studies Journal/Journal d'études sur la femme* [Acadia Univ.], 4, No. 1 (Fall/automne 1978), 150–52.
Smyth, Donna E. "Middle Ground: The

Novels of Carol Shields." In *Present Tense: A Critical Anthology.* Vol. IV of *The Canadian Novel.* Ed. John Moss. Toronto: NC, 1985, pp. 102–09.

Interviews/Entretiens

Cowan, Doris. "The Fairly Conventional World of Carol Shields: 'What is yielded from everyday life is extraordinary enough.'" *Books in Canada*, Jan. 1983, pp. 26–27.
Vauthier, Simon. "A Transatlantic Conversation with Carol Shields." *Études Canadiennes/Canadian Studies* [Univ. de Bordeaux III], No. 12 (juin 1982), pp. 65–74.

Reviews/Comptes rendus

Cody, Susan. Rev. of *A Fairly Conventional Woman. Quill & Quire*, Sept. 1982, p. 59.
Collins, Anne. "Can This Marriage Be Saved Again?". Rev. of *A Fairly Conventional Woman. Maclean's*, 18 Oct. 1982, p. 78.

Sibbald, Susan

Articles and Sections of Books/
Articles et sections de livres

Fowler, Marian E. "Portrait of Susan Sibbald: Writer and Pioneer." *Ontario History*, 66, No. 1 (March 1974), 51–64.

Silvera, Makeda

Reviews/Comptes rendus

Bannerji, Himani. Rev. of *Silenced: Talks with Working Class West Indian Women about Their Lives and Struggles as Domestic Workers in Canada. Canadian Women's Studies/les cahiers de la femme* [Centennial College], [post Nairobi], 7, Nos. 1–2 (Spring–Summer 1986), 220–21.

Smart, Elizabeth

Articles and Sections of Books/
Articles et sections de livres

Barr, Ann. "Mourned by the Rogues and Rascals." *London Observer.* Rpt. in *Brick* [Toronto], No. 27 (Spring 1986), pp. 61–62.

"Controversial Canadian Angered Mother with Book." *The Globe and Mail* [Toronto], 6 March 1986, p. A14.

French, William. "Sense of Mystery Surrounded Smart." *The Globe and Mail* [Toronto], 6 March 1986, p. D5.

Goddard, John. "An Appetite for Life." *Books in Canada,* June–July 1982, pp. 7–12.

——— . "A Life of Passion." *Books in Canada,* May 1986, p. 39.

Mallinson, Jean. "The Figures of Love: Rhetoric in *By Grand Central Station I Sat Down and Wept.*" *Essays on Canadian Writing,* No. 10 (Spring 1978), pp. 108–18.

McFadden, David. "Writer's Block: Scenes with Smart, Gibson's Gerunditis, and Young's Dream." *Quill & Quire,* March 1983, p. 45.

McMullen, Lorraine. "'Behold thou art fair, my love: behold thou art fair': The Language of Love in Elizabeth Smart's *By Grand Central Station I Sat Down and Wept.*" In *La femme, son corps et la religion: approches pluridisciplinaires.* Ed. Elisabeth J. Lacelle. Montréal: Bellarmin, 1983, pp. 184–93.

——— . "A Canadian Heloise: Elizabeth Smart and the Feminist Adultery Novel." *Atlantis: A Women's Studies Journal/ Journal d'études sur la femme* [Acadia Univ.], 4, No. 1 (Fall/automne 1978), 76–85.

——— . "Elizabeth Smart's Lyrical Novel: *By Grand Central Station I Sat Down and Wept.*" In *Modern Times: A Critical Anthology.* Vol. III of *The Canadian Novel.* Ed. John Moss. Toronto: NC, 1982, pp. 133–45.

Sand, Cy-Thea. "The Novels of Elizabeth Smart: Biological Imperialism and the Trap of Language." *Canadian Women's Studies/les cahiers de la femme* [Centennial College], [Belles lettres], 5, No. 1 (Fall/automne 1983), 11–14.

Wachtel, Eleanor. "Passion's Survivor." *City Woman,* Summer 1980, pp. 51–55.

Interviews/Entretiens

French, William. "Elizabeth Smart: A Hidden Author, a Hidden Novel." *The Globe and Mail* [Toronto], 20 Dec. 1975, p. 27.

Goddard, John. "An Appetite for Life." *Books in Canada,* June–July 1982, pp. 7–12.

Reviews/Comptes rendus

Sand, Cy-Thea. "The Trap of Language." Rev. of *By Grand Central Station I Sat Down and Wept. The Radical Reviewer,* No. 6 (Spring 1982), pp. 12–15.

Wachtel, Eleanor. "Stations of the Womb." Rev. of *Assumption of Rogues and Rascals. Books in Canada,* Oct. 1978, pp. 8–9.

Smyth, Donna E.

Reviews/Comptes rendus

Gerson, Carole. Rev. of *Quilt. Atlantis: A Women's Studies Journal/Journal d'études sur la femme* [Acadia Univ.], 9, No. 1 (Fall/automne 1983), 135–36.

Masters, Philinda. "Patchwork Lives." Rev. of *Quilt. Broadside: A Feminist Review* [Toronto], May 1983, p. 10.

Spies, Mary M. Rev. of *Quilt. Hysteria* [Kitchener, Ont.], 2, No. 3 (Spring 1983), 20.

Stanton, Julie

Articles and Sections of Books/
Articles et sections de livres

de Billy, Hélène. "Julie Stanton: 'Je n'ai plus

de cendre dans la bouche.'" *La Gazette des femmes,* 2, no 2 (juin 1980), 6–7.

Interviews/Entretiens

Bélanger, Claire. "Entrevue avec Julie Stanton." *Entrelles: revue féministe de l'outaouais,* [des créatrices en outaouais . . .], 2, no 4 (juil. 1980), 8–9.

Reviews/Comptes rendus

Alonzo, Anne-Marie. "La transparence des sexes." Compte-rendu de *À Vouloir vaincre l'absence. La vie en rose,* juin 1985, p. 55.
de Billy, Hélène. Compte rendu de *Ma fille comme une amante. La Gazette des femmes,* 3, no 2 (juil.–août 1981), 4.
La Palme Reyes, Marie. Compte rendu de *Je n'ai plus de cendre dans la bouche. Canadian Women's Studies/les cahiers de la femme* [Centennial College], 3, no 2 (1981), 116.
Messner, Céline. Compte rendu de *À Vouloir vaincre l'absence. Canadian Women's Studies/les cahiers de la femme* [Centennial College], [Affirmative action/Action positive], 6, no 4 (Winter/hiver 1985), 127.
Trépanier, Monique. Compte rendu de *Ma fille comme une amante. Entrelles: revue féministe de l'outaouais,* 3, no 3 (sept. 1981), 10.

Stevenson, Sharon

Articles and Sections of Books/
Articles et sections de livres

Blain, J. "Poet Sharon Stevenson: Transforming Politics & Prose. A Biographical Sketch." *HERizons: The Manitoba Women's News Magazine,* July 1985, p. 22.

Reviews/Comptes rendus

Grant, Linda. "Sharon Stevenson: Not Drowning but Waving." Rev. of *Gold*

Earrings. Kinesis, Oct. 1984, pp. 20, 28.

Stricklands (Susanna Moodie and Catharine Parr Traill) (See also/voir aussi Moodie, Susanna; and/et Traill, Catharine Parr)

Articles and Sections of Books/
Articles et sections de livres

Thomas, Clara. "Journeys to Freedom." *Canadian Literature,* [Poetry of P. K. Page], No. 51 (Winter 1972), pp. 11–19.
——— . "The Strickland Sisters: Susanna Moodie, 1803–1885; Catharine Parr Traill, 1802–1899." In *The Clear Spirit: Twenty Canadian Women and Their Times.* Ed. Mary Quayle Innis. Toronto: Canadian Federation of University Women/Univ. of Toronto Press, 1966, pp. 42–73.
Weaver, Emily P. "Pioneer Canadian Women: III — Mrs. Traill and Mrs. Moodie." *The Canadian Magazine of Politics, Science, Art and Literature* [Toronto], March 1917, pp. 473–76.

Summers, Myrna

Reviews/Comptes rendus

Carrington, Maureen. Rev. of *The Skating Party. Branching Out: Canadian Magazine for Women,* 2, No. 1 (Jan.–Feb. 1975), 40–41.

Swan, Susan

Reviews/Comptes rendus

Buitenhuis, Peter. Rev. of *The Biggest Modern Woman of the World. Queen's Quarterly,* 92 (Winter 1985), 844–45.
Read, Daphne. Rev. of *The Biggest Modern Woman in the World. Resources for Feminist Research/Documentation sur la*

recherche féministe, [Reviews Issue/
Comptes rendus], 14, No. 2 (July/juil.
1985), 28–29.

Szumigalski, Anne

Interviews/Entretiens

Hillis, Doris. "A Conversation with Anne
Szumigalski." *Dandelion*, 10, No. 1
(Spring–Summer 1983), 5–17.

Théoret, France

Articles and Sections of Books/
Articles et sections de livres

Corriveau, Hugues. "Des yeux qui écrivent."
Estuaire, [France Théoret: L'imaginaire
du réel], no 38 (hiver 1986), pp. 13–22.
Dupré, Louise. "Qui parle?". *Estuaire*,
[France Théoret: L'imaginaire réel], no 38
(hiver 1986), pp. 41–47.
Lamy, Suzanne. "Des résonances de la petite
phrase: 'Je suis un noeud' de France
Théoret." Dans *Féminité, subversion,
écriture*. Ed. Suzanne Lamy et Irène
Pagès. Montréal: Remue-ménage, 1983,
pp. 139–49.
Lejeune, Claire. "Clefs pour une correspon-
dance à quatre voix." *Estuaire*, [France
Théoret: L'imaginaire du réel], no 38
(hiver 1986), pp. 31–39.
Nepveu, Pierre. "Intérieurs d'une pensée."
Estuaire, [France Théoret: L'imaginaire
du réel], no 38 (hiver 1986), pp. 23–29.
Racine, Robert. "France Théoret: Bibliographie." *Estuaire*, [France Théoret: L'imaginaire du réel], no 38 (hiver 1986), pp.
119–31.
Smart, Patricia. "Quand la fille du bar se met
à parler: le piège de la représentation dans
la poésie de France Théoret." ACQL/
ALCQ, Univ. de Guelph, Guelph, Ont. 5
juin 1984. Emprunté ("Quand la fille du
bar se met à parler: la poésie de France
Théoret") dans *Dalhousie French Studies*,
[Numéro spécial: La poésie québécoise

depuis 1975], 1985, pp. 153–62.
———. "Un réalisme moderne: l'approche
du réel." *Estuaire*, [France Théoret: L'i-
maginaire du réel], no 38 (hiver 1986), pp.
55–71.

Interviews/Entretiens

Fournier, Danielle. "Entretien avec France
Théoret." MOEBIUS, no 23 (automne
1984), pp. 71–77.
Gaudet, Gérald. "Une écriture responsable."
Estuaire, [France Théoret: L'imaginaire
du réel], no 38 (hiver 1986), pp. 103–17.
Royer, Jean. "France Théoret: Les sciences
exactes de l'être." *Le Devoir* [Montréal],
15 mai 1982, pp. 19, 36. Repris dans *Ecrivains contemporains: Entretiens 3: 1980–
1983*. Par Jean Royer. Montréal: L'Hexagone, 1985, pp. 308–13.

Reviews/Comptes rendus

Alonzo, Anne-Marie. "France Théoret fois
trois." Compte-rendu de *Transit*. *La vie
en rose*, déc.–jan. 1984–85, p. 61.
Massé, Carole. "L'Écriture paradoxale."
Compte rendu de *Nous parlerons comme
on écrit*. *Canadian Women's Studies/les
cahiers de la femme* [Centennial College],
[Multiculture], 4, no 2 (Winter 1982),
97–98.
Yanacopoulo, Andrée. "Lettre de Montréal." Compte rendu de *Nous parlerons
comme on écrit*. *Spirale*, no 32 (mars
1983), p. 4.

Thériault, Marie-José

Articles and Sections of Books/
Articles et sections de livres

Moisan, Clément. "Marie José Thériault:
Lectures d'une oeuvre poétique." *Dalhousie French Studies*, [Numéro spécial:
La poésie québécoise depuis 1975], 1985,
pp. 135–47.

Interviews/Entretiens

Lord, Michel. "Marie-José Thériault. Interview." *Lettres québécoises*, no 40 (hiver 1985–86), pp. 40–44.

Thesen, Sharon

Reviews/Comptes rendus

Banting, Pamela. "Shifting Voices." Rev. of *Confabulations*. *Brick* [Toronto], No. 27 (Spring 1986), pp. 54–56.

Thomas, Audrey

Articles and Sections of Books/ Articles et sections de livres

Amussen, Robert. "Finding a Writer." *Room of One's Own*, [The Audrey Thomas Issue], 10, Nos. 3–4 (March 1986), 63–67.

Archer, Anne. "Real Mummies." *Studies in Canadian Literature*, 9, No. 2 (1984), 214–23.

Bellamy, Robin V. H. "Audrey Thomas: A Select Bibliography." *Room of One's Own*, [The Audrey Thomas Issue], 10, Nos. 3–4 (March 1986), 154–75.

Butling, Pauline. "The Cretan Paradox, or Where the Truth Lies in *Latakia*." *Room of One's Own*, [The Audrey Thomas Issue], 10, Nos. 3–4 (March 1986), 105–10.

——— . "Thomas and Her Rag-Bag." *Canadian Literature*, [B.C. Writers/Reviews], No. 102 (Autumn 1984), pp. 195–99.

Coldwell, Joan. "Natural Herstory and *Intertidal Life*." *Room of One's Own*, [The Audrey Thomas Issue], 10, Nos. 3–4 (March 1986), 140–49.

Davidson, Arnold. "Reading between the Texts in Audrey Thomas' *Munchmeyer and Prospero on the Island*." *American Review of Canadian Studies*, 15, No. 4 (Winter 1985), 421–31.

Gottlieb, Lois C., and Wendy Keitner. "Narrative Technique and the Central Female Character in the Novels of Audrey Thomas." *World Literature Written in English* [Univ. of Guelph], 21 (Summer 1982), 364–73.

Howells, Coral Ann. "No Sense of an Ending: *Real Mothers*." *Room of One's Own*, [The Audrey Thomas Issue], 10, Nos. 3–4 (March 1986), 111–23.

Keitner, Wendy. See/voir Gottlieb, Lois C., and Wendy Keitner.

Quigley, Ellen. "Redefining Unity and Dissolution in *Latakia*." *Essays on Canadian Writing*, No. 20 (Winter 1980–81), pp. 201–19.

Shaw, Jenny. "Letter to Edinburgh." *Room of One's Own*, [The Audrey Thomas Issue], 10, Nos. 3–4 (March 1986), 81–85.

Sherrin, Robert G. "In Esse." *Room of One's Own*, [The Audrey Thomas Issue], 10, Nos. 3–4 (March 1986), 68–74.

Thomas, Audrey. "My Craft and Sullen Art: The Writers Speak: Audrey Thomas." *Atlantis: A Women's Studies Journal/ Journal d'études sur la femme* [Acadia Univ.], 4, No. 1 (Fall/automne 1978), 152–54.

Wachtel, Eleanor. "The Guts of *Mrs. Blood*." *Books in Canada*, Nov. 1979, pp. 3–6.

——— . "The Image of Africa in the Fiction of Audrey Thomas." *Room of One's Own*, 2, No. 4 (1977), 21–28.

——— . Introduction. *Room of One's Own*, [The Audrey Thomas Issue], 10, Nos. 3–4 (March 1986), 3–6.

Theses and Dissertations/Thèses

Dorscht, Susan Rudy. "Blown Figures and Blood: Toward a Feminist/Post Structuralist Reading of Audrey Thomas' Writing." M.A. Thesis New Brunswick 1985.

Interviews/Entretiens

Bowering, George. "Songs & Wisdom: An Interview with Audrey Thomas." *Open Letter*, [Three Vancouver Writers], Ser. 4, No. 3 (Spring 1979), pp. 7–31.

Coupey, Pierre, Gladys Hindmarch, Wendy

Pickell, and Bill Schermbrucker. "Interview: Audrey Thomas." *The Capilano Review*, No. 7 (Spring 1975), pp. 87–112.

Wachtel, Eleanor. "An Interview with Audrey Thomas." *Room of One's Own*, [The Audrey Thomas Issue], 10, Nos. 3–4 (March 1986), 7–62.

Reviews/Comptes rendus

Atwood, Margaret. Rev. of *Ten Green Bottles* and *Ladies & Escorts*. *The Globe and Mail* [Toronto], 16 April 1977, p. 25. Rpt. in *Second Words: Selected Critical Prose*. By Margaret Atwood. Toronto: House of Anansi, 1982, pp. 268–71. Rpt. (excerpt) in *Contemporary Literary Criticism: Excerpts from Criticism of the Works of Today's Novelists, Poets, Playwrights, Short Story Writers, Filmmakers, and Other Creative Writers*. Ed. Daniel G. Marowski. Vol. XXXVII. Detroit: Gale, 1986, 417.

Butling, Pauline. Rev. of *Latakia*. *Periodics*, Nos. 7–8 (Winter 1981), pp. 186–88.

Coldwell, Joan. "From the Inside." Rev. of *Mrs. Blood*. *Canadian Literature*, [Poetry of P. K. Page], No. 50 (Autumn 1971), pp. 98–99.

Godard, Barbara. "Dispossession." Rev. of *Blown Figures*. *Open Letter*, Ser. 3, No. 5 (Summer 1976), pp. 81–82. Rpt. (excerpt) in *Contemporary Literary Criticism: Excerpts from Criticism of the Works of Today's Novelists, Poets, Playwrights, and Other Creative Writers*. Ed. Dedria Bryfonski and Laurie Lanzen Harris. Vol. XIII. Detroit: Gale, 1979, 540–41.

——. Rev. of *Latakia*. *The Fiddlehead*, No. 126 (Summer 1980), pp. 121–23.

——. Rev. of *Real Mothers*. *The Fiddlehead*, No. 135 (Jan. 1983), pp. 110–14. Rpt. (excerpt) in *Contemporary Literary Criticism: Excerpts from Criticism of the Works of Today's Novelists, Poets, Playwrights, Short Story Writers, Filmmakers, and Other Creative Writers*. Ed. Daniel G. Marowski. Vol. XXXVII. Detroit: Gale, 1986, 420–22.

Hutcheon, Linda. "No Woman Is an Island." Rev. of *Intertidal Life*. *Canadian Literature*, [Italian-Canadian Connections], No. 106 (Fall 1985), pp. 94–98.

Kamboureli, Smaro. "How Desire Speaks the Self." Rev. of *Latakia*. *Brick* [Ilderton, Ont.], No. 10 (Fall 1980), pp. 19–21.

Laurence, Margaret. "Audrey Thomas Writes Another Fine Novel." Rev. of *Blown Figures*. *The Gazette* [Montreal], 26 April 1975, p. 55. Rpt. ("*Blown Figures*: A Review") in *Room of One's Own*, [The Audrey Thomas Issue], 10, Nos. 3–4 (March 1986), 99–102.

MacKinley-Hay, Linda. Rev. of *Real Mothers*. In *Canadian Book Review Annual: 1981*. Ed. Dean Tudor and Ann Tudor. Toronto: Simon & Pierre, 1983, pp. 188–89.

Maika, Pat. "The Best Revenge." Rev. of *Real Mothers*. *The Radical Reviewer*, No. 5 (Winter 1981–82), p. 11.

Norcross, Gail. "Inner and Outer Landscapes." Rev. of *Latakia*. *The Radical Reviewer*, No. 6 (Spring 1982), pp. 8–9.

Prins, Marie. Rev. of *Latakia*. *Status of Women News/Statut de la femme*, [The World's Women], 6, No. 3 (Summer 1980), 22–23.

Rooke, Constance. Rev. of *Latakia*. *Canadian Women's Studies/les cahiers de la femme* [Centennial College], [Law and Politics/La loi et la politique], 2, No. 4 (1980), 108.

Wachtel, Eleanor. "Contemporary Triangles." Rev. of *Real Mothers*. *Saturday Night*, April 1982, pp. 51–52. Rpt. in *Contemporary Literary Criticism: Excerpts from Criticism of the Works of Today's Novelists, Poets, Playwrights, Filmmakers, and Other Creative Writers*. Ed. Daniel G. Marowski. Vol. XXXVII. Detroit: Gale, 1986, 419–20.

Tostevin, Lola Lemire

Reviews/Comptes rendus

McCaffery, Steve. "The Scene of the Cicatrice." Rev. of *Color of Her Speech*. *Brick*

[Toronto], No. 25 (Fall 1985), pp. 43–44.

Traill, Catharine Parr (See also/voir aussi Stricklands)

**Articles and Sections of Books/
Articles et sections de livres**

Ballstadt, Carl P. A. "Catharine Parr Traill (1802–1899)." In *Canadian Writers and Their Works*. Ed. Robert Lecker, Jack David, and Ellen Quigley. Fiction Series. Vol. I. Downsview, Ont.: ECW, 1983, 149–93.

Tregebov, Rhea

**Articles and Sections of Books/
Articles et sections de livres**

Doyle, Judith. "Rhea Tregebov." In her *In a Different Voice: Conversations with Women Artists and Filmmakers*. Toronto: Funnel, 1986, pp. 11–14.

Uguay, Marie

Books/Livres

Royer, Jean. *Marie Uguay: la vie, la poésie*. Montréal: Silence, 1982. 36 pp.

van Herk, Aritha

**Articles and Sections of Books/
Articles et sections de livres**

Batt, Sharon. "Aritha van Herk: Her Time and Place." *Branching Out: Canadian Magazine for Women*, [Special Issue on Women and Art], 5, No. 2 (1978), 26–29.
Pedwell, Susan. "Aritha van Herk Finds Magic Again." *The Globe and Mail* [Toronto], 2 Dec. 1980, p. 15.

Reviews/Comptes rendus

Boland, Viga. ". . . Such an Excellent Novel." Rev. of *Judith*. *Canadian Author & Bookman*, 54, No. 3 (May 1979), 34–35.
Dawe, Alan. "A Smashing Good Read." Rev. of *The Tent Peg*. *The Vancouver Sun*, 13 March 1981, p. L38.
French, William. "Aritha van Herk Becomes Radicalized. But What of the Power of Hormones?". Rev. of *The Tent Peg*. *The Globe and Mail* [Toronto], 21 Feb. 1981, p. E14.
Hill, Douglas. "Gritted Teeth on the Pig Farm." Rev. of *Judith*. *Saturday Night*, Nov. 1978, pp. 67–68.
Hoskins, Cathleen. "Hammering a Polemical Peg." Rev. of *The Tent Peg*. *Maclean's*, 16 March 1981, pp. 53–54.
Kirkwood, Hilda. "Travelling Woman." Rev. of *No Fixed Address: An Amorous Journey*. *The Canadian Forum*, Aug.–Sept. 1986, pp. 40–41.
Laurence, Jocelyn. "Is This the Best That Young Novelists Can Offer?". Rev. of *The Tent Peg*. *The Toronto Star*, 21 Feb. 1981, p. F10.
Manson, Eileen. "Mythic Heroines Inspiration for van Herk Tales." Rev. of *The Tent Peg*. *The Gazette* [Montreal], 21 March 1981, p. 124.
McGoogan, Kenneth. "Naughty New Heroine Proves van Herk Still Refusing to Conform." Rev. of *No Fixed Address: An Amorous Journey*. *Quill & Quire*, June 1986, p. 34.
McMullen, Lorraine. "Circe in Canada." Rev. of *Judith*. *Journal of Canadian Fiction*, Nos. 28–29 (1980), pp. 253–56.
Van Varseveld, Gail. "Worship Thy Father?". Rev. of *Judith*. *Branching Out: Canadian Magazine for Women*, 6, No. 2 (1979), 43–44.
Wachtel, Eleanor. "Barefoot in the Kitchen." Rev. of *The Tent Peg*. *Books in Canada*, March 1981, pp. 16–17.
Williamson, David. "The Novel Creaks with Symbols." Rev. of *The Tent Peg*. *Winnipeg Free Press*, 21 Feb. 1981, p. L4.

Villemaire, Yolande

Articles and Sections of Books/
Articles et sections de livres

Blouin, Louise, Yolande Villemaire, et Bernard Pozier. "Dossier Yolande Villemaire." APLF: *Atelier de Production littéraire des forges* [Trois-Rivières], nos 19–20 (printemps 1985), pp. 4–33.

Lamy, Suzanne. "Subversion en rose." Dans *Féminité, subversion, écriture.* Ed. Suzanne Lamy et Irène Pagès. Montréal: Remue-ménage, 1983, pp. 107–18.

Pozier, Bernard. Voir/see Blouin, Louise, Yolande Villemaire, et Bernard Pozier.

Robert, Lucie. "Bibliographie de Yolande Villemaire." *voix & images: littérature québécoise,* [Yolande Villemaire], no 33 (printemps 1986), pp. 455–62.

Royer, Jean. "Yolande Villemaire." *Les deux rives* [Paris], no 1 (printemps–été 1984), pp. 19–21.

Terretti, Andrée. "Lettre à ange amazone." *Les deux rives* [Paris], no 1 (printemps–été 1984), p. 24.

Villemaire, Yolande. "performantes." *Jeu: cahiers de théâtre,* [Théâtre-femmes], no 16 (1980), pp. 175–77.

———. Voir aussi/see also Blouin, Louise, Yolande Villemaire, et Bernard Pozier.

Interviews/Entretiens

Giguère, Suzanne, et Marie-Claude Trépanier. "Yolande Villemaire." *Lettres québécoises,* no 40 (hiver 1985–86), pp. 50–52.

Robert, Lucie. "Entrevue avec Yolande Villemaire." *voix & images: littérature québécoise,* [Yolande Villemaire], no 33 (printemps 1986), pp. 390–405.

Royer, Jean. "Yolande Villemaire: La vie en prose." *Le Devoir* [Montréal], 7 mars 1981, pp. 19, 20. Repris dans *Ecrivains contemporains: Entretiens 3: 1980–1983.* Par Jean Royer. Montréal: L'Hexagone, 1985, pp. 170–80.

Trépanier, Marie-Claude. Voir/see Giguère, Suzanne, et Marie-Claude Trépanier.

Reviews/Comptes rendus

David, Carole. "Le Corps blessé de Wonder Woman." Compte-rendu d'*Ange Amazone. Spirale,* no 28 (oct. 1982), p. 6.

Dumont, Monique. Compte rendu de *La Vie en prose. La vie en rose,* mars 1981, p. 46.

Fournier, Danielle. Compte rendu de *La Constellation du cygne,* par Yolande Villemaire; et *Hommes et Femmes,* par Annie Leclerc. MOEBIUS, [Écritures/Littérature], no 26 (automne 1985), pp. 120–22.

Klein-Lataud, Christine. Compte rendu de *Belles de nuit. Resources for Feminist Research/Documentation sur la recherche féministe,* [Women and Language/Les Femmes et le langage], 13, no 3 (Nov./nov. 1984), 61.

LaRue, Monique. "Le texte derviche." Compte rendu de *La Vie en prose. Spirale,* no 13 (nov. 1980), p. 4.

Stanton, Julie. Compte rendu de *La Vie en prose. La Gazette des femmes,* 2, no 9 (mai 1981), 4.

Waddington, Miriam

Articles and Sections of Books/
Articles et sections de livres

"But It's No Snap — Housework, Poetry Blend as 'Outside Interest Needed.'" *The Gazette* [Montreal], 4 Feb. 1955, Sec. 1, p. 10.

Jacobs, Maria. "The Personal Poetry of Miriam Waddington." CV/II, 5, No. 1 (Autumn 1980), 26–33.

MacCulloch, Claire. "'The Nineteen Thirties Are Over': The Changing Face of Miriam Waddington's Poetry, with a Complete Bibliography." *Alive* [Guelph, Ont.], No. 31 (1973), pp. 39–46.

Moritz, Albert. "From a Far Star: 'I don't have the place in Canadian literature that I deserve,' says Miriam Waddington. 'I'm a Jew, a Woman, and I hate all this about blood and knives.'" *Books in Canada,* May 1982, pp. 5–8.

Ricou, L. "Miriam Waddington: A Checklist 1936–1975." *Essays on Canadian Writing*, No. 12 (Fall 1978), pp. 162–91.

Ricou, Laurie. "Miriam [Dworkin] Waddington: An Annotated Bibliography." In *The Annotated Bibliography of Canada's Major Authors*. Ed. Robert Lecker and Jack David. Vol. VI. Toronto: ECW, 1985, 287–388.

Stevens, Peter. "Miriam Waddington (1917–)." In *Canadian Writers and Their Works*. Ed. Robert Lecker, Jack David, and Ellen Quigley. Introd. George Woodcock. Poetry Series. Vol. V. Toronto: ECW, 1985, 279–329.

Wachtel, Eleanor. "Miriam Waddington in Vancouver." *Room of One's Own*, 3, No. 1 (1977), 2–7.

Waddington, Miriam. "Exile: A Woman and a Stranger Living Out the Canadian Paradox." *Maclean's*, March 1974, pp. 40–43.

———. "'My Craft and Sullen Art': The Writers Speak. Is There a Feminine Voice in Literature?'". *Atlantis: A Women's Studies Journal/Journal d'études sur la femme* [Acadia Univ.], 4, No. 1 (Fall/automne 1978), 145–47.

"Women in the Arts Have Tough Sledding." *Scarborough Mirror*, 6 April 1966, p. 28.

Interviews/Entretiens

Jenoff, Marvyne. "Miriam Waddington: An Afternoon." *Waves*, 14, Nos. 1–2 (Fall 1985), 4–12.

Matyas, Cathy. "Miriam Waddington." In *Profiles in Canadian Literature*. Ed. Jeffrey M. Heath. Vol. IV. Toronto: Dundurn, 1982, 9–16.

Pearce, Jon. "Bridging the Inner and Outer: Miriam Waddington." In his *Twelve Voices: Interviews with Canadian Poets*. Ottawa: Borealis, 1980, pp. 175–87.

Reviews/Comptes rendus

Djwa, Sandra. "Letters in Canada: 1981. Poetry." Rev. of *The Visitants*. *University of Toronto Quarterly*, 51 (Summer 1982), 348.

Morley, Patricia. "Talking to All of Us . . . Yet a Word for the Women." Rev. of *The Price of Gold*. *The Ottawa Journal*, 11 Sept. 1976, p. 44.

Rooke, Constance. "Second Launching." Rev. of *The Visitants*. *Canadian Literature*, [Caribbean Connections], No. 95 (Winter 1982), pp. 116–18.

Vanstone, Gail. Rev. of *Mister Never*. *Canadian Women's Studies/les cahiers de la femme* [Centennial College], 1, No. 3 (Spring/printemps 1979), 109.

Wallace, Bronwen

Reviews/Comptes rendus

Carey, Barbara. Rev. of *Common Magic*. *Poetry Canada Review*, 7, No. 2 (Winter 1985–86), 39, 41.

Warland, Betsy

Articles and Sections of Books/Articles et sections de livres

Parks, Joy. "Speaking the Unspeakable." *HERizons: The Manitoba Women's News Magazine*, July–Aug. 1985, pp. 26–27.

Reviews/Comptes rendus

Herringer, Barbara. "Charting the Poet's Passage." Rev. of *A Gathering Instinct*. *The Radical Reviewer*, No. 6 (Spring 1982), p. 22.

Watson, Sheila

Articles and Sections of Books/Articles et sections de livres

Godard, Barbara. "'Between One Cliché and Another': Language in *The Double Hook*." *Studies in Canadian Literature*, 3 (Summer 1978), 149–65. Rpt. in *Sheila Watson and* The Double Hook. Ed.

George Bowering. Ottawa: Golden Dog, 1985, pp. 159–76.

Theses and Dissertations/Thèses

Bowering, Angela. "Illumination in *The Double Hook*: Figures Cut in Sacred Ground." Diss. Simon Fraser 1982.

Webb, Phyllis

**Articles and Sections of Books/
Articles et sections de livres**

Frey, Cecelia. "Phyllis Webb: An Annotated Bibliography." In *The Annotated Bibliography of Canada's Major Authors*. Ed. Robert Lecker and Jack David. Vol. VI. Toronto: ECW, 1985, 389–448.

Hulcoop, John. "Webb's *Water and Light*." *Canadian Literature*, [Mothers and Daughters], No. 109 (Summer 1986), pp. 130–59.

Thesen, Sharon. Introduction. In *Selected Poems: The Vision Tree*. By Phyllis Webb. Vancouver: Talonbooks, 1982, pp. 9–20.

Wachtel, Eleanor. "Intimations of Mortality: Once Threatened by 'the terrible abyss of despair,' Phyllis Webb Has Moved Beyond Mysticism and Anarchy to a Curiously Domestic Isolation." *Books in Canada*, Nov. 1983, pp. 8–9, 11–15.

Interviews/Entretiens

Fitzgerald, Judith. "No Longer a CanLit Goddess of Gloom: Phyllis Webb Clears the Air." *The Globe and Mail* [Toronto], 11 May 1983, p. 19.

Reviews/Comptes rendus

Mandel, Ann. "The Poetry of Last Things." Rev. of *Wilson's Bowl*. *Essays on Canadian Writing*, No. 26 (Summer 1983), pp. 85–91.

Weinzweig, Helen

Interviews/Entretiens

Bauer, Nancy. "Nancy Bauer Interviews Helen Weinzweig." *The Fiddlehead*, No. 132 (April 1982), pp. 12–17.

Reviews/Comptes rendus

Bolick, Merle Wallis. Rev. of *Basic Black with Pearls*. *Canadian Women's Studies/ les cahiers de la femme* [Centennial College], [Belles lettres], 5, No. 1 (Fall/ automne 1983), 35–36.

Crawley, Ennis. Rev. of *Basic Black with Pearls*. *Queen's Quarterly*, 88 (Autumn 1981), 563–65.

Klovan, Peter. "Canadian Gothic." Rev. of *Basic Black with Pearls*. *Canadian Literature*, [Contemporary Quebec Fiction], No. 88 (Spring 1981), pp. 186–87.

Weiss, Kate

Interviews/Entretiens

Thompson, Peggy. "Trust and Risk." *Room of One's Own*, 8, No. 2 (1983), 70–77.

Wetherald, Ethelwyn

**Articles and Sections of Books/
Articles et sections de livres**

Garvin, John. "Canadian Poets VII: Ethelwyn Wetherald." *Public Health Journal*, Oct. 1914, pp. 636–40.

Wilson, Ethel

**Articles and Sections of Books/
Articles et sections de livres**

Collins, Alexandra. "Who Shall Inherit the Earth? Ethel Wilson's Debt to Wharton, Glasgow, Cather, and Ostenso." The

Ethel Wilson Symposium, Univ. of Ottawa, Ottawa. 25 April 1982. Printed ("Who Shall Inherit the Earth? Ethel Wilson's Kinship with Wharton, Glasgow, Cather and Ostenso") in *The Ethel Wilson Symposium*. Ed. Lorraine McMullen. Reappraisals: Canadian Writers, No. 8. Ottawa: Univ. of Ottawa Press, 1982, pp. 61–72.

Fisher, D. M. "Government Defines Obscenity." *Quill & Quire*, Aug.–Sept. 1959, p. 22.

Gelfant, Blanche. "The Hidden Mines in Ethel Wilson's Landscapes (or, An American Cat among Canadian Falcons)." *Canadian Literature*, [Wilson, Laurence, Gallant, Glassco], No. 93 (Summer 1982), pp. 4–23.

Howard, Irene. "Shockable and Unshockable Methodists in *The Innocent Traveller*." *Essays on Canadian Writing*, No. 23 (Spring 1982), pp. 107–34.

Livesay, Dorothy. "Ethel Wilson: West Coast Novelist." *Saturday Night,* 26 July 1952, pp. 20, 36.

McComb, Bonnie Martyn. "Ethel Wilson: An Annotated Bibliography." In *The Annotated Bibliography of Canada's Major Authors*. Ed. Robert Lecker and Jack David. Vol. v. Downsview, Ont.: ECW, 1984, 415–80.

———. "Ethel Wilson: A Bibliography 1919–1977." Part i. *West Coast Review,* 14, No. 1 (June 1979), 38–43.

———. "Ethel Wilson: A Bibliography 1919–1977." Part ii. *West Coast Review,* 14, No. 2 (Oct. 1979), 49–57.

———. "Ethel Wilson: A Bibliography 1919–1977." Part iii. *West Coast Review,* 14, No. 3 (Jan. 1980), 58–64.

———. "Ethel Wilson: A Bibliography 1919–1977." Part iv. *West Coast Review,* 15, No. 1 (June 1980), 67–72.

McLay, Catherine. "Ethel Wilson's Lost Lady: *Hetty Dorval* and Willa Cather." *Journal of Canadian Fiction,* No. 33 (1981–82), pp. 94–106.

McLay, Catherine M. "The Initiation of Mrs. Golightly." *Journal of Canadian Fiction,* 1, No. 3 (Summer 1972), 52–55.

Rpt. (excerpt) in *Contemporary Literary Criticism: Excerpts from Criticism of the Works of Today's Novelists, Poets, Playwrights, and Other Creative Writers*. Ed. Dedria Bryfonski and Laurie Lanzen Harris. Vol. XIII. Detroit: Gale, 1980, 609–10.

McMullen, Lorraine. "The Divided Self." *Atlantis: A Women's Studies Journal/ Journal d'études sur la femme* [Acadia Univ.], 5, No. 2 (Spring/printemps 1980), 54–55.

———. "Ethel Wilson 1888–1980." *Canadian Literature*, [Faces of Realism/Facing Realities], No. 89 (Summer 1981), pp. 182–84.

———. Introduction. In *The Ethel Wilson Symposium*. Ed. Lorraine McMullen. Reappraisals: Canadian Writers, No. 8. Ottawa: Univ. of Ottawa Press, 1982, pp. 1–5.

Mitchell, Beverley. "Ethel Wilson (1888–1980)." In *Canadian Writers and Their Works*. Ed. Robert Lecker, Jack David, and Ellen Quigley. Introd. George Woodcock. Fiction Series. Vol. VI. Toronto: ECW, 1985, 183–238.

———. "'On the *Other* Side of the Mountains': The Westering Experience in the Fiction of Ethel Wilson." In *Women, Women Writers, and the West*. Ed. Laurence L. Lee and Merrill Lewis. Troy, N.Y.: Whitson, 1979, pp. 219–29.

Smyth, Donna E. "Maggie's Lake: The Vision of Female Power in *Swamp Angel*." In *Modern Times: A Critical Anthology*. Vol. III of *The Canadian Novel*. Ed. John Moss. Toronto: NC, 1982, pp. 159–65.

———. "Strong Women in the Web: Women's Work and Community in Ethel Wilson's Fiction." The Ethel Wilson Symposium, Univ. of Ottawa, Ottawa. 25 April 1982. Printed in *The Ethel Wilson Symposium*. Ed. Lorraine McMullen. Reappraisals: Canadian Writers, No. 8. Ottawa: Univ. of Ottawa Press, 1982, pp. 87–95.

Stouck, David. "An Annotated Index to the Ethel Wilson Papers at the University of British Columbia." The Ethel Wilson

Symposium, Univ. of Ottawa, Ottawa. 26 April 1982. Printed in *The Ethel Wilson Symposium*. Ed. Lorraine McMullen. Reappraisals: Canadian Writers, No. 8. Ottawa: Univ. of Ottawa Press, 1982, pp. 147–52.

———. "The Ethel Wilson Papers." The Ethel Wilson Symposium, Univ. of Ottawa, Ottawa. 25 April 1982. Printed in *The Ethel Wilson Symposium*. Ed. Lorraine McMullen. Reappraisals: Canadian Writers, No. 8. Ottawa: Univ. of Ottawa Press, 1982, pp. 47–59.

Urbas, Jeannette. "Perquisites of Love." *Canadian Literature*, [Lovers and Losers], No. 59 (Winter 1974), pp. 6–15.

Theses and Dissertations/Thèses

Clarke, Helen Marguerite. "Related Themes in the Fiction of Ethel Wilson." M.A. Thesis British Columbia 1964.

Reviews/Comptes rendus

Lane, Georgie. "'Hetty Dorval Wrote Itself' Says Author of New Novel." *The Vancouver Sun,* 9 May 1947, p. 19.

Wiseman, Adele

Articles and Sections of Books/ Articles et sections de livres

Morley, Patricia. "Wiseman's Fiction: Out of Pain, Joy." *Etudes Canadiennes/Canadian Studies* [Univ. de Bordeaux III], No. 4 (juin 1978), pp. 41–50.

Reviews/Comptes rendus

Brady, Elizabeth. Rev. of *Old Woman at Play. Fireweed: A Women's Literary & Cultural Journal,* No. 2 (Spring 1979), pp. 83–86.

Engel, Marian. "The Dollmaker." Rev. of *Old Woman at Play. Branching Out: Canadian Magazine for Women,* [Special Fiction Issue], 6, No. 3 (1979), 42.

Greenstein, Michael. "Adele Wiseman (1928–)." In *Canadian Writers and Their Works*. Ed. Robert Lecker, Jack David, and Ellen Quigley. Introd. George Woodcock. Fiction Series. Vol. VI. Toronto: ECW, 1985, 241–72.

McIntyre Sheila. Rev. of *Old Woman at Play. Canadian Women's Studies/les cahiers de la femme* [Centennial College], 1, No. 3 (Spring/printemps 1979), 107.

Morley, Patricia. "Artist at Play: Wiseman's Theory of Creativity." Rev. of *Old Woman at Play. Atlantis: A Women's Studies Journal/Journal d'études sur la femme* [Acadia Univ.], 6, No. 1 (Fall/ automne 1980), 104–09.

Redekop, Magdalene. Rev. of *Old Woman at Play. Status of Women News/Statut de la femme,* 5, No. 3 (March 1979), 22.

Wood, Joanna

Articles and Sections of Books/ Articles et sections de livres

"Literary Notes." *The Canadian Magazine of Politics, Science, Art and Literature* [Toronto], Feb. 1901, pp. 388–90.

Wyatt, Rachel

Interviews/Entretiens

Grady, Wayne. "Interview with Rachel Wyatt." *Books in Canada,* Aug.–Sept. 1982, pp. 32–33.

Images of Women in Men's Writing/ La Représentation des femmes chez les écrivains masculins (Articles and Sections of Books/Articles et sections de livres and/et Theses and Dissertations/Thèses)

Articles and Sections of Books/ Articles et sections de livres

Alonzo, Anne-Marie. "De palabres et d'exotisme." *La vie en rose*, nov. 1985, p. 51.

Anderson, Karen. "Shrews and Lambs: Images of Montagnais — Naskapi and Huron Women in the Writing of the 17th Century Jesuits." Canadian Research Institute for the Advancement of Women/ Institut canadien pour l'avancement des femmes, Montréal. Nov. 1984. Emprunté dans *Femmes: images, modèles/ Women: images, role-models, Actes du Colloque 1984/Proceedings of the 1984 Conference*. Ed. Evelyne Tardy. Ottawa: CRIAW/ ICRAF, 1985, pp. 84–90.

Barrett, Caroline, et Marie José des Rivières. "La femme dans la littérature populaire québécoise (1945–1965)." *Revue de l'Université d'Ottawa/University of Ottawa Quarterly*, [Conférence des femmes-écrivains en Amérique], 50 (jan.–mars/ Jan.–March 1980), 99–108.

Bowen, Gail. "Guides to the Treasure of Self: The Function of Women in the Fiction of Robertson Davies." *Waves*, 5, No. 1 (Fall 1976), 64–77.

Collet, Paulette. "La quarantaine, âge de l'abdication ou du renouveau pour la femme dans le théâtre de Marcel Dubé." *Canadian Drama/L'Art dramatique canadien* [Univ. de Waterloo], 5 (Fall/ automne 1979), 144–63.

——. "Women in Tremblay's Dramatic Works." York Univ./Univ. of Toronto, Women's Studies Colloquium, Ontario Institute for Studies in Education, Toronto. Oct. 1978.

de Venster, Dagmar. "Leonard Cohen's Women." In *Mother Was Not a Person*. Ed. Margret Andersen. Montreal: Black Rose, 1972, pp. 96–97.

des Rivières, Marie José. Voir aussi/see also Barrett, Caroline, et Marie José des Rivières.

Djwa, Sandra. "Response: The Fear of Women in Prairie Fiction: An Erotics of Space." Crossing Frontiers, Univ. of Alberta/Idaho State Univ., Banff, Alta. 14 April 1978. Printed in Crossing *Frontiers: Papers in American and Canadian Western Literature*. Ed. Dick Harrison. Edmonton: Univ. of Alberta Press, 1979, pp. 84–88.

Doumic, René. "La jeune fille dans le roman." *La Minerve* [Montréal], 8 août 1898, p. 6.

Falardeau, Jean-Charles. "La mère dans le roman canadien-français." *Recherches sociographiques*, 5, no 3 (sept. 1964), 385–88.

Genuist, Monique. "Mille Milles et la femme dans *Le Nez qui voque*." *Atlantis: A Women's Studies Journal/Journal d'études sur la femme* [Acadia Univ.], 2, no 2, Pt. I (Spring/printemps 1977), 56–63.

Kroetsch, Robert. "Fear of Women in Prairie Fiction: Erotics of Space." Crossing Frontiers, Univ. of Alberta/Idaho State Univ., Banff, Alta. 14 April 1978. Printed in *The Canadian Forum*, Oct.–Nov. 1978, pp. 22–27. Rpt. in Crossing *Frontiers: Papers in American and Canadian Western Literature*. Ed. Dick Harrison. Edmonton: Univ. of Alberta Press, 1979, pp. 73–83. Rpt. ("The Fear of Women in Prairie Fiction: *An Erotics of Space*") in *Robert Kroetsch: Essays*. By Robert Kroetsch. Ed. Frank Davey and bpNichol. Introd. Frank Davey. [*Open Letter*, Ser. 5, No. 4 (Spring 1983)], pp. 47–55.

Laceline, Philippe. "La femme dans les romans d'André Langevin." *Letters et écritures* [Univ. de Montréal], 1, no 3 (mars 1964), 20–24.

McKenna, Isobel. "As They Really Were: Women in the Novels of Grove." *English*

Studies in Canada, 2 (Spring 1976), 109–16.

McMullen, Lorraine. "Women in Grove's Novels." *Inscape* [Univ. of Ottawa], [The Grove Symposium], 11, No. 1 (Spring 1974), 67–76. Rpt. in *The Grove Symposium.* Ed. John Nause. Reappraisals: Canadian Writers, No. 1. Ottawa: Univ. of Ottawa Press, 1974, pp. 67–76.

Onley, Gloria. "Breaking through Patriarchal Nets to the Peaceable Kingdom: An Ecosystemic Review of Several Ideas, Books, and Events." *West Coast Review,* 8, No. 3 (Jan. 1974), 43–50.

Pedneault, Hélène. Voir/see Trépanier, Marie-Claude, et Hélène Pedneault.

Royer, Jean. "Robert Baille: Ma mère littéraire." Entretien avec Robert Baille. *Le Devoir* [Montréal], 5 mars 1983, pp. 17, 32. Repris dans *Ecrivains contemporains: Entretiens 3: 1980–1983.* Par Jean Royer. Montréal: L'Hexagone, 1985, pp. 223–29.

Saint-Martin, Lori. "Mise à mort de la femme et 'libération' de l'homme: Godbout, Aquin, Beaulieau." *voix & images: littérature québécoise,* 10, no 1 (automne 1984), 107–17.

Trépanier, Marie-Claude, et Hélène Pedneault. "Appeler un chat un chat." Entretien avec Michel Tremblay. *La vie en rose,* nov. 1985, pp. 42–45.

Trofimenkoff, Susan Mann. "Les femmes dans l'oeuvre de Groulx." *Revue d'histoire de l'Amérique française,* 32 (déc. 1978), 385–98.

Urbas, Jeannette. "La Représentation de la femme chez Godbout Aquin et Jasmin." *Laurentian University Review/Revue de l'Université Laurentienne,* [The Social and Political Novel in English Canada/Le roman engagé au Canada français], 9, no 1 (Nov. 1976), 103–14.

Verduyn, Christl. "L'image de la femme dans l'oeuvre de Gérard Bessette." Dans *Lectures de Gérard Bessette.* Ed. Jean-Jacques Hamm. Montréal: Québec/Amérique, 1982, pp. 99–114.

Worthington, Bonnie. "Ryga's Women." *Canadian Drama/L'Art dramatique canadien* [Univ. of Waterloo], 5 (Fall 1979), pp. 139–43.

Theses and Dissertations/Thèses

Bossanne, Brigitte Germaine. "Images de la femme dans l'oeuvre de Jacques Godbout." M.A. Thesis Manitoba 1979.

Coulombe-Dionne, Mannon. "Etudes comparative du thème de la femme dans 'l'âge de ma parole' de Roland Giguère, 'L'homme rapaillé' de Gaston Miron et 'Séquences de l'aile' de Fernand Ouellette." Thèse de maîtrise Ottawa 1972.

Crépeau, Jean-François. "L'Univers féminin dans l'oeuvre de Marcel Dubé." Thèse de maîtrise McGill 1974.

des Rivières, Marie José. "La Répresentation de la femme dans le roman d'espionnage *Les Aventures étranges de l'agent IXE-13.*" Thèse de maîtrise Laval 1978.

Eddie, Christine. "L'evolution des personnages féminins de *Rue des Pignons [de Louis Morisset et Mia Riddeg].*" Thèse de maîtrise Laval 1980.

Ford, Barbara. "L'oeuvre romanesque d'André Langevin: la perception de la femme chez les personnages masculins." M.A. Thesis Western Ontario 1972.

Fournier, Louise G. "La femme dans les romans d'Yves Thériault." M.A. Thesis Dalhousie 1977.

Gauthier, Nicole. "La féminité et ses représentations fantasmatiques dans le roman québécois masculin." Thèse de maîtrise Québec à Montréal 1981.

Keays, Suzanne Marie Turenne. "Le Rôle des femmes dans le théâtre de Michel Tremblay." M.A. Thesis McMaster 1979.

Kreipans-McGrath, Veneranda. "Love and Loathing: The Role of Woman in Irving Layton's Vision." M.A. Thesis Concordia 1981.

Parkin, Allan. "A Study of Women in Hugh Garner." M.A. Thesis Queen's 1973.

Pesando, Frank. "The Women in the Prairie Novels of Frederick Philip Grove." M.A. Thesis York 1972.

Rideout, Elliott Christopher. "The Women in the Novels of Frederick Grove." M.A. Thesis Alberta 1969.

Rudakoff, Judith Debra. "The Women in *Forever Yours, Marie-Lou*." M.A. Thesis Alberta 1977.

Images of Men/La Représentation des hommes (Articles and Sections of Books/Articles et sections de livres, and/et Reviews/Comptes rendus)

Articles and Sections of Books/ Articles et sections de livres

Bailey, Nancy I. "The Masculine Image in Lives of Girls and Women." *Canadian Literature*, [The Moral Novel], No. 80 (Spring 1979), pp. 113–20.

Burton, Lydia, and David Morley. "A Sense of Grievance: Attitudes toward Men in Contemporary Fiction." *The Canadian Forum*, Sept. 1975, pp. 57–60.

Campbell, Sheila. "Wes Wakeham and the Masculine Mystique." *Room of One's Own,* 1, No. 4 (Winter 1976), 24–32.

Lalonde, Michèle. "Le mythe du père dans la littérature québécoise." *Interprétation,* 3, nos. 1–2 (jan.–juin 1969), 215–26.

Michaud, Carole. "Testicules et peau d'homme." *Le Québec littéraire,* 1 (1974), 79–86.

Saint-Onge, Paule. "Les hommes d'ici." *Incidences* [Univ. d'Ottawa], no 5 (avril 1964), pp. 13–17.

van Lent, Peter. "Absence and Departure: The Male Mystique in French-Canadian Literature before 1950." *The American Review of Canadian Studies*, 16, No. 1 (Spring 1986), 17–23.

Zonailo, Carolyn. "Male Stereotypes in *The Diviners* and *The Edible Woman*." *Room of One's Own,* 3, No. 1 (1977), 70–72.

Reviews/Comptes rendus

"L'homme est absent de la littérature canadienne-française." Compte rendu du colloque organisé par la Sociéte d'Etudes et de Conférences. *Le Devoir* [Montréal], 20 avril 1965, p. 7.

Journalism/Journalisme (Books/ Livres, Articles and Sections of Books/Articles et sections de livres, Theses and Dissertations/Thèses, and/et Reviews/Comptes rendus)

Books/Livres

Le Cercle des Femmes Journalistes. *Vingt-cinq à l'une.* Montréal: La Presse, 1976. 189 pp.

Des Ormes, Renée. *Robertine Barry en littérature: Françoise, pionnière du journalisme féminin au Canada, 1863–1910.* Québec: L'Action sociale, 1949. 159 pp.

Articles and Sections of Books/ Articles et sections de livres

Bettinotti, Julia. "Féminisme et presse féminine au Québec." Dans *Féminité, subversion, écriture.* Ed. Suzanne Lamy et Irène Pagès. Montréal: Remue-ménage, 1983, pp. 9–14.

Bettinotti, Julia, et Jocelyn Gagnon. *"Que c'est bête, ma belle!". Etudes sur la presse féminine au Québec.* Montréal: Soudeyns/Donzé, 1983. 143 pp.

Boivin, Aurélien, et Kenneth Landry. "Françoise et Madeleine, pionnières du journalisme féminin au Québec." *voix et images: études québécoises,* 4 (déc. 1978), 233–43.

de Guise, Anne. "*La Nouvelle Barre du jour*: La complicité." *La vie en rose,* juin–juil.–août 1982, p. 68.

Dupont, Sylvie, et Claudine Vivier. "*La vie en rose*: un petit 24 pages de grandes ambitions." *Des luttes et des rires de femmes,* 3, no 5 (juin–juil.–août 1980), 35–36.

Frost, Wendy. "Lesbiantics: A Rich and Varied Brew." Rev. of *Fireweed: A Feminist Quarterly,* [Lesbian Issue], No. 13 (1982). *The Radical Reviewer: A Feminist Journal of Critical & Creative Work,* Nos. 7–8 (1982), p. 1.

Gagnon, Jocelyn. Voir/see Bettinotti, Julia, et Jocelyn Gagnon.

Jean, Michèle. "Bilan de Têtes de pioche." *Des luttes et des rires de femmes,* 3, no 1 (oct. 1979), 29–30.

Kerr, Kandace. "Early Feminist Journalists: Pt. I." *Kinesis,* Nov. 1984, p. 11.

———. "Early Feminist Journalists: Pt. II." *Kinesis,* Dec.–Jan. 1984–85, p. 25.

Landry, Kenneth. Voir/see Boivin, Aurélien, et Kenneth Landry.

Lemoine, Christine. "La presse au Canada: au lieu de movement des femmes." *Des luttes et des rires de femmes,* 3, no 5 (juin–juil.–août 1980), 40–43.

MacDonald, Ingrid. "Publishing Priorities." *Broadside: A Feminist Review* [Toronto], June 1986, p. 7.

Manathorne, Jacquie. "Le Colloque sur les périodiques féministes: un succès." *Communiqu'Elles,* 11, no 5 (sept. 1985), 17–18.

O'Leary, Véronique, et Louise Toupin. "*Québécoises debouttes!*: pour qu'hier serve à demain." *Des luttes et des rires de femmes,* 3, no 5 (juin–juil.–août 1980), 30–33.

"Readings from Current Literature: Women in Journalism." *The Week: A Canadian Journal of Politics, Literature, Science and Arts* [Toronto], 3 June 1893, p. 712.

Saint-Jean, Armande. "*Les Têtes de pioche*: pour qu'hier serve à demain." *Des luttes et des rires de femmes,* 3, no 5 (juin–juil.–août 1980), 29.

Sirois, Denise. "Entrelles." *Des luttes et des rires de femmes,* 3, no 5 (juin–juil.–août 1980), 34.

Toupin, Louise. Voir/see O'Leary, Véronique, et Louise Toupin.

Vipond, Mary. "The Image of Women in Canadian Mass Circulation Magazines in the 1920s." *Modernist Studies: Literature and Culture 1920–1940,* [Women in the Literature and Culture of the Twenties and Thirties], 1, No. 3 (1974–75), 5–14.

Vivier, Claudine. Voir/see Dupont, Sylvie, et Claudine Vivier.

Weaver, Emily P. "Pioneer Canadian Women VII — 'Kit,' the Journalist." *The Canadian Magazine of Politics, Science, Art and Literature* [Toronto], Aug. 1917, pp. 275–79.

Wilson, Susannah J. "The Changing Image of Women in Canadian Mass Circulating Magazines, 1930–1970." CRIAW Conference, Halifax, N.S. Nov. 1976. Printed in *Atlantis: A Women's Studies Journal/ Journal d'études sur la femme* [Acadia Univ.], 2, No. 2, Pt. II (Spring/printemps 1977), 33–44.

Wolfe, Morris. "Of Ms. and Men in Publishing." *Books in Canada*, May 1975, pp. 4–5.

Wyman, Georgina. "The Day Women Took Over the Toronto *Globe*." *Branching Out: Canadian Magazine for Women,* 1, No. 1 (March–April 1974), 22–23, 39–40.

Theses and Dissertations/Thèses

Bourret, Guy. "Bio-bibliographie de Madame veuve Charles Gill." Thèse en bibliothéconomie Montréal 1944.

Chassé, Gertrude. "Bio-bibliographie de Françoise (Mlle Robertine Barry)." Thèse en bibliothéconomie Montréal 1945.

Cloutier, Laurette. "Bio-bibliographie de Madame Raoul Dandurand (née Joséphine Marchand)." Thèse en bibliothéconomie Montréal 1942.

Courchesne, Ginette. "Laure Hurteau, journaliste: étude bio-bibliographique." Thèse de maîtrise Montréal 1975.

De Matos Andrade, Maria-Eugenia. "Biographie et bibliographie descriptive de Madeleine (1875–1943)." Thèse de D.E.S. Montréal 1969.

Miles, Barbara Anne. "Madeleine [Huguenin] et *La Revue moderne*: sa contribution à la vie littéraire et culturelle de Québec." Thèse de maîtrise Western Ontario 1982.

Plante, Juilette. "Madeleine Journaliste." Thèse de maîtrise Ottawa 1962.

Reviews/Comptes rendus

Beauchamp, Colette. "Une réimpression qui s'imposait." Compte rendu de *Québécoises deboutes!*. *Spirale*, no 35 (juin 1983), p. 11.

Compte rendu de *Québécoises Deboutte!*, vol. II. *Spirale*, no 35 (juin 1983), p. 11.

Mouré, Erin. "Another Look at *Tessera*." *Kinesis*, Oct. 1984, p. 21.

Feminist Presses/Les Presses féministes (Articles and Sections of Books/Articles et sections de livres)

Articles and Sections of Books/ Articles et sections de livres

Desjardins, Louise. See/voir Raoult, Marie-Madeleine, and Louise Desjardins.

Nuse, Betsy. See/voir Oughton, Libby, with Betsy Nuse.

Oughton, Libby, with Betsy Nuse. "The Spirit of Ragweed." *Broadside: A Feminist Review* [Toronto], Aug.–Sept. 1986, p. 8.

Parks, Joy. "Riches from Ragweed." *HERizons: The Manitoba Women's News Magazine*, July–Aug. 1985, pp. 24–25.

Pike, Lois. "A Selective History of Feminist Presses and Periodicals in English Canada." In *In the Feminine: Women and Words/Les Femmes et les mots: Conference Proceedings 1983*. Ed. Ann Dybikowski, Victoria Freeman, Daphne Marlatt, Barbara Pulling, and Betsy Warland. Edmonton: Longspoon, 1985, pp. 209–17.

Raoult, Marie-Madeleine, and Louise Desjardins. "The Raison d'être for Pleine Lune." In *In the Feminine: Women and Words/Les Femmes et les mots: Conference Proceedings 1983*. Ed. Ann Dybikowski, Victoria Freeman, Daphne Marlatt, Barbara Pulling, and Betsy Warland. Edmonton: Longspoon, 1985, pp. 201–08.

Wolfe, Margie. "Feminist Publishing in Canada." *Canadian Women's Studies/les cahiers de la femme* [Centennial College], 2, No. 2 (1980), 11–14.